I0813006

POSTCARD HISTORY SERIES

Morgan County

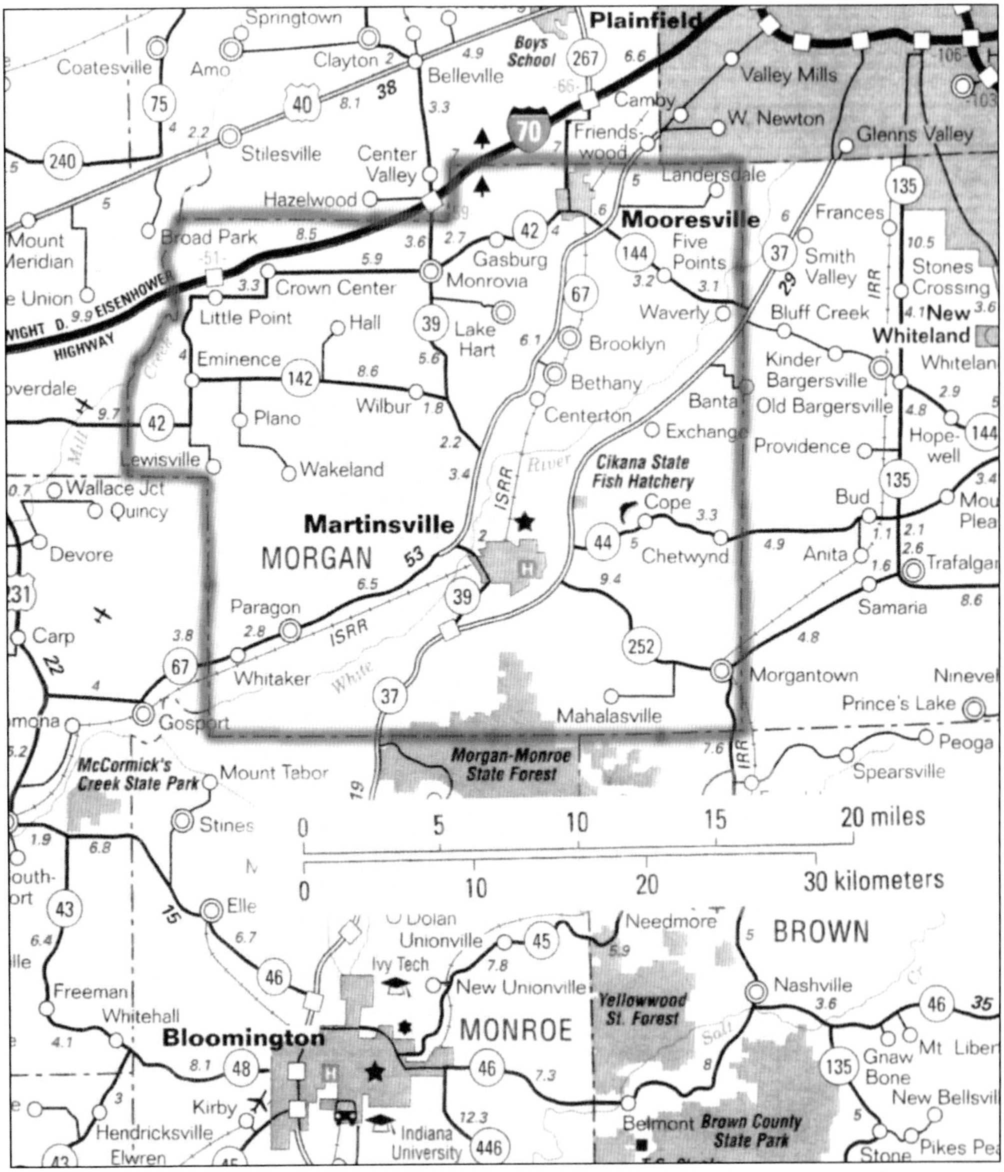

MORGAN COUNTY, 2006. Seen here is a map of Morgan County showing the locations of towns and villages depicted in the vintage postcards featured in this book.

On the front cover: **INDIANAPOLIS SOUTHERN (LATER ILLINOIS CENTRAL) DEPOT AT MORGANTOWN, 1909.** Running north and south through the east end of Morgantown, the Illinois Central Railroad was constructed in 1906, as was this depot. "My dear little darling," an absent mother writes, "I hope you and papa are getting along fine. Don't eat the bread I baked if it is not good. . . . Kiss papa for me and mama will be home Tuesday."

On the back cover: **MORGAN COUNTY COURTHOUSE, MARTINSVILLE, *C.* 1910.** The pre-Civil War-era courthouse has long been the anchor of downtown Martinsville. In this view, horses and buggies are tethered to the hitching rail surrounding the lawn.

POSTCARD HISTORY SERIES

Morgan County

Joanne Raetz Stuttgen and Curtis Tomak

ARCADIA
PUBLISHING

ISBN 978-0-7385-5120-3

Published by Arcadia Publishing
Charleston SC, Chicago IL, Portsmouth NH, San Francisco CA

Printed in the United States of America

Library of Congress Catalog Card Number: 2006939090

For all general information contact Arcadia Publishing at:
Telephone 843-853-2070
Fax 843-853-0044
E-mail sales@arcadiapublishing.com
For customer service and orders:
Toll-Free 1-888-313-2665

Visit us on the Internet at www.arcadiapublishing.com

We dedicate this book to local historians, both past and present, who have provided a record of earlier times through their research, memories, writings, compilations, and collections.

Contents

ACKNOWLEDGMENTS

We are indebted to the generosity of many postcard collectors who graciously shared their collections with us. Some are friends we have known for a long time (and bid against at auctions). Others are people we had never before met but who answered our call for postcards. Still others include eBay sellers who e-mailed us scans of cards when we somewhat sheepishly asked. Without their contributions, this book, and a possible Martinsville book to come, would never have come to life. Thank you to the following people, institutions, and organizations: Academy of Hoosier Heritage, Dianna Atkins, Cathy Counsilman Bonner, Del Chafey, Irma S. Coates, Ruth Connell, Michael Gorham, Sharon Platt Kain, Kevin Kent, Bill Kirk, Pam Lanham, Peggy LaPlante, Mooresville Public Library, Morgan County Historic Preservation Society, Morgan County Public Library, Tim and Camilla Morris, Don and Joyce Robinson, Joe Seiter, Harley Sheets, Keith Steinway, Joanne Raetz Stuttgen, Curtis Tomak, Frances Tutterow, Donna Walker, and Jeanne Weaver.

Furthermore, we are beholden to the following local residents and historians whose passion for and commitment to preserving and recording the past have enriched this book immeasurably: Albert "Dutch" Allen, Stella Avery, Janet Cowen, Alma Fraker, Patsy Harker Freed, Mae Gano, Almira Harvey Hadley, Gordon Hadley, Becky Hardin, Lena Hensley, Henrietta Hickman, John E. Hurt Sr., Lloyd James, Noble K. Littell, Don and Donna McGuire, Mary E. Monical, Charlie Nelson, Wanda Potts, Robert Prather, Claude M. Renner, Clara S. Richardson, Rachel Ruona, Margaret Sedwick, Mary E. Murphy Taylor, Phyllis Walker, Jeanne Weaver, and Henry Youngblood.

Introduction and History of Postcards

This is a book about postcards, but even more, it is a book about the history of Morgan County as illustrated by postcards.

Morgan County was established in 1822 and is located in south-central Indiana, immediately southwest of Indianapolis. It is a rural area of about 409 square miles with a population of approximately 70,000. Martinsville (population about 13,000) is the county seat and the largest town, and Mooresville is the only other sizeable town. There have been numerous towns and communities in Morgan County. Among those shown on present-day maps are Bethany, Brooklyn, Centerton, Eminence, Hall, Lewisville, Little Point, Mahalasville, Martinsville, Monrovia, Mooresville, Morgantown, Paragon, and Waverly. Those are the ones for which we have seen postcards and the ones represented in this book.

Many more postcards are available for Martinsville than for any other Morgan County location. A substantial number are known for Mooresville and Bethany Park, but postcards for other locations occur in noticeably smaller numbers with only a few or no cards known for some places. As a result, this publication could have been heavily weighted toward Martinsville. However, this is a Morgan County book, and since it has a size limit and postcards from other places are less often seen, we emphasized non-Martinsville postcards. However, a nice selection of uncommon Martinsville cards is included, and we hope to feature many more in a later Martinsville postcard book. Over 200 postcards are pictured in this book. Dates given in the picture captions refer to the postmark date with circa dates being an estimate based upon the type of postcard.

Joanne proposed doing this book and invited me to participate. The undertaking greatly benefits from her extensive knowledge of Morgan County history and her research experience. My postcard collection was a starting point for the book. Together we put much effort into locating other postcards and have had good success with that. Those who contributed are listed in the acknowledgments, and we are very grateful to them.

The formal term for the study and collecting of postcards is *deltiology*, which derives from a Greek word referring to a small writing tablet. Over the years, the terms *postcard* (*post card*) and *postal card* have been used in various ways and contexts. However, in a technical sense *postcard* has come to mean a privately printed card to which a postage stamp is affixed, whereas *postal card* refers to a government-printed card that has a preprinted stamp.

Deltiology has become one of the most popular collecting activities in the United States. This is evidenced by the large and continually growing number of postcard collectors, dealers, and organizations such as the Indianapolis Postcard Club. Organized in 1975, it has about 115 members, holds monthly meetings, and now hosts two shows per year where postcards are bought, sold, traded, and exhibited. The volume of postcard business conducted on eBay further attests to the interest in and demand for postcards.

People collect postcards for various reasons. Some collections reflect an interest in a particular topic. Examples are interurban and railroad trains and depots, sports, high schools, Route 66, restaurants, comic cards, occupations, archaeology, politics, parks, postal history, famous people, drugstores, theaters, royalty, holiday and greeting cards, children, advertising, courthouses, and animals.

Many collections are based upon an interest in the history of certain places or events, memories, experiences, associations with people and places, and/or personal and family history. For example, someone may collect just the city of Wabash, anything Morgan County, or a combination of hometown, current place of residence, and father's hometown. Some places, such as French Lick and West Baden, may be collected just because they are interesting or unusual.

There are many postcards that are so attractive that they are desirable as objects of art. Often cards are sought that have been illustrated by a particular artist with those that are signed (printed signature) being more desirable. Some search for postcards manufactured by a particular company or taken by a specific photographer. For instance, the white-, gray-, and silver-bordered view cards (see page 16, bottom) made by the Wayne Paper Box and Printing Corporation of Fort Wayne during the early 1930s to the late 1940s are a favorite of some collectors. Others, for example, may collect the fine real-photo postcards made by J. Inbody of Elkhart during the 1907 to 1915 time period.

Some people are interested in postal history and collect old postcards because of their cancel marks and postmarks from post offices that no longer exist. The image on the front of the card or the type of card is usually of little or no real importance.

Collections may also focus on certain categories of postcards as exemplified by the following four kinds of cards.

Real-photo postcards are cards that are actual black-and-white photographs printed onto photographic paper having a postcard back (see page 15, top). They are quite popular because of the quality of the image. Although actual photographic postcards of one kind or another have continued to be produced, what are typically thought of as real-photo postcards date from approximately 1900 into the 1920s.

View cards are postcards that basically show scenes or views of such things as towns, buildings, and landscapes (see page 77). This is a standard and popular kind of card. The time span for what are regarded as view cards is from the 1890s to the present.

A multiview postcard is a card that has from 2 to at least 19 separate views on it (see page 81, top). Typically the views are images of individual view cards for a particular place. Examples are multiviews of towns or university buildings. Multiviews are collectible cards with the general time span of vintage examples being from the 1890s into the 1930s.

Pennant postcards are generic postcards that have a picture of a pennant on the front (see page 55, bottom). Often the name of a town is printed on the pennant, and typically the card also has an image of the town, people, or cartoon characters and a witty line or two about the town. They basically date from about 1907 to 1915.

Although there may be a primary reason for the composition of a postcard collection, many collections result from a combination of factors. Some are based upon an interest in history combined with an association with a particular area. Halloween cards may be collected because of the subject matter, beautiful colors, and artistic quality.

It takes more than an interest in a topic or a place to collect postcards. Some people collect many different kinds of things related to their subject area but do not have much interest in postcards. However, many people think that postcards themselves are so nice and so enjoyable to collect that they concentrate on them to satisfy their area of interest basically to the exclusion of other things. For instance, it may be that a person does not have much interest in photographs pertaining to their subject area or is not really interested in collecting relevant trade cards or blotters even though the images or text on them are as good or better than on postcards. Assembling an outstanding postcard collection becomes an important goal that is reinforced by the good feeling that comes from a sense of accomplishment.

A number of postcard companies distributed postcards that advertised their products. One side of the card is a sample of a type of postcard being advertised, and the other side has ordering and price information. This is exemplified by a printed white-border view postcard of mine produced by the Auburn Postcard Manufacturing Company of Auburn, Indiana, during the 1915–1930 period. The stated price for 500 copies of the printed view cards is $3.75 and that for 100 "full size photo post cards" of local views is $1.50.

Some postcard photographers put their name on the front of their postcards and/or advertised their business on the back. For instance, "J. Inbody, post card artist, Elkhart, Ind." is on the back of a card of mine postmarked 1907. Another example is M. L. Photo, which signed as such on the front of 1907–1915 real-photo postcards and often had some version of "M. L. Photo Company, Chicago" on the back. M. L. Photo produced good quality cards of many places in Indiana, including some towns in Morgan County.

Morgan County photographers who produced postcards during the first two decades of the 20th century are well represented in this book. They include Mooresville's Jarvis P. Calvert; Morgantown's Granville E. Davis, Roscoe C. Karst, and evidently a photographer named Whitaker; and Waverly's Joseph Counsilman. The latter is the father of James "Doc" Counsilman, the famous Indiana University swimming coach. There were also postcard photographers in Martinsville, but none of their cards appear in this book.

In addition to professional photographers, it was a common practice for anyone to take photographs of family members, homes, places, and events and have them printed as postcards. Beginning about 1906, this was aided by the availability of small affordable cameras for postcard photography.

Postcards came into use during the last half of the 19th century as a convenient means of sending a brief message. The earliest postcards were privately published. Evidently the first card that qualifies as a postcard in the United States is the Lipman Postal Card, designed and copyrighted by John Charlton and H. L. Lipman of Philadelphia in 1861. Not many of these cards are known. The oldest mailed example is dated October 25, 1870, and that card is the earliest known mailed American postcard.

The U.S. government went into the postcard business in 1873 when the U.S. postal service began the production of prestamped 1¢ mailing cards referred to as postal cards. From 1873 until 1898, only the U.S. government could produce the 1¢ cards. During this time, privately published cards with a written message were required, like letters, to have a 2¢ postage stamp affixed to them.

On May 19, 1898, the Private Mailing Card Act became federal law. This act permitted privately published mailing cards with a written message to be mailed domestically for 1¢ like the government-printed cards but required that a postage stamp be used. The private cards had to have the words "Private Mailing Card Authorized by Act of Congress of May 19, 1898" printed on the back (address/postage side) to distinguish them from government cards. As before, the message on government cards and on privately published cards was to be confined to the front.

The December 24, 1901, order of the U.S. postal service rescinded much of the 1898 act and allowed privately published cards to have Post Card (Postcard) printed on the back instead of Private Mailing Card. As before, the back of government and private cards was an undivided area to be used solely for the address. Although undivided backs were the norm prior to 1902, the period from about 1902 to 1907 is considered to be the undivided-back period (or era). The message was still to be confined to the front in a space provided at the side or the bottom of the card and/or written anywhere on the front, including over the picture. It was during this period that real-photo postcards came into prominence.

As of March 1, 1907, the U.S. postal service permitted the back of postcards to be divided by a vertical line with the message to the left and the address to the right of the line (see page 122). This initiated the divided-back period, which, for the purpose of postcard history, is considered to last until 1915 (the beginning of World War I). During this time, hundreds of millions of postcards were mailed each year in the United States. People not only used postcards for messages but also generally viewed the cards as quite desirable as souvenirs and pictorial records. Collecting postcards (both unused and mailed) and keeping them in albums had become a craze. People exchanged cards as collectibles, and sometimes the message on a card included a request to be sent a view card in return. This period, plus the preceding few years, is commonly referred to as the golden age of postcards. During this time, Germany was the world leader in postcard production, largely due to its superior printing and production technology, and most U.S. postcards were printed in Germany.

World War I brought the postcard business with Germany to an end, and then most American postcards were made in the United States. In an effort to reduce production costs by saving ink, postcards manufactured from about 1915 to 1930 had a white border around the front (see page 14, bottom). Although white borders continued, the period from about 1915 to 1930 is termed the white border period.

Beginning about 1930, great quantities of postcards were printed with brightly colored inks on paper having a high rag content and a linenlike textured look (see page 20, top). Although the image covers the entire card on many linen postcards, they often have a white border, a carryover from the previous period. Also it is not unusual for a white-bordered linen card to have the same view as appeared earlier on a postcard from the white border period. The linen period is considered to date from about 1930 to 1950, although linens were being made well into the 1950s.

Chrome (photochrome) postcards (see page 112) are the familiar glossy-colored photographic postcards of recent times. They first appeared in 1939 and by the late 1940s had become the most common or the standard type of postcard. The chrome period overlaps the linen period and is considered to extend from about 1940 to the present time.

Let me conclude with a word about postage rates for the time span with which we are most concerned. From the passage of the Private Mailing Card Act in 1898 until 1952, the rate was 1¢, except during the World War I years when postage was raised to 2¢. The penny postcard continued until December 31, 1951, at which time postage was raised to 2¢, and rates have continued to increase since then.

This book was written because of our interest in postcards as pictorial records of the past and our strong interest in Morgan County history. We hope you find the book to be as enjoyable, interesting, and informative to read as it has been for us to prepare it.

—Curtis Tomak

One

Martinsville

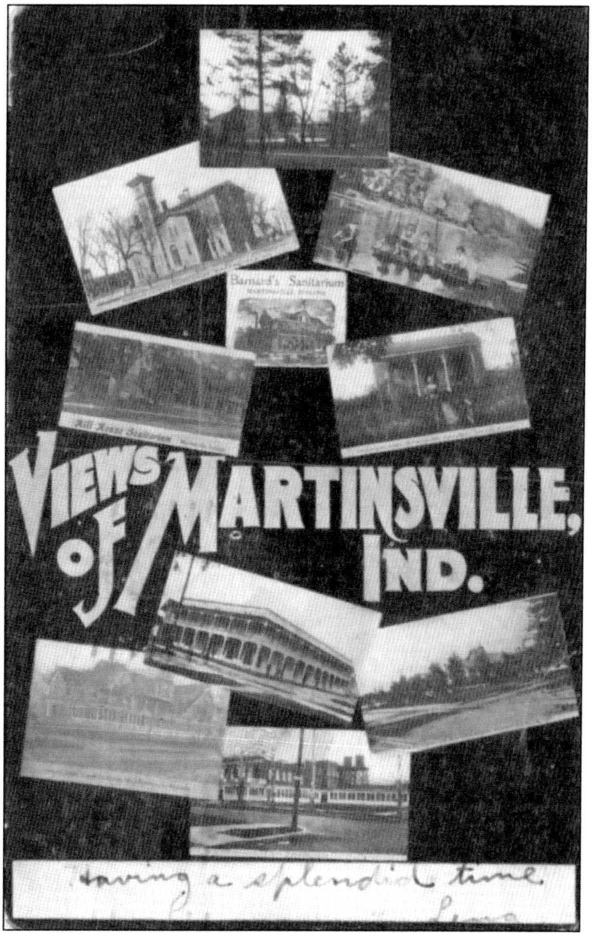

Martinsville Multiview, 1908. Clockwise from the top are Home Lawn Sanitarium, Blue Bluffs Resort, Celestina Phelps (also known as "Aunt Tiny," she was the inspiration for a character in *Lovey Mary*, a popular novel), Martinsville Sanitarium, Colonial Sanitarium, Highland Sanitarium, National Sanitarium, Hill House Sanitarium, Morgan County Courthouse, and Barnard Sanitarium.

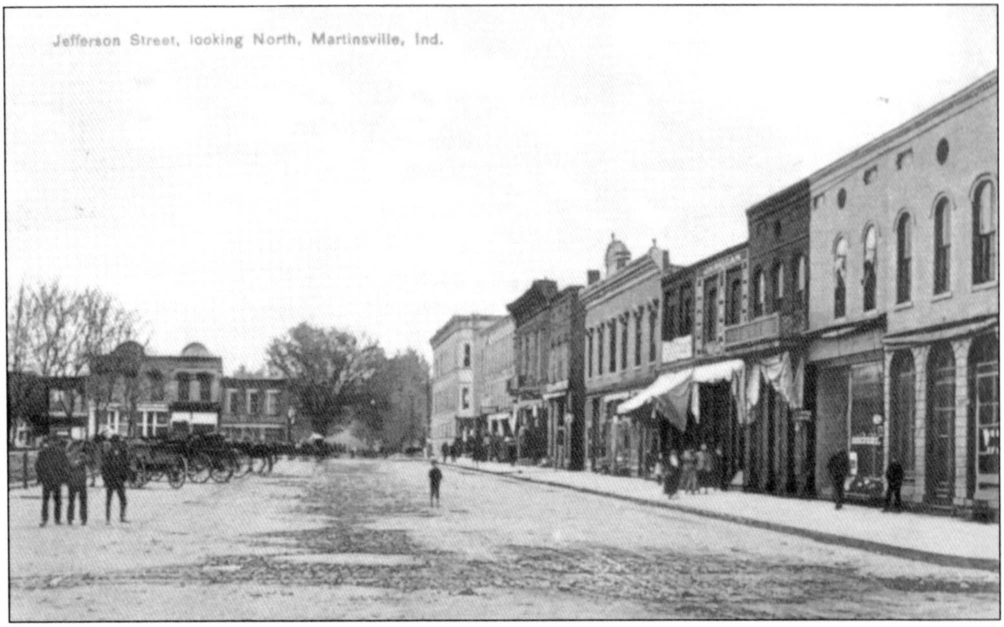

EAST SIDE OF COURTHOUSE SQUARE, JEFFERSON STREET, LOOKING NORTH FROM WASHINGTON STREET, 1909. At the far right is the Singleton building, home of the Martinsville Post Office; much later it was Newberry's department store. The three-story Independent Order of Odd Fellows (IOOF) building at the northeast corner of Morgan and Jefferson Streets is easily picked out. The two buildings at the north end of Jefferson would be extensively remodeled as a bank and Toner's department store, respectively.

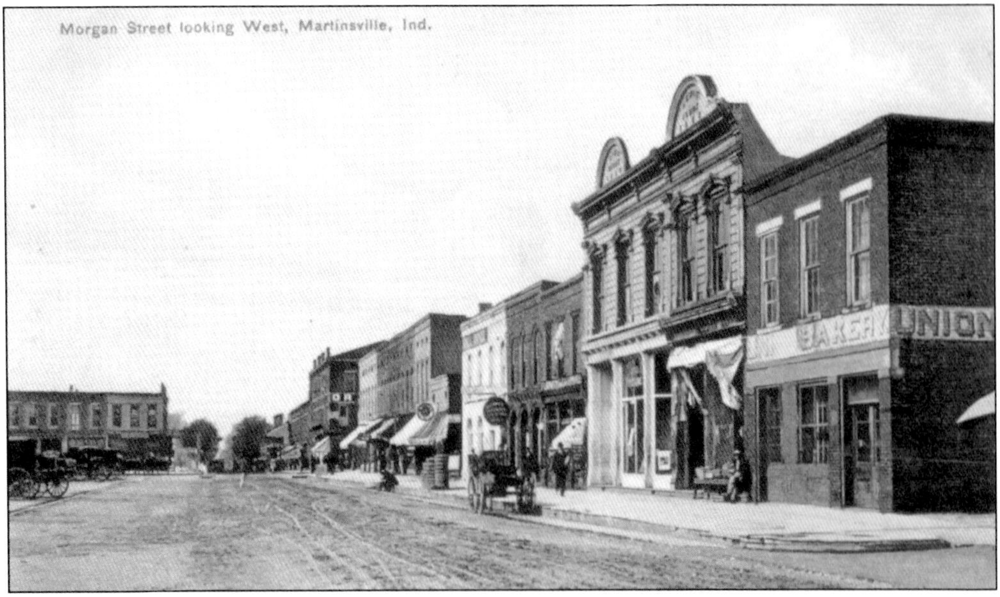

NORTH SIDE OF COURTHOUSE SQUARE, MORGAN STREET, LOOKING WEST FROM JEFFERSON STREET, C. 1908. At near right is Leb Matthews's Union Bakery. Within a few years after this postcard was published, the white building at mid-block was remodeled as Citizens National Bank, which closed during the Depression. At the west end of the block is the Union Block built by Norman T. Cunningham in 1866.

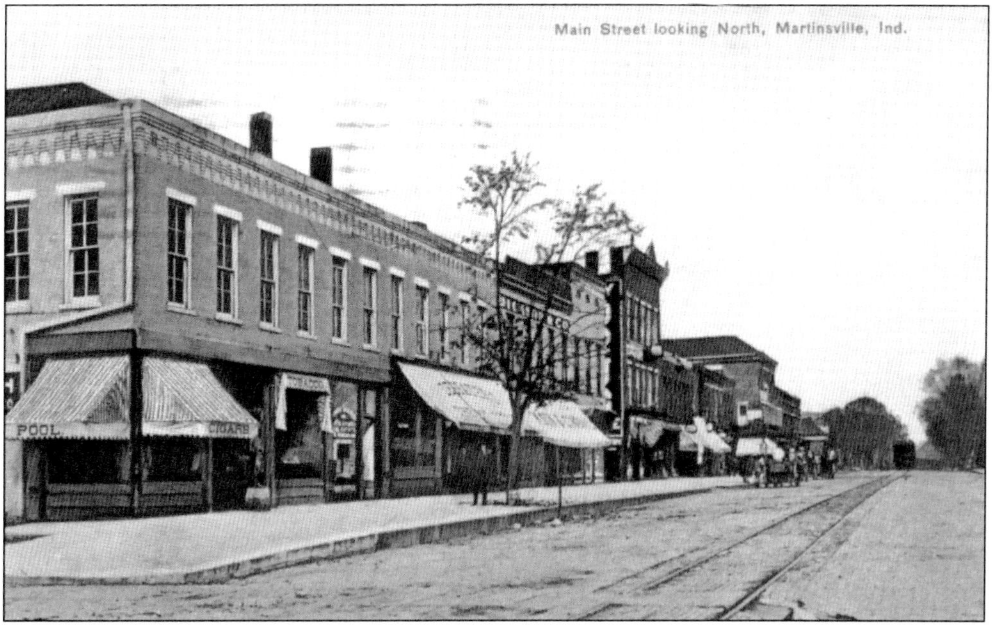

WEST SIDE OF COURTHOUSE SQUARE, MAIN STREET, LOOKING NORTH FROM WASHINGTON STREET, 1908. In the former hotel building on the corner is a pool hall and cigar store and David and Ben Dessauer's clothing store. Dickson's menswear store is behind the tree. The Modern Woodmen of America lodge is on the third floor of the building north of the alley; this floor was later removed. Interurban tracks run down the center of Main Street.

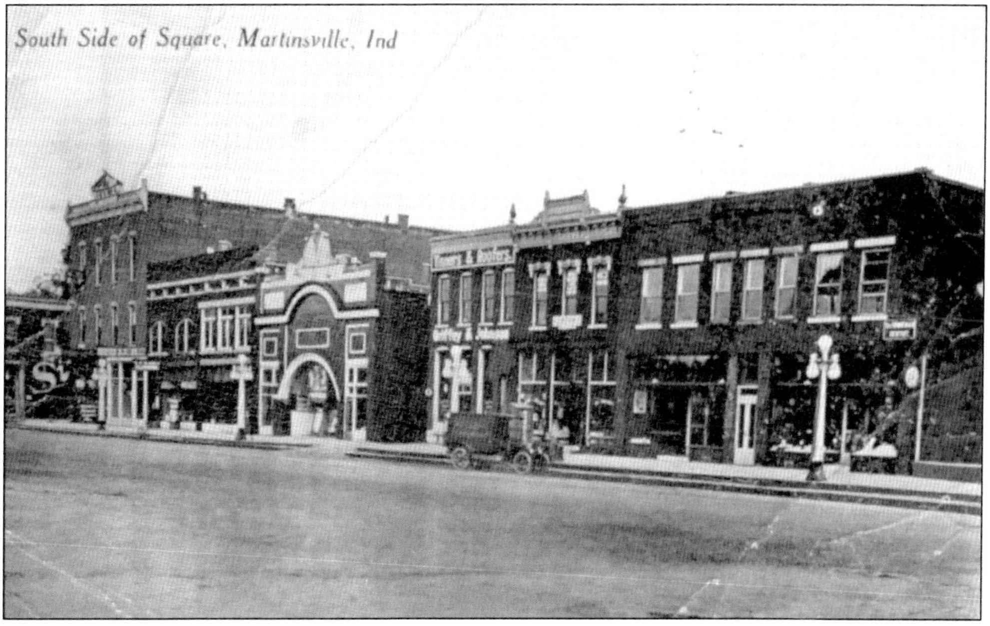

SOUTH SIDE OF COURTHOUSE SQUARE, WASHINGTON STREET, LOOKING EAST FROM MAIN STREET, *C.* 1915. The last to reach full maturity, the south side features the Stevens building at right, built as a private residence about 1847. Just east of the alley, Switow's Dream Theatre, built in 1914, was the finest movie palace of its day. This postcard is among the rarest and most coveted of all known Martinsville views.

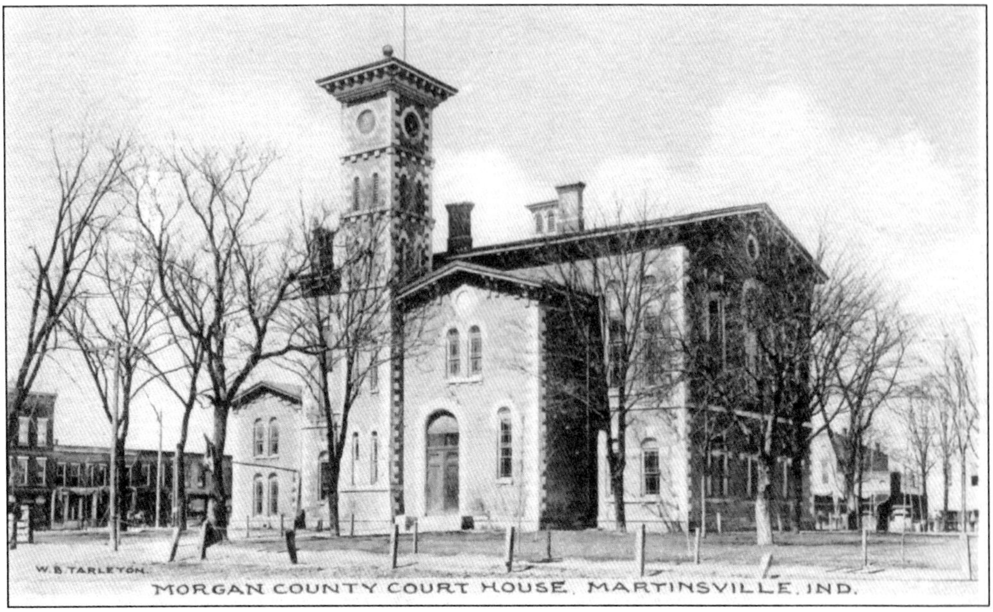

MORGAN COUNTY COURTHOUSE, C. 1906. This undivided-back card shows a very early view of the Italianate courthouse—one of the oldest in the state—built by Perry M. Blankenship between 1857 and 1859. Partial views of Main and Morgan Streets can be seen in the background. This card was published and sold by drugstore owner William B. Tarleton.

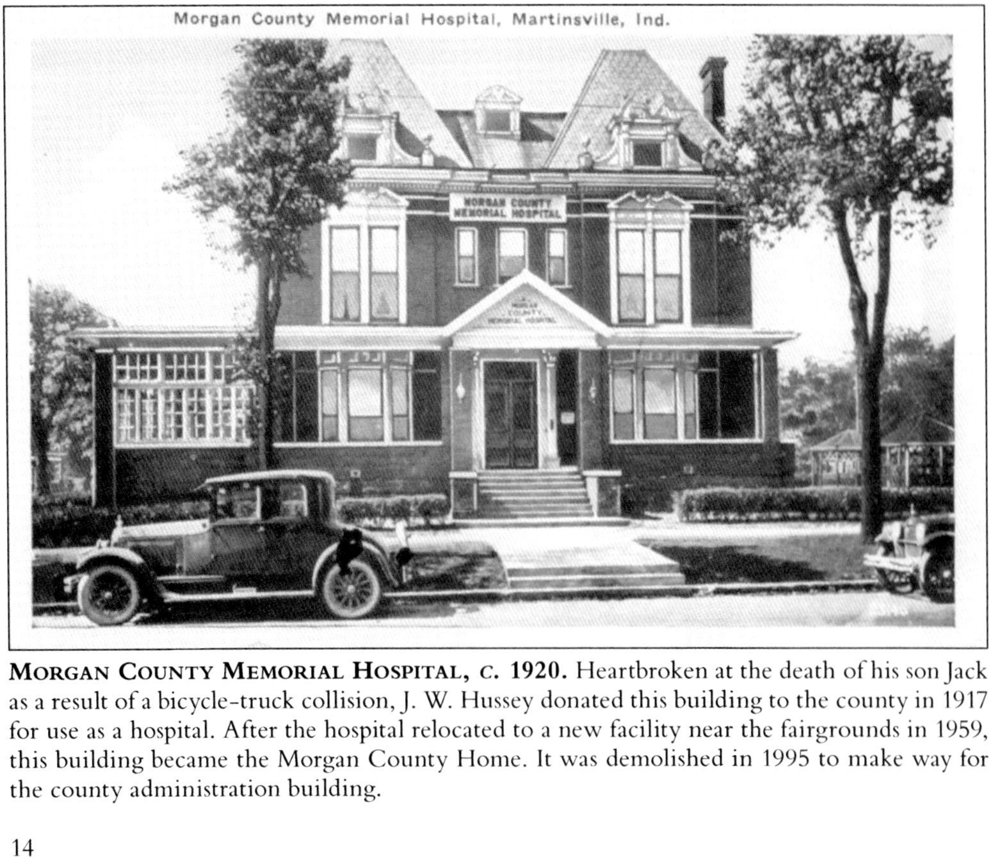

MORGAN COUNTY MEMORIAL HOSPITAL, C. 1920. Heartbroken at the death of his son Jack as a result of a bicycle-truck collision, J. W. Hussey donated this building to the county in 1917 for use as a hospital. After the hospital relocated to a new facility near the fairgrounds in 1959, this building became the Morgan County Home. It was demolished in 1995 to make way for the county administration building.

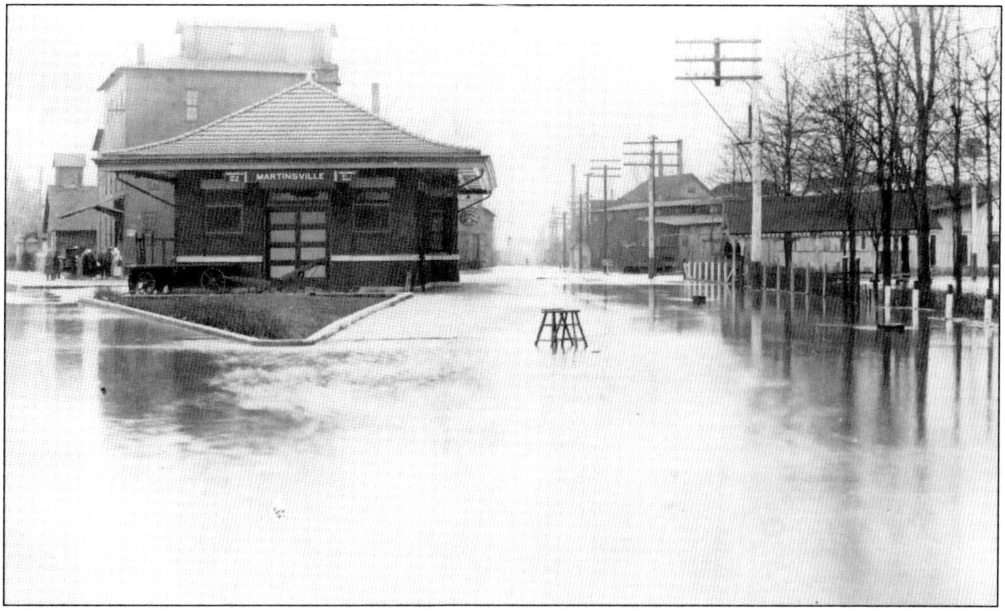

VANDALIA DEPOT, 1913. The flood of 1913 submerged Martinsville's low-lying northwest side. Here is a view of Marion Street (at left) and the Vandalia Railroad looking south. Towering above the depot is Branch Grain and Seed Company. The open structure at right is the train wait station belonging to the Martinsville Sanitarium. Behind it, one block to the south, is Barnard Sanitarium.

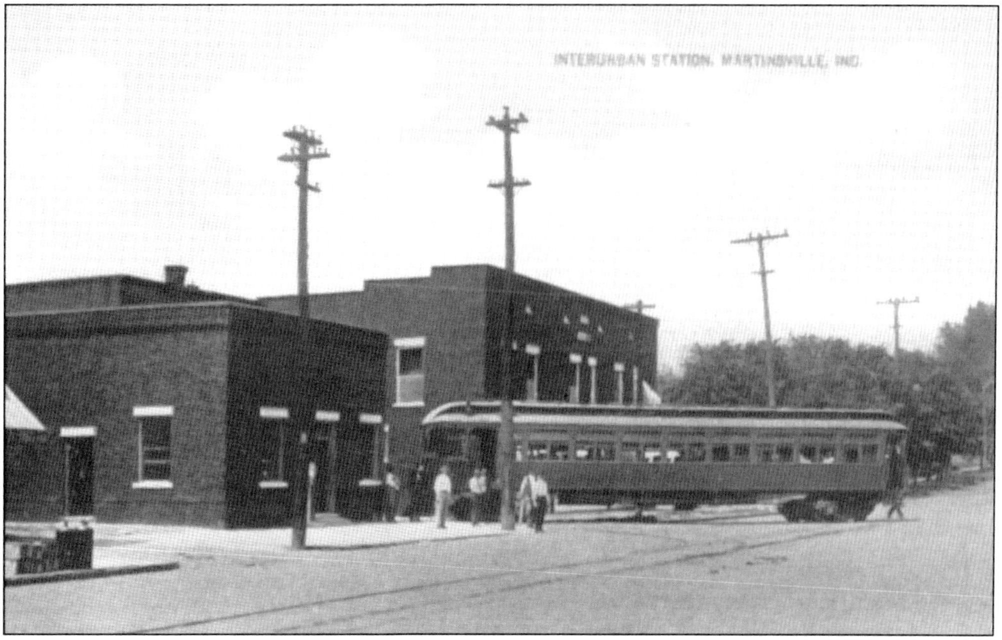

INTERURBAN STATION, *c.* 1915. A familiar sight in Martinsville between 1902 and 1930 was the electricity-powered interurban pulling in and out of its berth on North Main Street. Passengers and freight could reach the state capitol in record time, at speeds approaching 40–50 miles per hour. The brick building at left is the ticket and wait station. The Eslinger Hotel is behind the car.

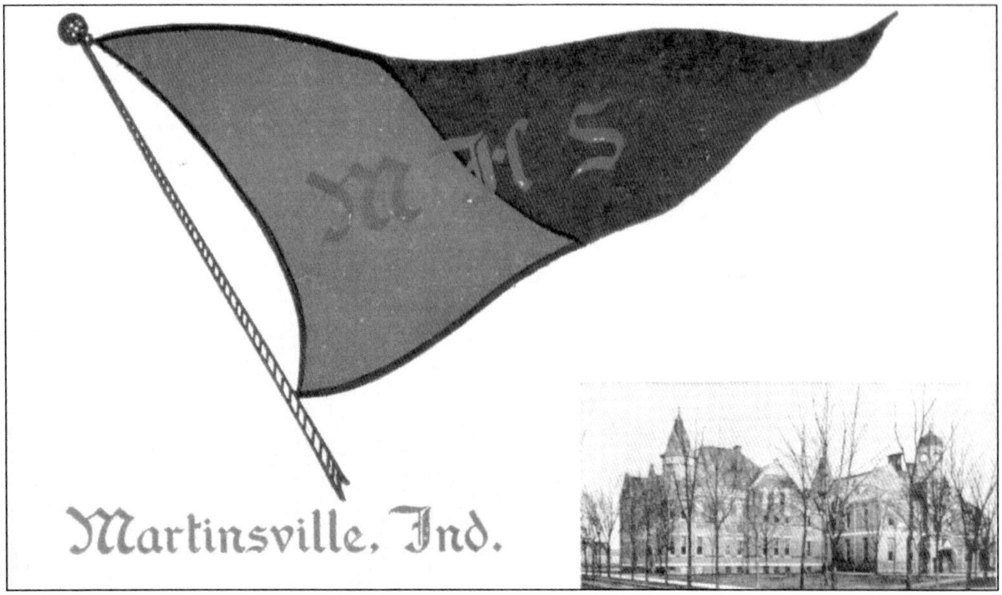

OLD MARTINSVILLE HIGH SCHOOL ON PENNANT CARD, 1910. Occupying the current site of Central School, this high school was replaced in 1913 by the building shown below. Irvin Paul, a 1910 graduate and the sender of this card published by Fuselman's News Stand, writes to the J. W. Throckmorton family of Franklin, "Dear Relatives: For your beautiful gift I thank you more than I can tell you."

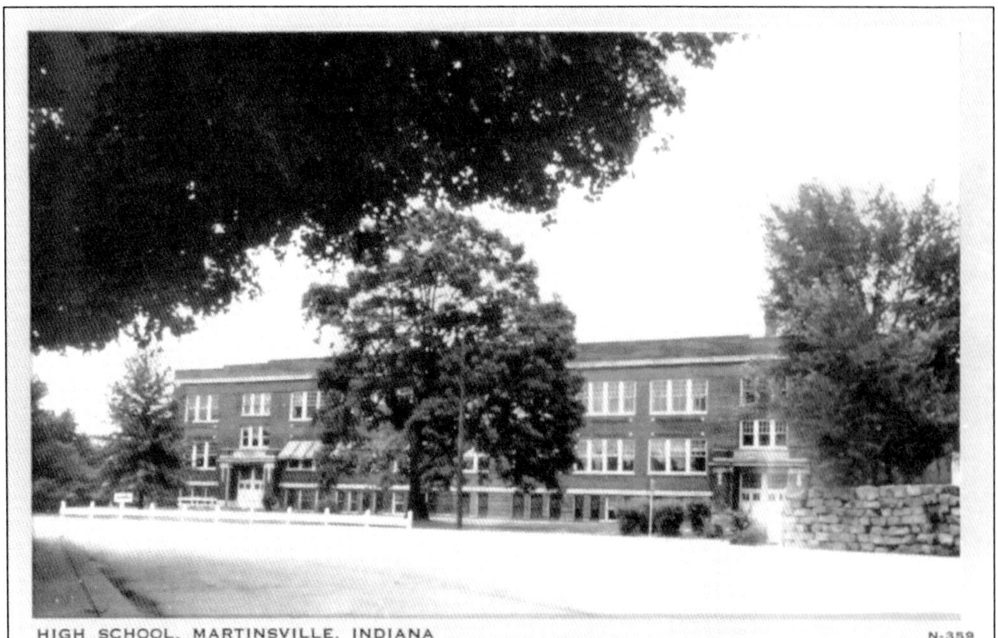

NEW MARTINSVILLE HIGH SCHOOL, *C.* 1940. Anchoring the corner of Main and Garfield Streets, this neoclassical-style building was in use from 1913 to December 1976. A 5,000-seat basketball gymnasium was completed in 1924. Although the gymnasium remains as a local landmark, the high school was demolished in 1978. This card is an example of the silver-border cards produced by the Wayne Paper Box and Printing Corporation of Fort Wayne.

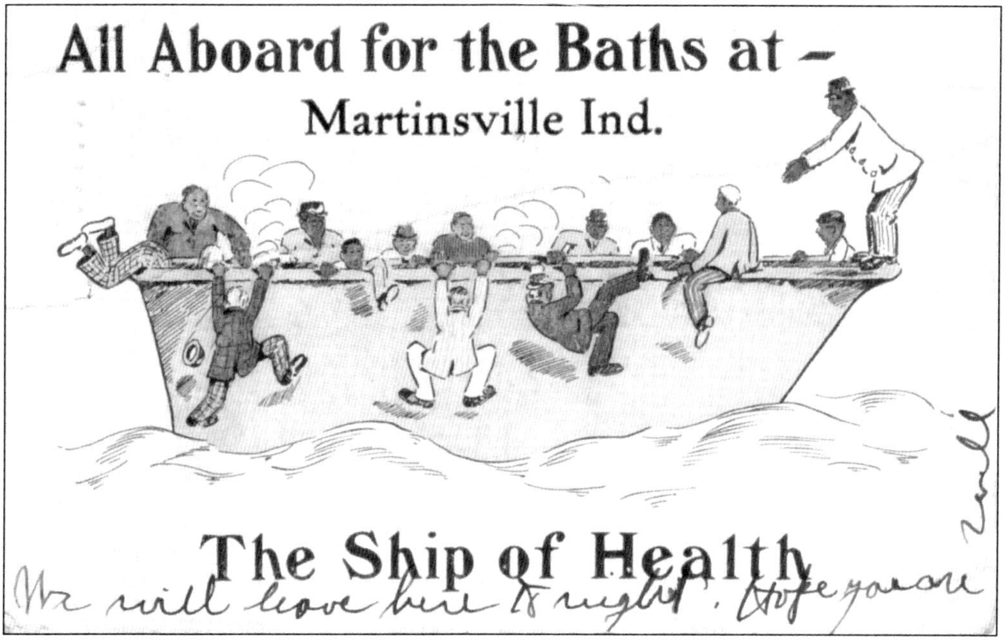

ALL ABOARD FOR THE BATHS, *C.* 1906. Martinsville was famous for its sanitariums in operation from 1888 to 1968. Water was discovered by accident in 1882. Within 20 years, a dozen spas were attracting guests from across the country. Closings accelerated during the 1940s and 1950s as it became evident that the water's health benefits were not as miraculous as once believed.

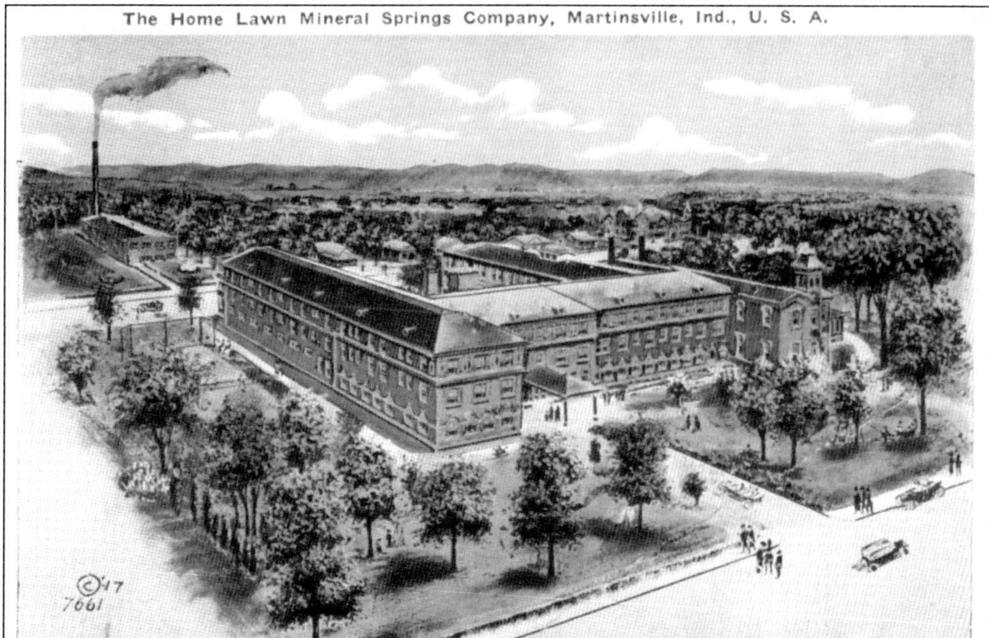

HOME LAWN SANITARIUM, 1917. Located on East Washington Street, the Home Lawn was Martinsville's largest and finest sanitarium. Established in 1889, it was owned by the Walter Kennedy family from 1918 until it closed in 1968. "Am feeling much better," this card's sender writes. "Think the baths are wonderful and the eats so good. Ed would not have to worry about my appetite now."

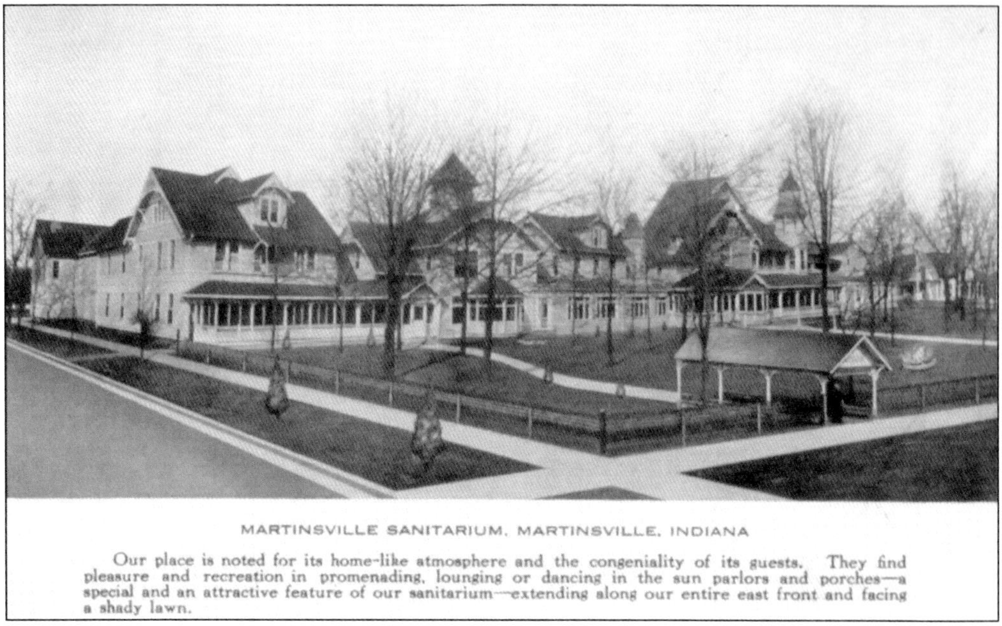

MARTINSVILLE SANITARIUM, *C.* 1915. Established on West Harrison Street in 1898 when two neighboring sanitariums merged, the Martinsville Sanitarium was purchased by Walter Kennedy in 1916. An ambitious expansion was completed in 1926. Kennedy donated the sanitarium in 1957 to the Disciples of Christ for use as a senior residential care center. The caption on the back of this card reads, "Mineral Baths—A health and pleasure resort, where Rheumatism Meets its Waterloo."

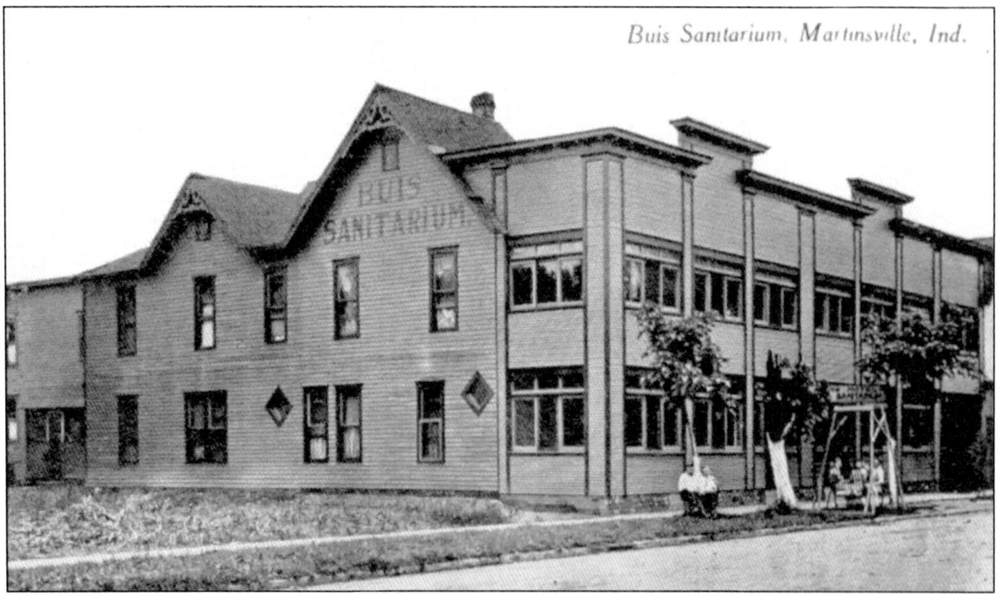

BUIS SANITARIUM, *C.* 1915. The Buis Sanitarium operated for a mere four years, from 1915 to 1919, at the southeast corner of Pike and Marion Streets. In 1920, it reopened as the Southern Sanitarium catering to the black servants of white sanitarium guests. Local opposition led to its closure six years later. The building was then demolished. This postcard is rare and commands a high price whenever it surfaces at auction.

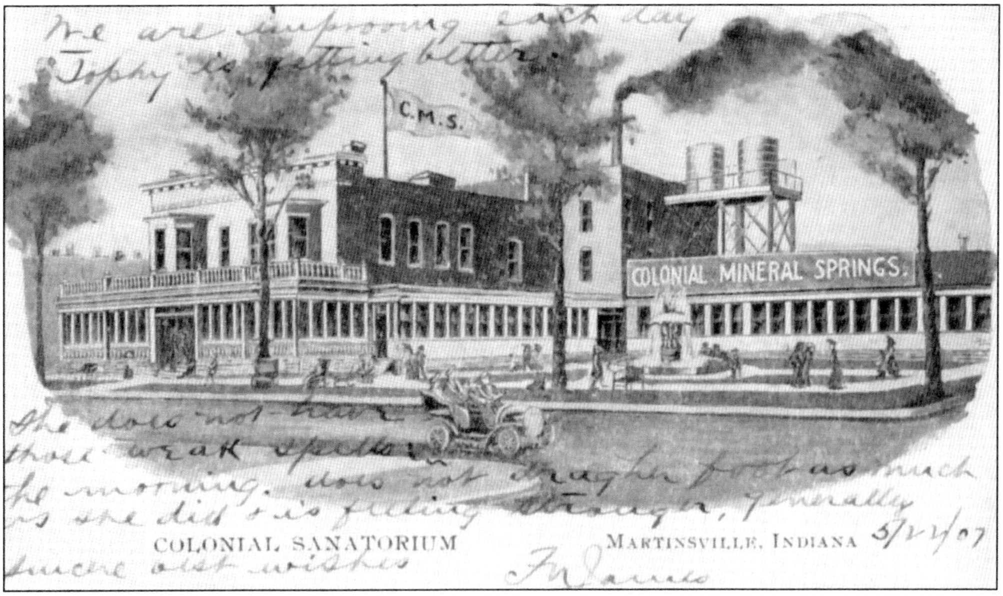

COLONIAL SANITARIUM, 1907. HomeBank occupies the former West Washington Street site of the Colonial Sanitarium, completed in 1906. The sanitarium was sold and renamed several times before finally closing in 1962. It was razed the following year. The sender's message appears on the front of this early undivided-back postcard.

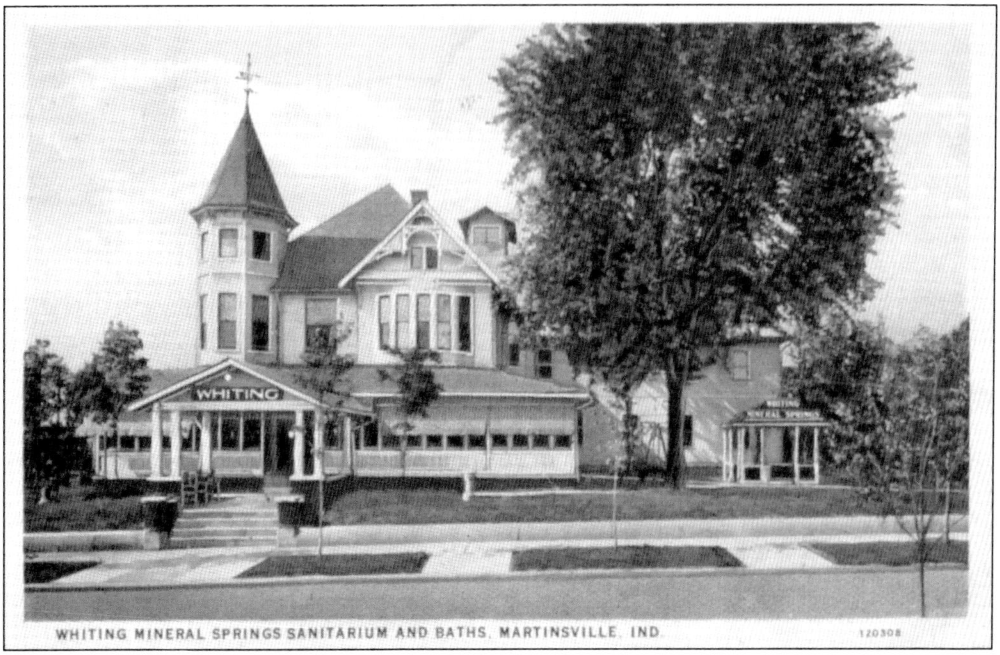

WHITING SANITARIUM, 1928. About this West Harrison Street sanitarium, in business from 1923 to 1949, the sender complains, "The picture does not represent the place I am confined. I am at a dilapidated and pretty monotonous place as yet. . . . Drinking of this mineral water does me good as it does many people. This small town is not much known in Gary—Perhaps some profession is against it. When I mentioned it to the Dr. I was the recipient of a derisive laugh. But I am going to recommend it to those who are similarly afflicted."

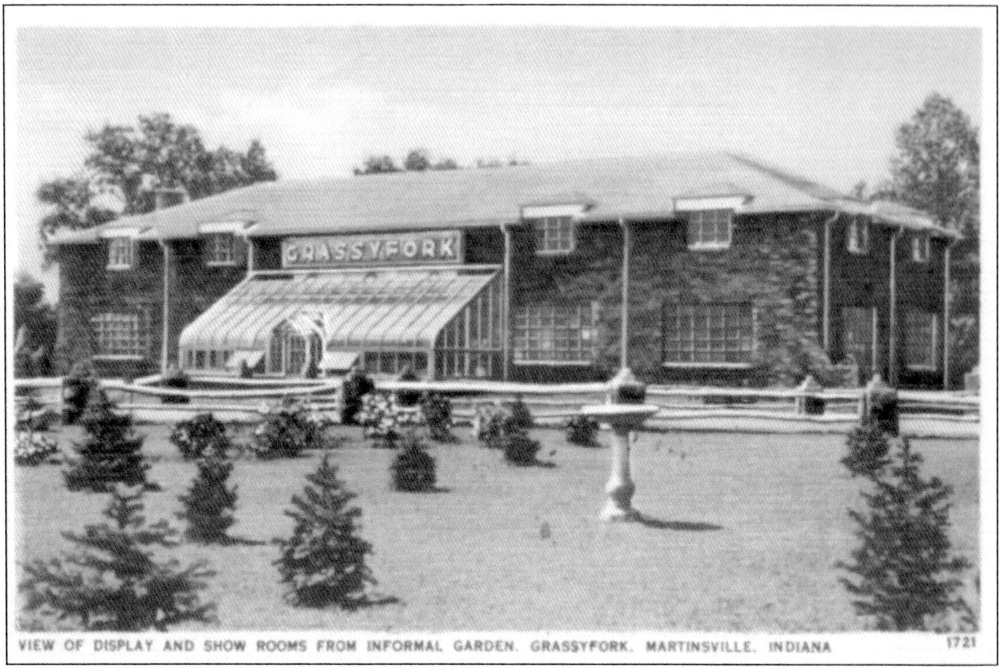

GRASSYFORK FISHERIES, *c.* 1940. What began with Eugene Shireman's inheritance of swampy farmland became by World War II the largest producer of goldfish in the world. Grassyfork, located on the Dixie Highway (now East Morgan Street), was one of Martinsville's most significant industries. The beauty of the landscaped grounds and surrounding ponds attracted hundreds of visitors out for a drive in the country.

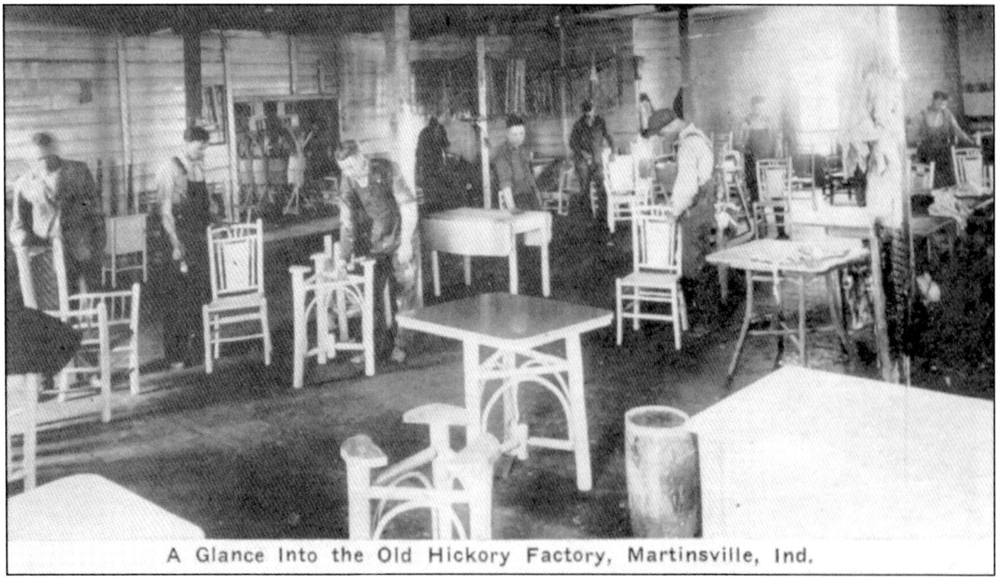

OLD HICKORY FURNITURE COMPANY, *c.* 1920. Old Hickory (1898–1978) was the major manufacturer of Indiana rustic hickory chairs and other furniture. Its Cherry Street factory employed several generations of Martinsville residents. Today the popularity of Martinsville-made Old Hickory pieces is tremendous, and collectors (like postcard collectors) are willing to pay premium prices for hard-to-find items.

Two

Mooresville

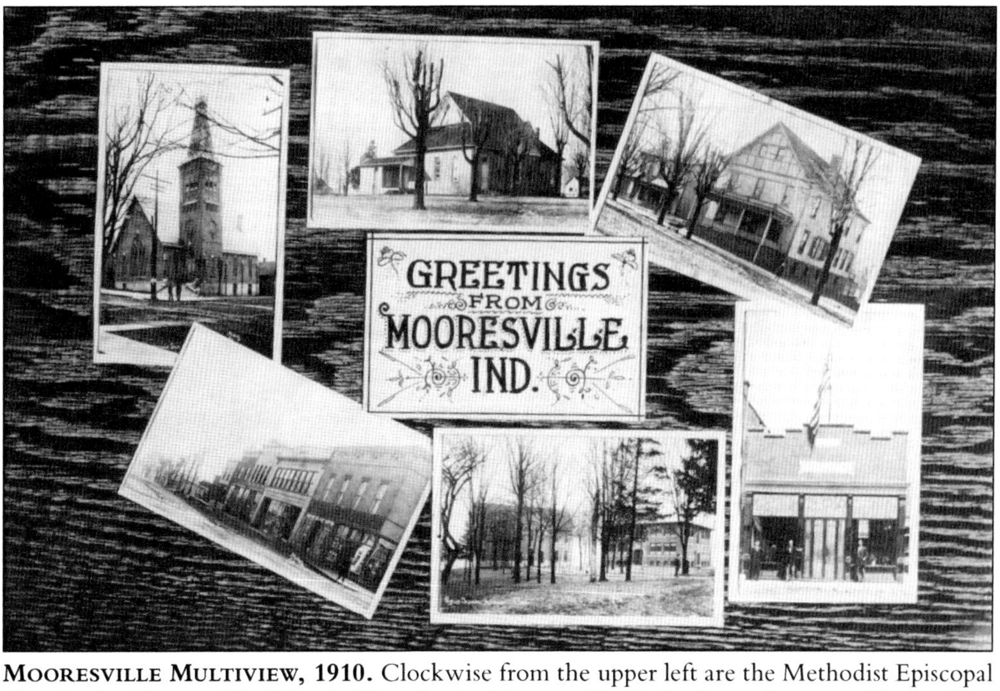

Mooresville Multiview, 1910. Clockwise from the upper left are the Methodist Episcopal church, the Mooresville Friends Church, the Mooresville Sanitarium, the post office on East Main Street built in 1909, the old and new public schools, and the south side of Main Street looking east from Indiana Street.

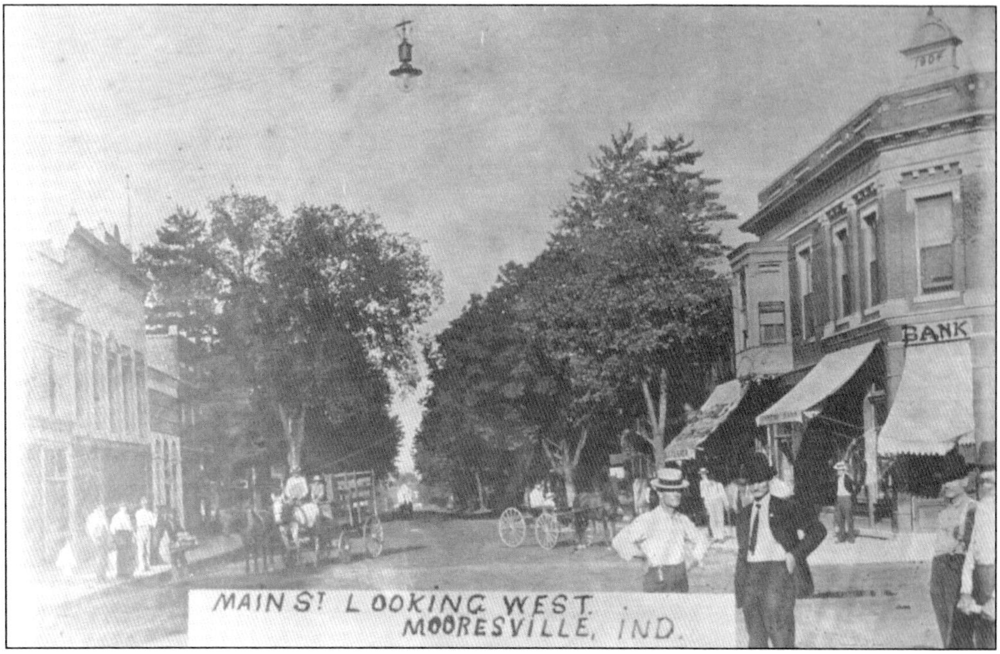

Main Street, Looking West from Indiana Street, 1912. A single electric light illuminates the main intersection. The roads are not yet paved, but new concrete sidewalks offer a convenience to pedestrians. At right is Farmers State Bank, built in 1873 and remodeled to the appearance above in 1904. The buildings at left are better seen in the two postcards that follow.

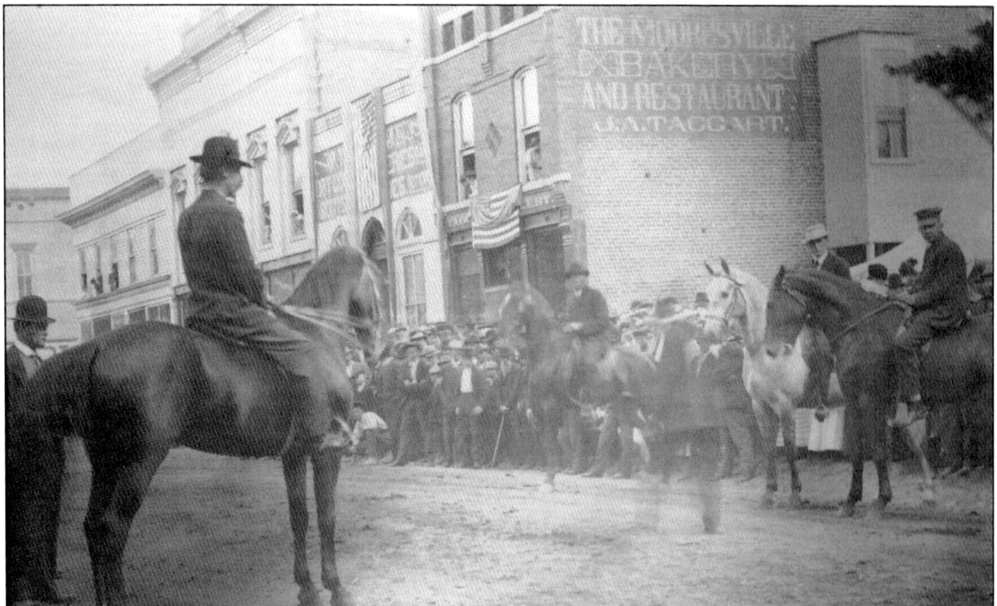

J. A. Taggart's Bakery, West Main Street, c. 1910. John A. Taggart, a native of the Isle of Man, and his wife Lena established a bakery in Mooresville in 1888. Eight years later, they moved into this new two-story brick building, now 15 West Main Street. It has been a bakery and/or eating establishment throughout its history. Nothing is known about the event onlookers have gathered to see.

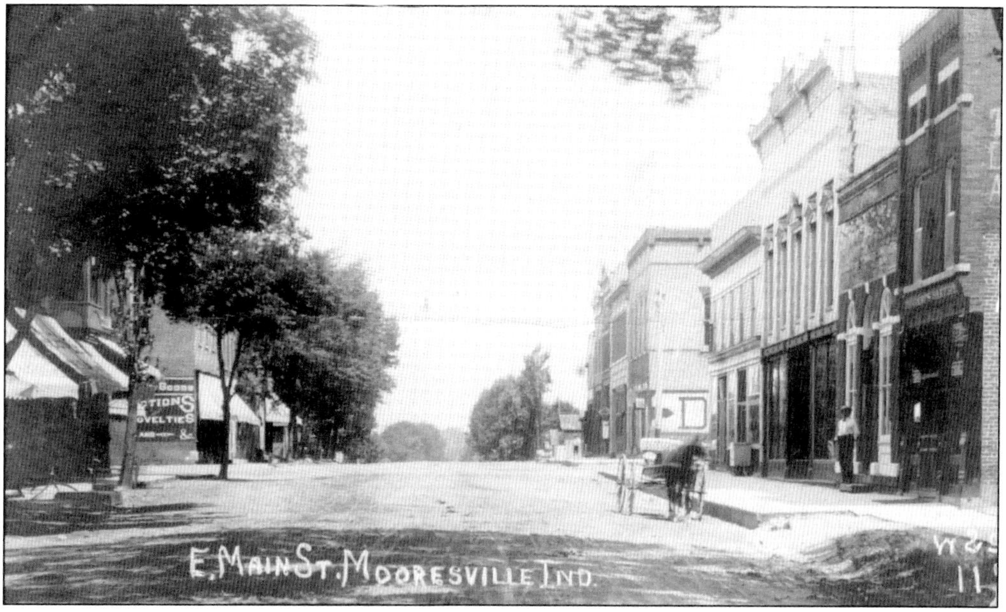

Main Street, Looking East, c. 1910. At near right is Taggart's Bakery. Then, in order from west to east, are Pace Thompson's dry goods store, the undertaking and furniture business of Frank E. Carlisle and Daniel Gilbert, and the frame Lindley Block, which burned on December 27, 1925. Across Indiana Street is George Bass's drugstore. The sign painted on the building at left center identifies Pleas Mills's dry goods store.

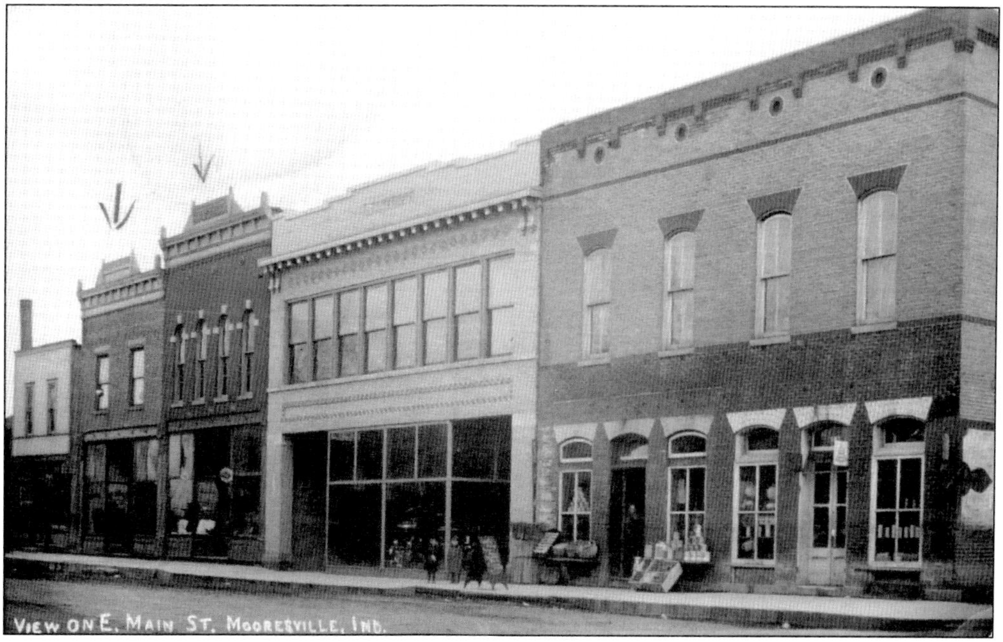

South Side of Main Street, Looking East from Indiana Street, 1908. George Scruggs sent this postcard to Mrs. S. Scruggs in O'Fallon, Illinois, with this message: "The buildings with the arrows are the ones we do business in." Scruggs owned and operated a dry goods store here from 1891 to 1921. The G. A. Keller hardware store is at center. Burch Grocery and Bass Drugstore occupy the building in the foreground.

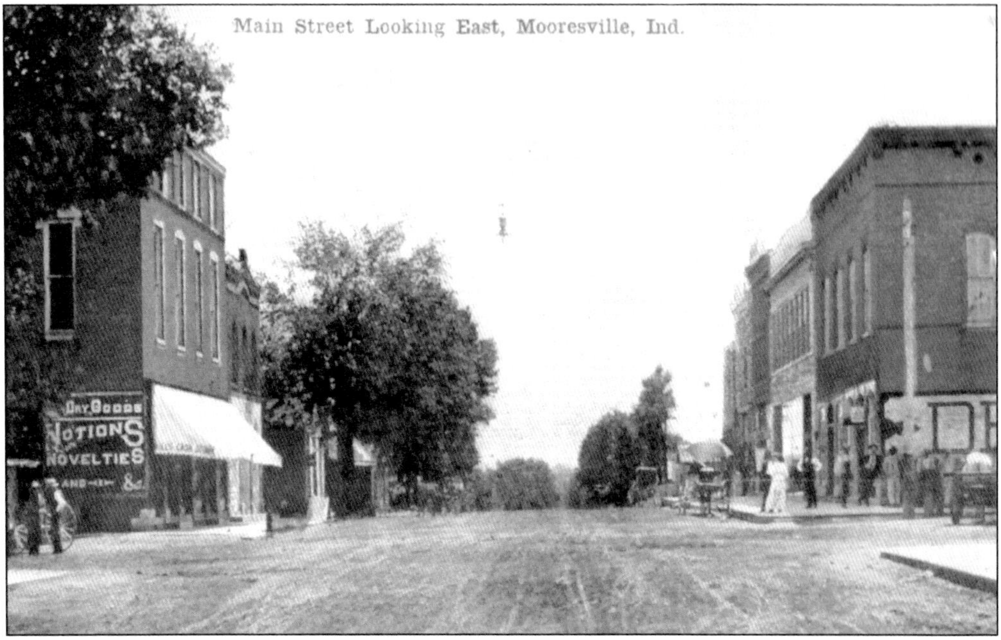

MAIN STREET, LOOKING EAST FROM INDIANA STREET, C. 1910. At left is Pleas Mills's dry goods store. When built around 1870, this building had three floors; the topmost was the IOOF lodge. The sender of this card wrote in August 1910, "We are going to have Old Settlers here Tuesday 9th. Better come down. We have great times down here at Old Settlers. We even have a merry-go-round. Lots of fun."

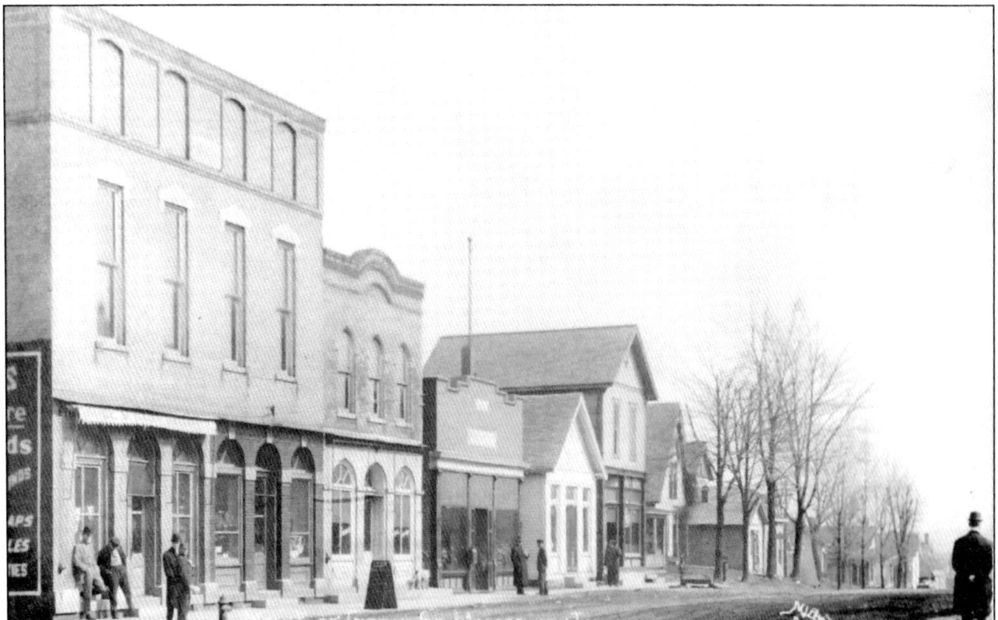

NORTH SIDE OF MAIN STREET, LOOKING EAST FROM INDIANA STREET, C. 1915. East of Mills's dry goods store on the corner—a sunny spot for loafers—is a pool hall and the new Mooresville Post Office, built in 1909 by James L. Matthews. Sam Wade replaced the gable-front frame buildings with the existing brick storefronts between 1925 and 1946.

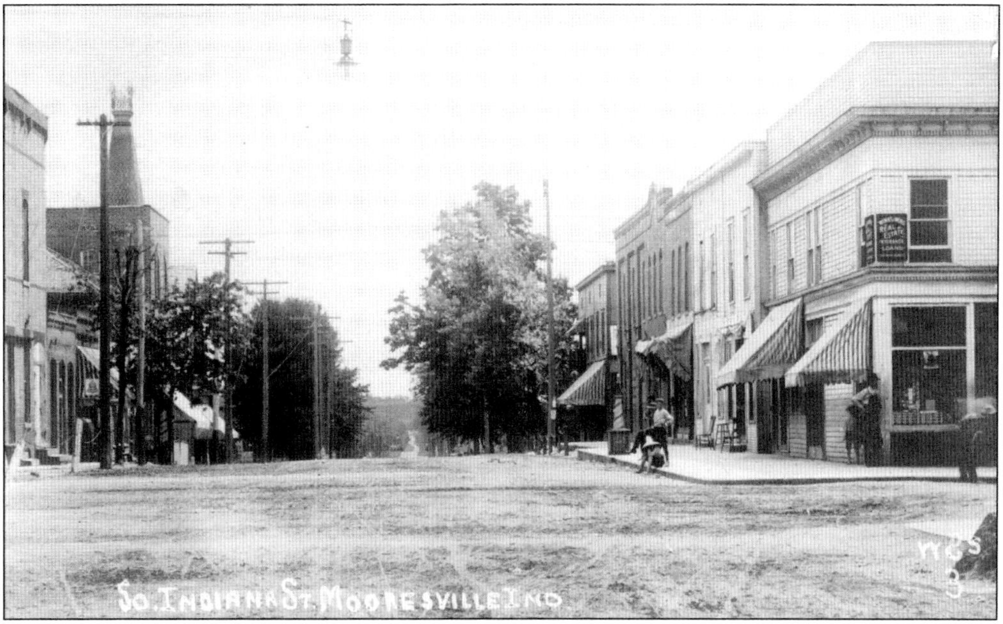

Indiana Street, Looking South from Main Street, c. 1910. A sign on the second story of the Lindley Block at front right advertises the real estate and insurance business of Orlando Winks and Benjamin Wing. In the white frame building to the south is a barbershop; a barber pole is found on the sidewalk out front. Across the street, the telephone exchange occupies the second floor of the three-story building partially hidden by the tree.

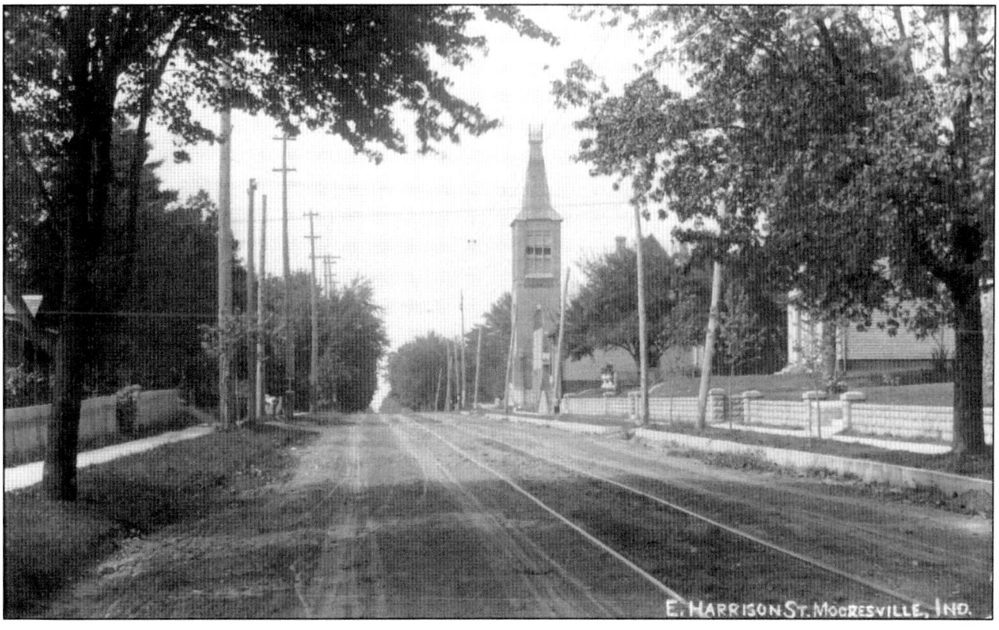

Harrison Street, Looking West from Clay Street, c. 1910. The Methodist Episcopal Church steeple dominates this scene. Some of the cottages at the right were removed and replaced by the church's educational annex. The block wall remains, however, marking the location of the home and gallery of photographer Jarvis P. (J. P.) Calvert. Note the interurban tracks running down the center of Harrison Street.

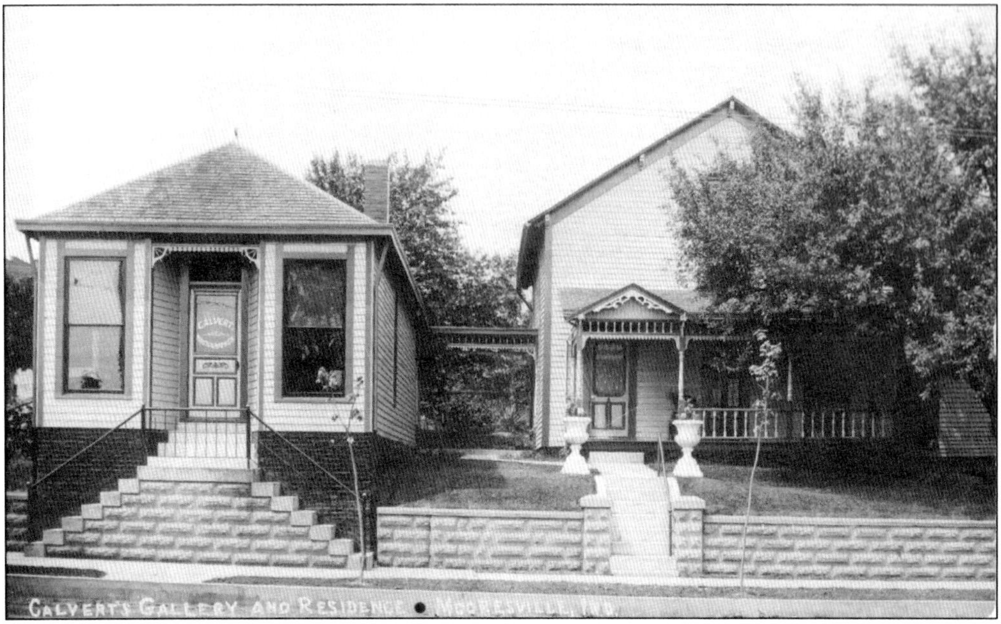

J. P. CALVERT'S GALLERY AND RESIDENCE, WEST HARRISON STREET, *c.* 1910. Active in Mooresville from 1867 to 1917, J. P. Calvert used this real-photo postcard for advertising. On the reverse is printed, "Accept my compliments and best wishes for your future welfare and sometime when you are feeling fine come again and have an excellent portrait of yourself made. J. P. Calvert. The photographer in your town."

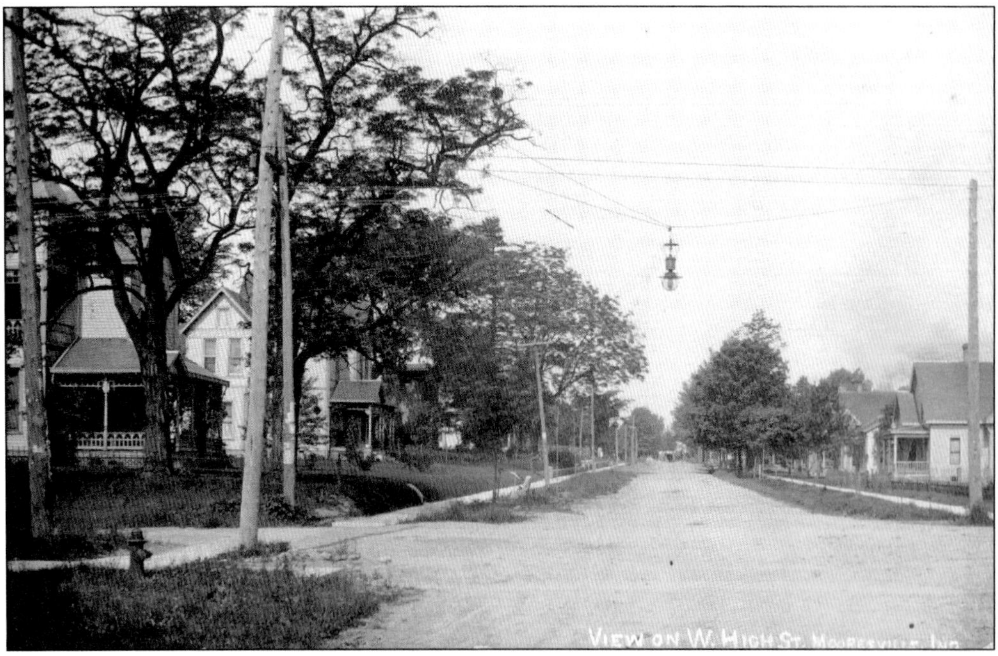

HIGH STREET, LOOKING WEST FROM INDIANA STREET, *c.* 1910. At the near left is the home of Alonzo Wheeler, father of the noted Indiana artist Clifton Wheeler. A mural painted by Clifton remains on an interior wall. The modest cottages on the north side of High Street were replaced by more imposing residences in the decade after Calvert took this photograph.

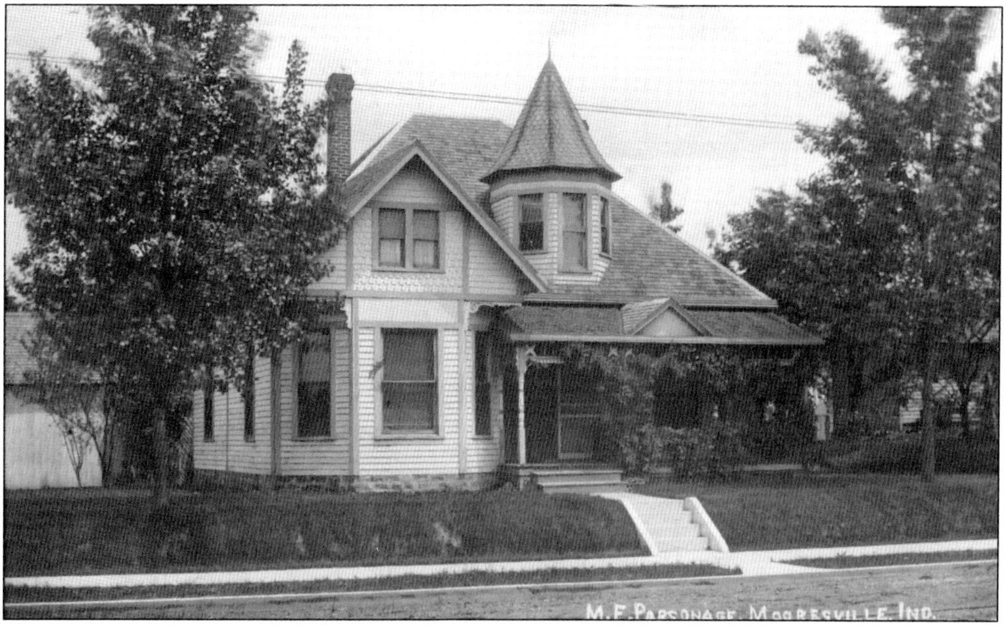

METHODIST EPISCOPAL PARSONAGE, 1909. The home of the Methodist Episcopal minister and his family, this demure Queen Anne cottage stood—and still stands—at the northeast corner of West Harrison and Jefferson Streets, one block west of the church. It was built about 1895. Across Harrison Street, directly opposite the parsonage, is the Christian church shown in the postcard below.

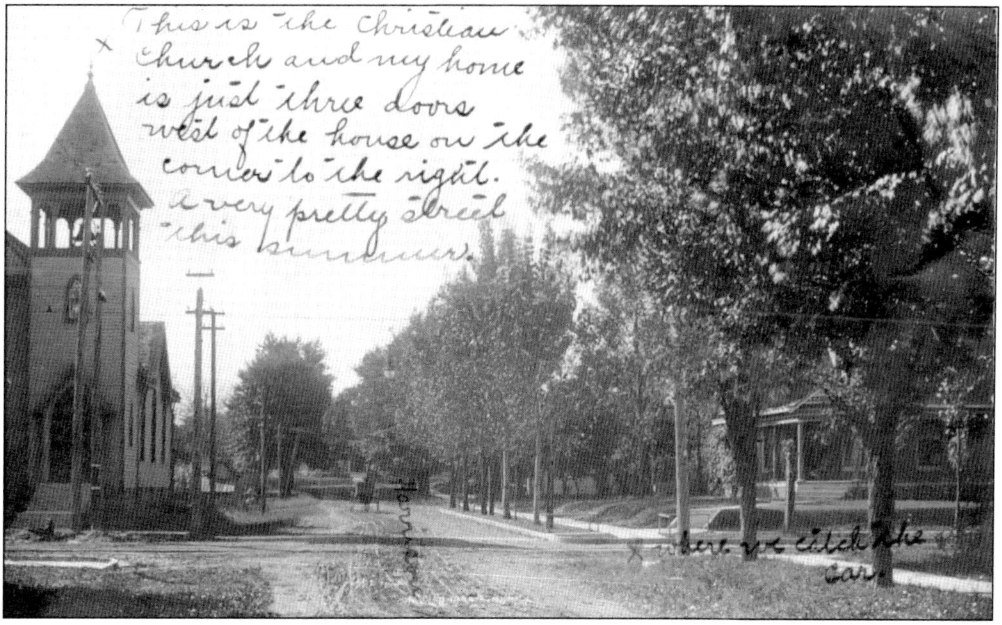

JEFFERSON STREET, LOOKING SOUTH FROM HARRISON STREET, C. 1910. The interurban power station was located on Harrison Street about two blocks west of this intersection. An *X* marks the spot where the writer catches the car. "This is the Christian church," she informs the recipient of this card, "and my home is just three doors west of the house on the corner to the right. A very pretty street this summer."

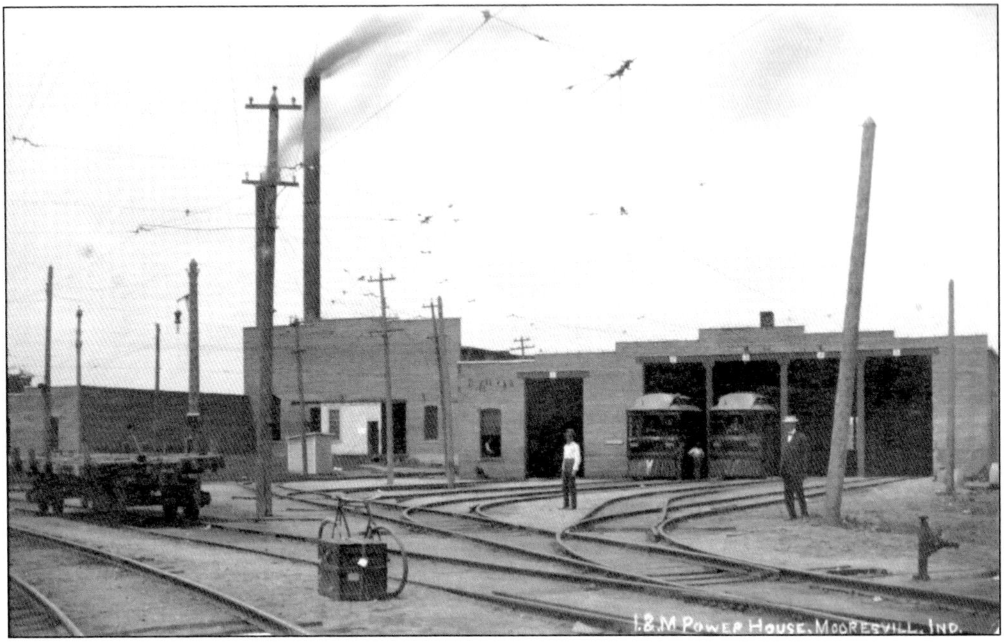

INTERURBAN POWERHOUSE, 1907. Located on Harrison Street just east of White Lick Creek were the power station, carbarn, shop, and storeroom of the Indianapolis and Martinsville line of the Terre Haute, Indianapolis, and Eastern Traction Company (THI&ET). The first Indianapolis–Mooresville run occurred in 1902; a year later, the first Mooresville–Martinsville run was made. Discontinuation of the line in 1930 was precipitated by a loss of revenue blamed on competition by buses and automobiles.

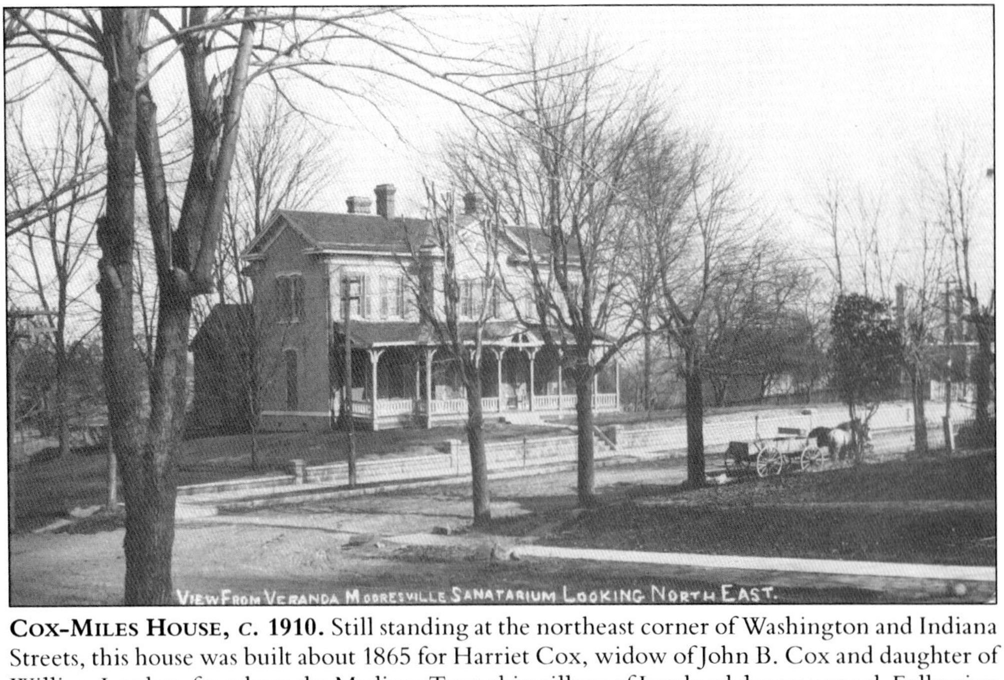

COX-MILES HOUSE, *c.* 1910. Still standing at the northeast corner of Washington and Indiana Streets, this house was built about 1865 for Harriet Cox, widow of John B. Cox and daughter of William Landers, for whom the Madison Township village of Landersdale was named. Following her death in 1911, it became the home of Jefferson Miles and later his son, Louis.

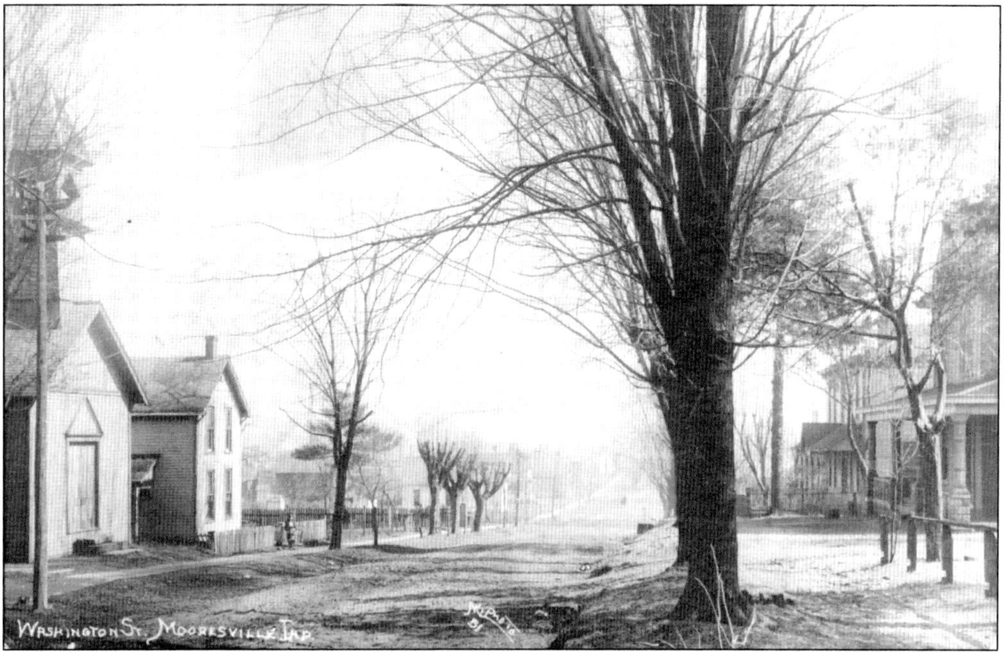

WASHINGTON STREET, ONE-HALF BLOCK EAST OF INDIANA STREET, 1912. Only the Fogleman house, built for John and Mary Fogleman in 1872 and seen at far right, remains today to identify this view. The church at near left was built in 1896 as the Methodist Protestant church.

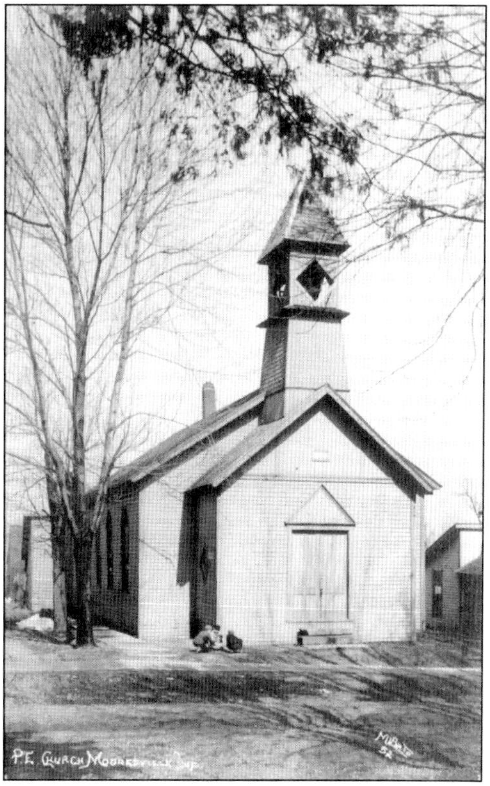

METHODIST PROTESTANT CHURCH, *c.* 1915. In 1940, the Methodist Protestant congregation was reorganized as Calvary Methodist. Ten years later it disbanded. The church building was torn down in 1969 and replaced with the existing building at 40 East Washington Street occupied by New Life in Christ Church.

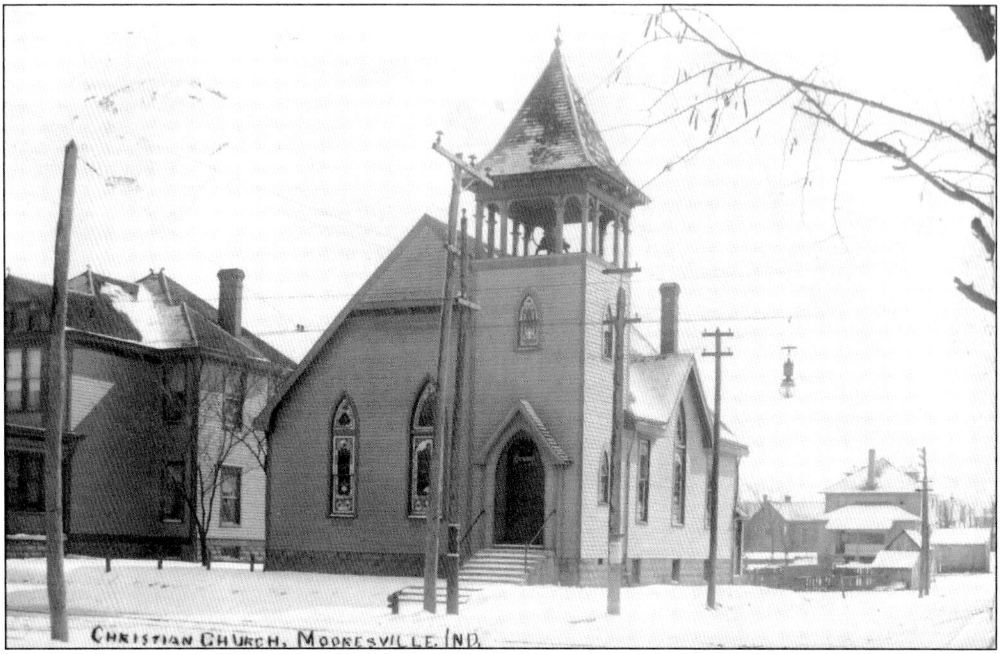

CHRISTIAN CHURCH, 1910. Dedicated in 1904, this modest Gothic Revival worship center at the southeast corner of Harrison and Jefferson Streets was built with funds raised from revivals, sewing bees, dinners, and bake sales put on by church women, as well as faith-filled private donations. Fifty years later, the congregation moved into a new church building on North Indiana Street.

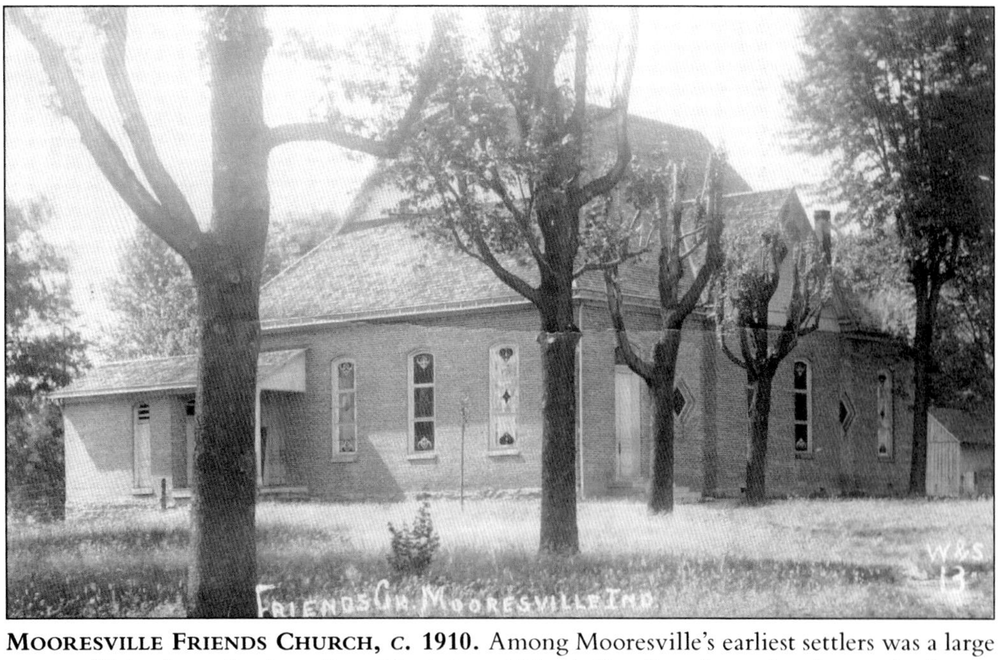

MOORESVILLE FRIENDS CHURCH, *c.* 1910. Among Mooresville's earliest settlers was a large group of Friends, or Quakers, from Virginia and North Carolina. Several early meetinghouses in outlying areas served these believers until 1869–1870, when this meetinghouse was built at the corner of Main and Monroe Streets. It remains in use today.

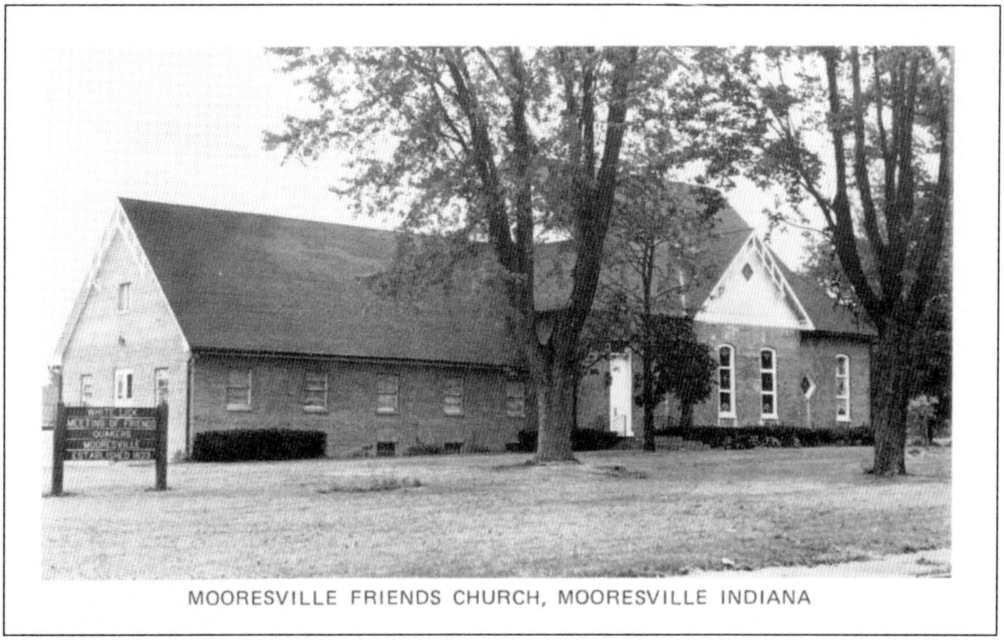

FRIENDS CHURCH ANNEX, *c.* 1960. The original brick meetinghouse received its first addition in 1893. In 1955, the large social and educational annex shown at left was completed. The classrooms, library, stage and dressing rooms, kitchen and dining room, and original parlor and office rooms have served the Mooresville Friends well until the present day.

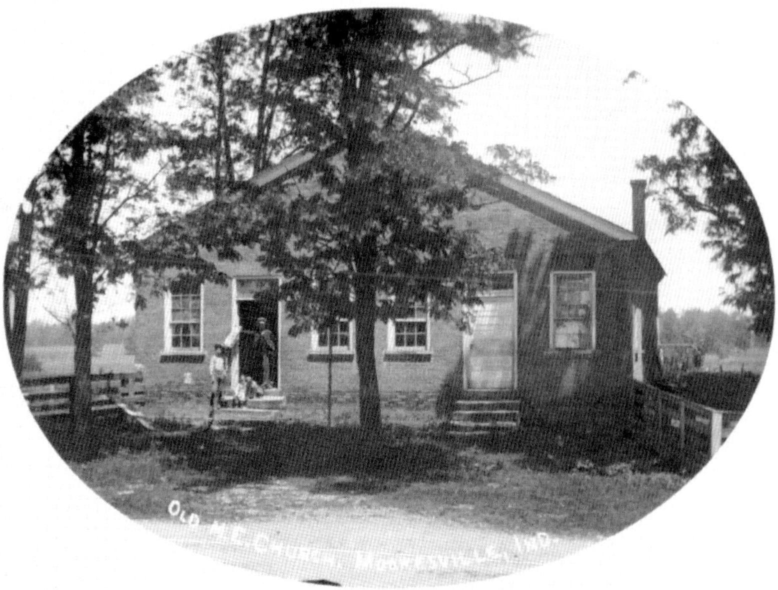

OLD METHODIST EPISCOPAL CHURCH, 1908. Once located on the site of the old Mooresville town cemetery on West Washington Street, this brick and timber church was used from 1839 to 1883. The congregation was organized in 1821 and served by circuit riders until 1855, when it received its first resident minister. The cemetery's earliest burial occurred in 1829. The interment of Mooresville founder Samuel Moore, who died in 1889, was the last.

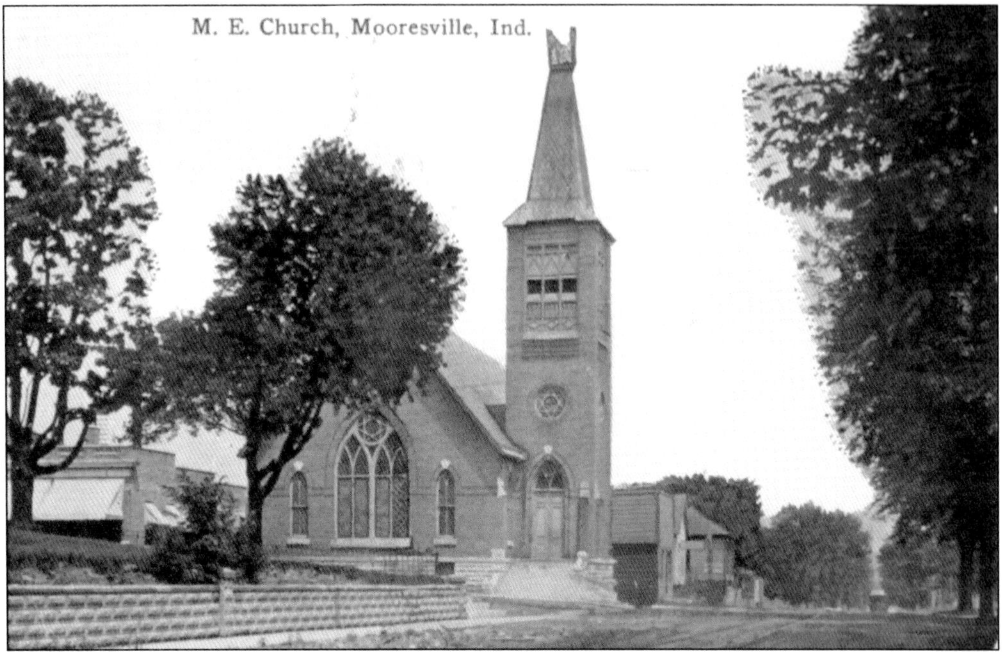

Methodist Episcopal Church, 1914. The tall steeple and Gothic pointed windows of the Methodist Episcopal church reflect the believer's yearning for God. The cornerstone was laid in April 1882, with dedication following in February 1883. An annex stretching east along the north side of Harrison Street was completed in 1924.

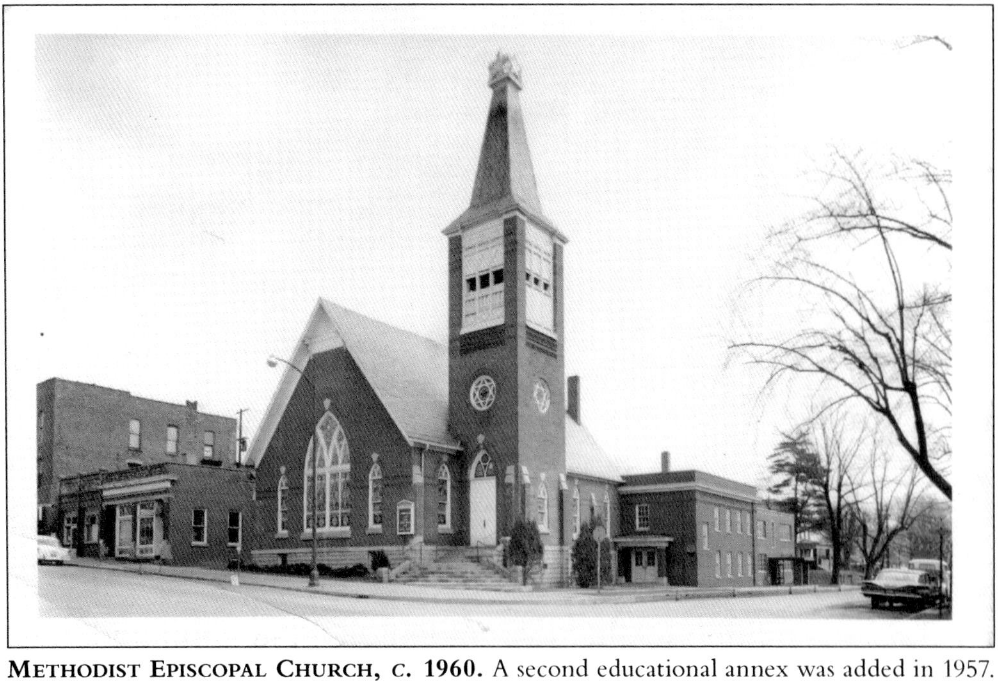

Methodist Episcopal Church, c. 1960. A second educational annex was added in 1957. After the Methodists moved into a new church complex on Indianapolis Road in 2001, the Town of Mooresville purchased the landmark building and renovated it for use as the Mooresville Government Center. A dedication ceremony and public reception was held in 2006.

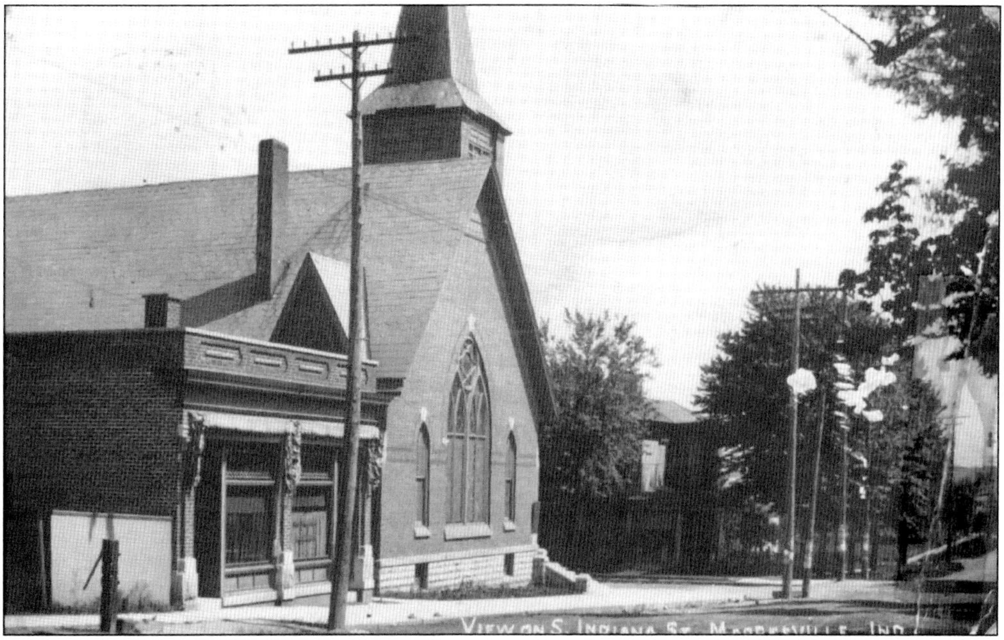

NORTHEAST CORNER OF INDIANA AND HARRISON STREETS, *C.* 1909. North of the church is the office of Dr. William L. Thompson, built in 1907. Across Harrison Street to the south is the James L. Matthews house, which in 1931 became a funeral home operated by Elmer F. Harvey. It was here in 1934 that the funeral of John Dillinger was held. Thousands of people wanting a glimpse of the famous gangster formed a line that circled the block.

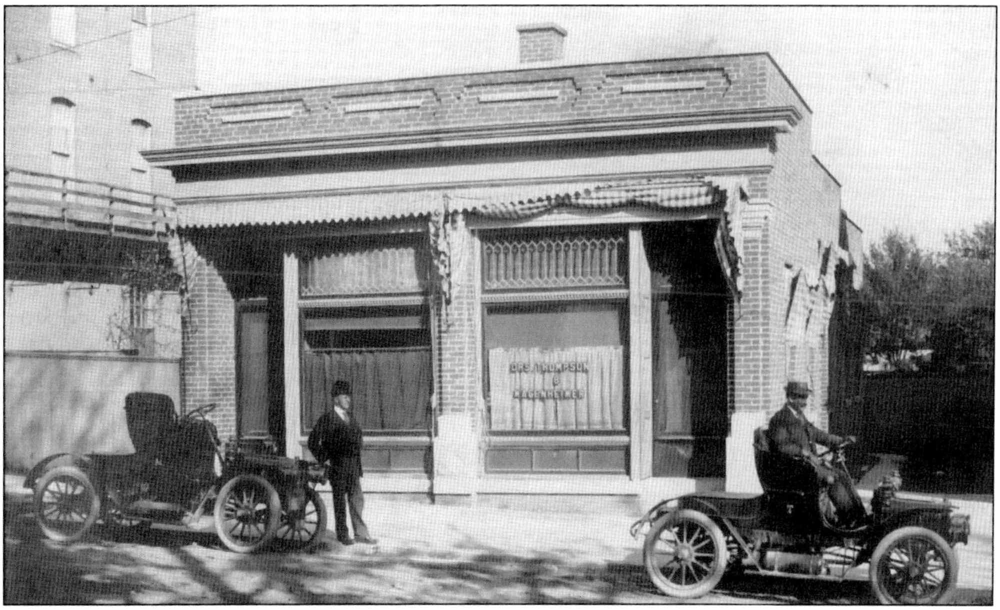

OFFICE OF DR. THOMPSON AND DR. MAGENHEIMER, *C.* 1909. Dr. William L. Thompson was joined in 1908 by Dr. Valentine Magenheimer, Thompson's former apprentice and an 1895 graduate of the Indiana Medical College who had been practicing in Waverly. Initials on the automobiles designate their owners. Magenheimer stands at left, and Thompson is seated at right. Magenheimer is the brother-in-law of Joseph Counsilman, who photographed the Waverly views in this book.

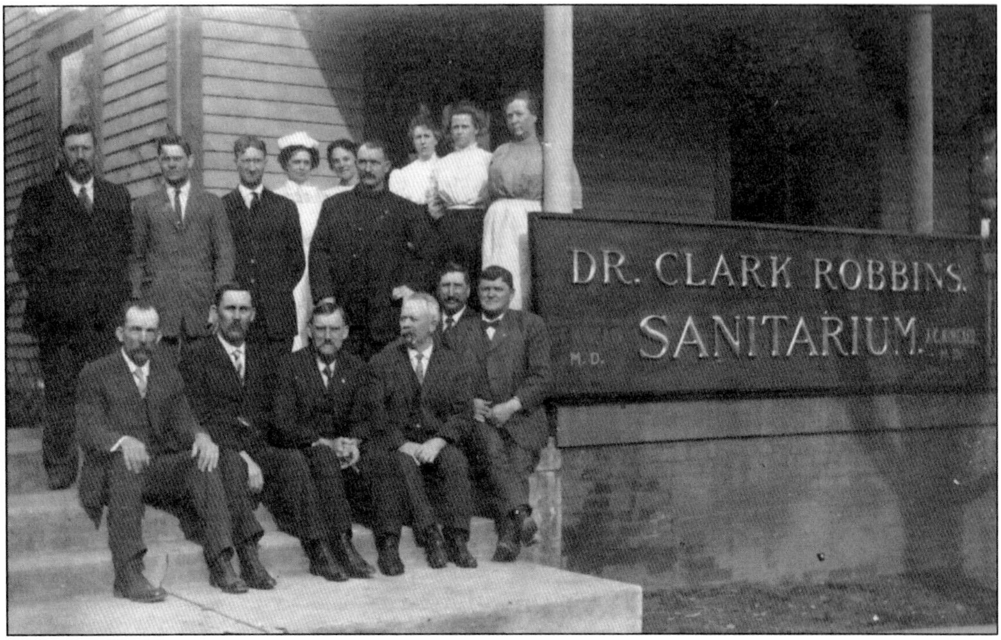

DR. CLARK ROBBINS SANITARIUM, C. 1910. The practice of medicine played a significant role in Mooresville's history. Born in 1836 in Morgan County, Dr. Clark Robbins doctored in Brooklyn, Martinsville, and Mooresville before opening a private sanitarium specializing in rectal problems in 1881. The building shown was constructed on the southwest corner of Indiana and Washington Streets in 1900.

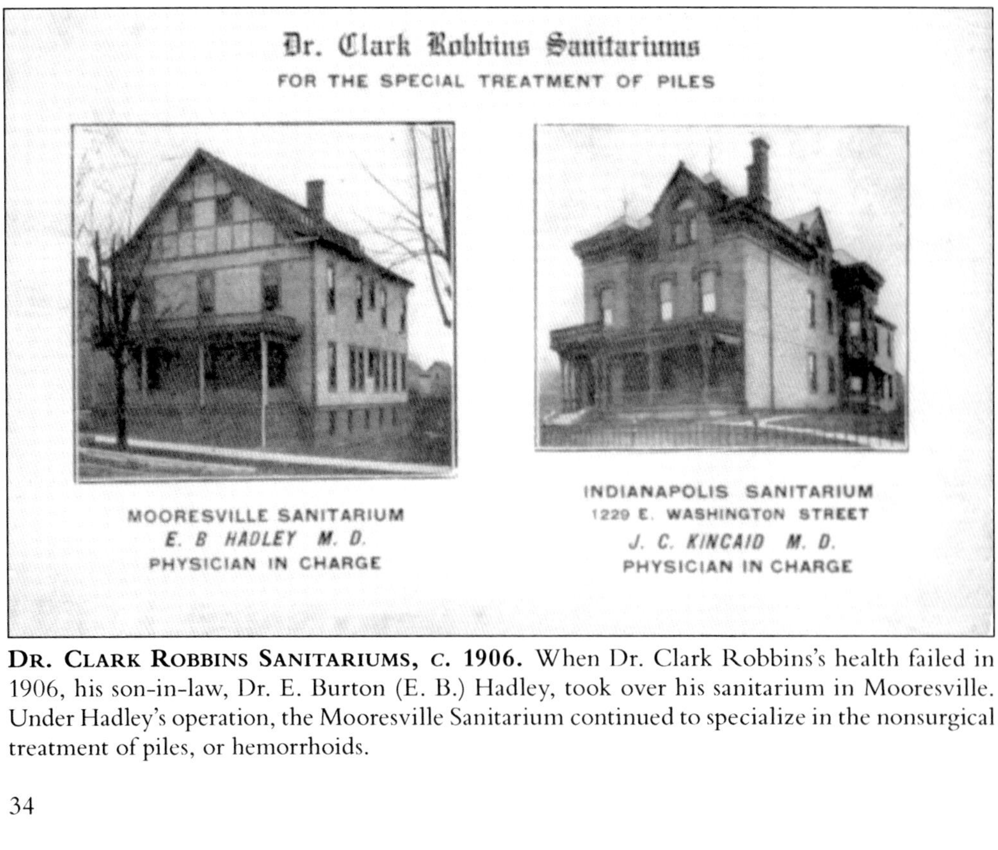

DR. CLARK ROBBINS SANITARIUMS, C. 1906. When Dr. Clark Robbins's health failed in 1906, his son-in-law, Dr. E. Burton (E. B.) Hadley, took over his sanitarium in Mooresville. Under Hadley's operation, the Mooresville Sanitarium continued to specialize in the nonsurgical treatment of piles, or hemorrhoids.

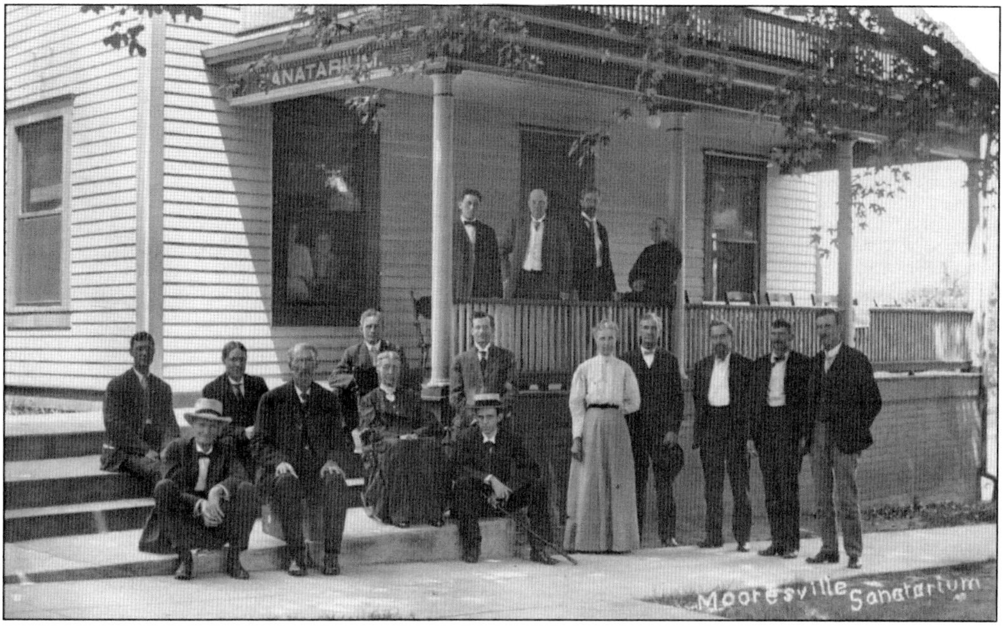

MOORESVILLE SANITARIUM, JULY 18, 1907. Dr. E. B. Hadley is the man in the white shirt and vest standing on the porch. Others on the porch are, from left to right, Dr. William Streng, Dr. Fred Hadley, and Melissa Robbins, the widow of Dr. Clark Robbins, the sanitarium's founder. Seen through the window are Edith Hadley Shirley, the daughter of E. B. Hadley and the granddaughter of the Robbinses, and Ann Baker. The others are unidentified patients.

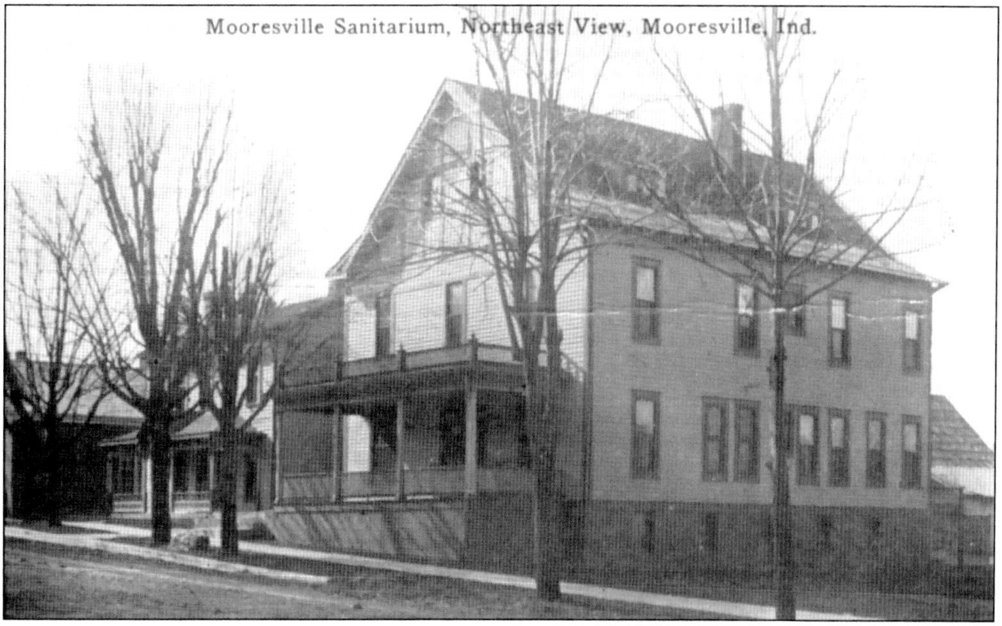

GREETINGS FROM MOORESVILLE SANITARIUM, JUNE 1916. The message on the back of this postcard reads, "Dear Fern: I have really awakened again, and how are you getting on. I am nurse here in this sanitarium that I am sending you. Have been here since middle of March. Like my work just fine and will write you a letter soon. With love. I have made a mark where my room is. Goldie."

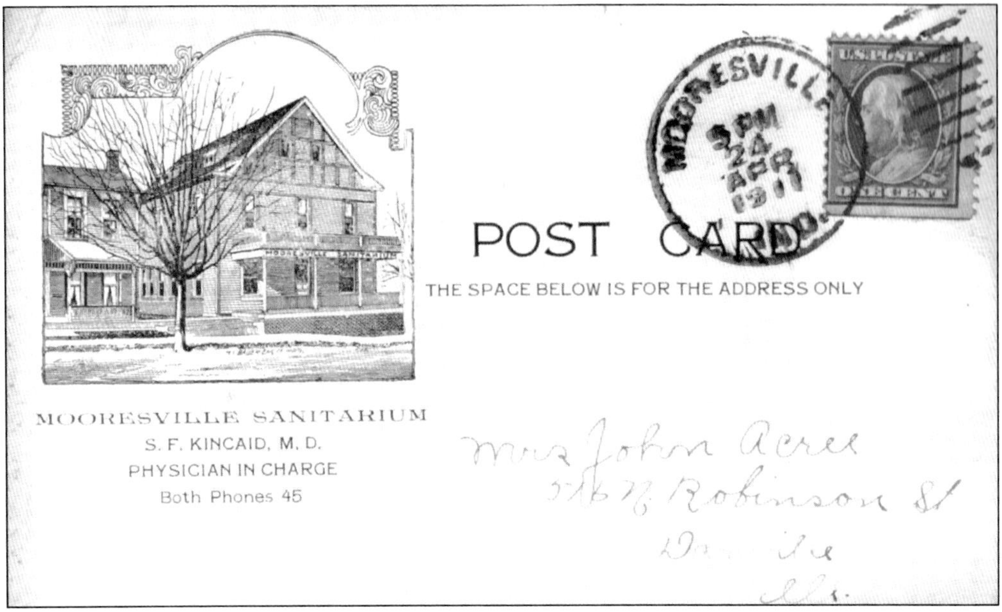

MOORESVILLE SANITARIUM, 1911. The Hadleys sold the sanitarium about 1909. One subsequent owner was Dr. S. F. Kincaid. He in turn sold it in 1916 to Jonathon "Jot" Comer, who had practiced medicine at both Waverly and Bargersville. The sanitarium prospered under Comer's ownership. Tragedy struck on October 5, 1936, however, when the building burned to the ground.

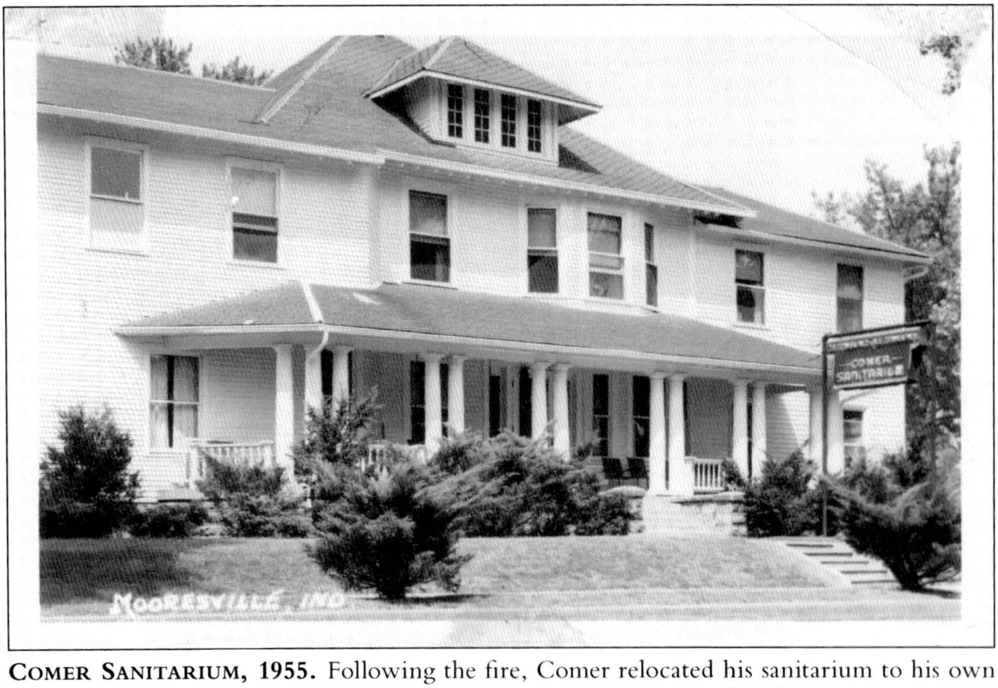

COMER SANITARIUM, 1955. Following the fire, Comer relocated his sanitarium to his own home, the former Henry Conduitt house at the corner of Morgan and Indiana Streets. He later took as a partner Dr. William Kendrick. In 1961, Kendrick became sole owner, and the sanitarium was renamed Kendrick Hospital. A note on the back of this card reads, "Hospital where Billie is at for rectal operation Nov. 20-1955."

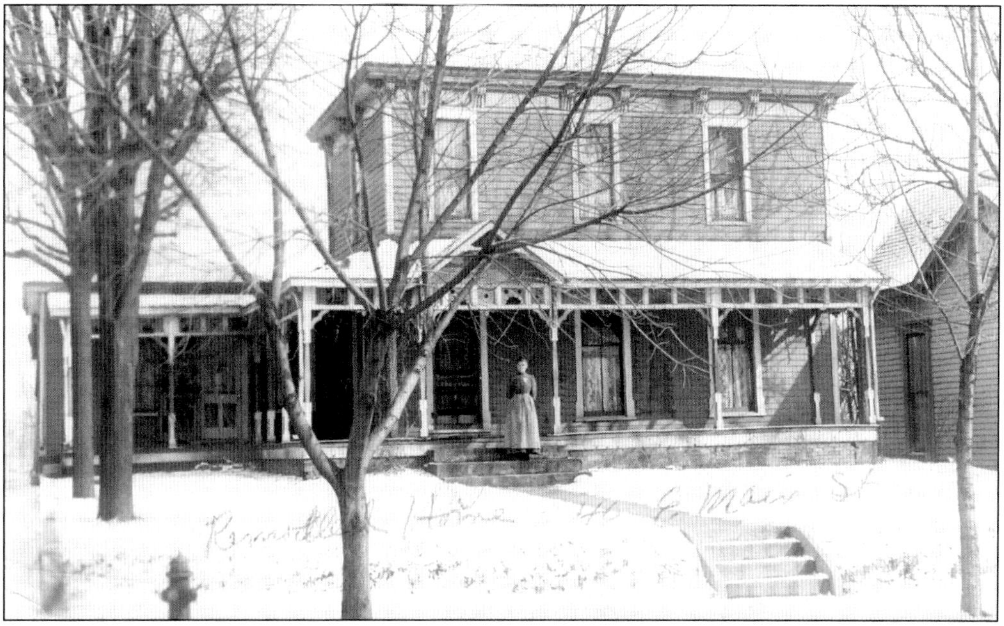

PACE THOMPSON HOUSE, 40 EAST MAIN STREET, C. 1910. The original house was remodeled (as the note across the front of this card indicates) with the addition of the second story. The house no longer exists. Pace Thompson operated a dry goods store on West Main Street from about 1895 to 1916. An advertisement in the 1909 Mooresville High School annual identifies his merchandise as "notions, hats, caps, shoes, carpets, window shades, and groceries."

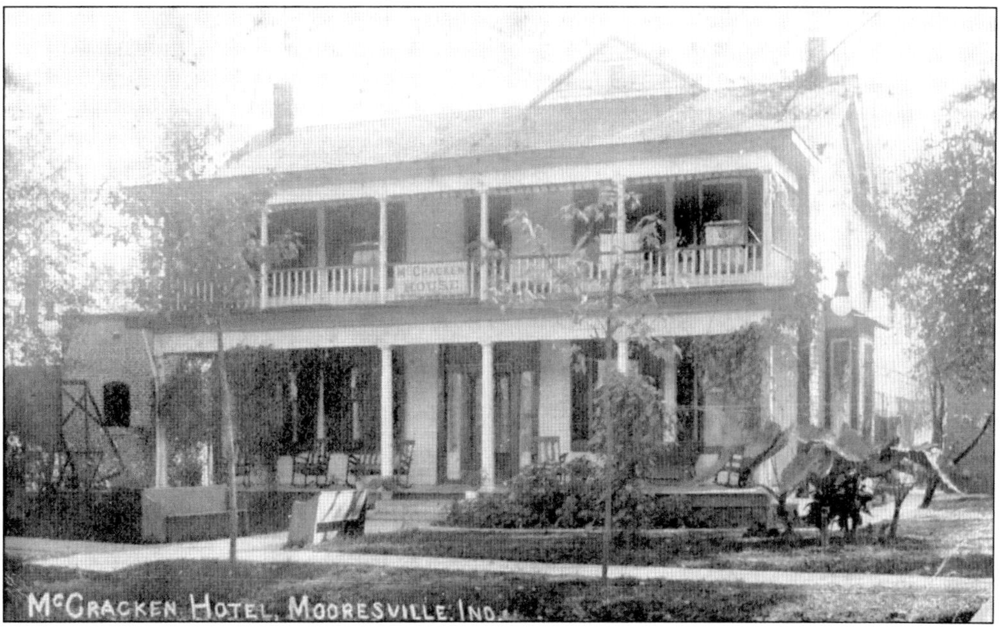

MCCRACKEN HOTEL IN SUMMER, 1912. Located on the south side of West Main Street across from Mooresville's Carnegie library, this popular hotel was built about 1870. It was operated by Wilkinson and Sarah McCracken for 45 continuous years, followed by their daughter, Eliza Crawford. On Sundays, Indianapolis residents rode the interurban to Mooresville to dine on the hotel's celebrated fried chicken dinners. The hotel was torn down in 1951.

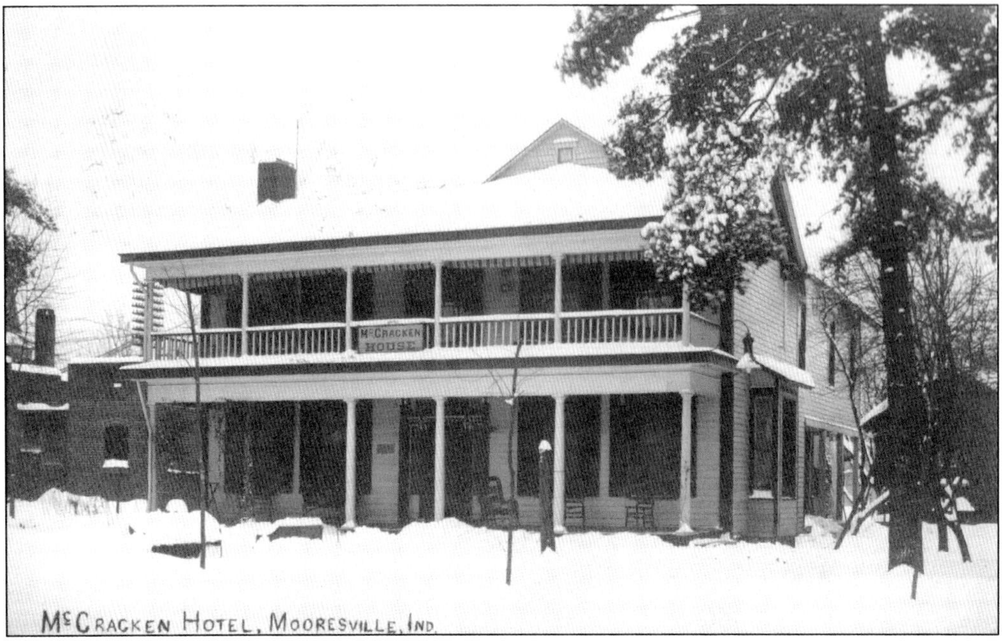

McCracken Hotel in Winter, 1912. The message on this card mailed to Florida reads, "If you will turn this card over you can see how it looks in Mooresville at the present time. The snow is about a foot deep on the level and has drifted until it is about waist deep right in the public square and is turning cold again. The trains and cars have not been running to-day."

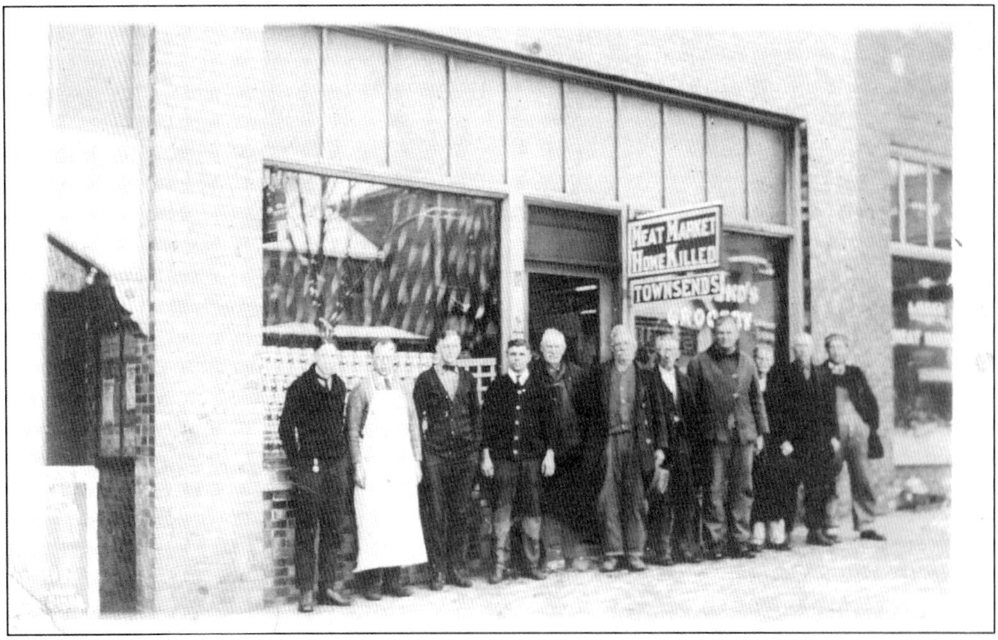

Hobart Townsend's Grocery, East Main Street, 1920 or 1921. Identified in pencil on the back of this postcard are, from left to right, Edward Townsend, Ernest Shireman, Hobart Townsend, Pleas Holmes, Ch—— S——, John Parker, Sammy Heath and son, a Mr. Plunkett in the back, Wm. Hanes, and Chester King. The sign above their heads reads, "Meat Market Home Killed." Townsend's Grocery was located in the G. A. Keller building.

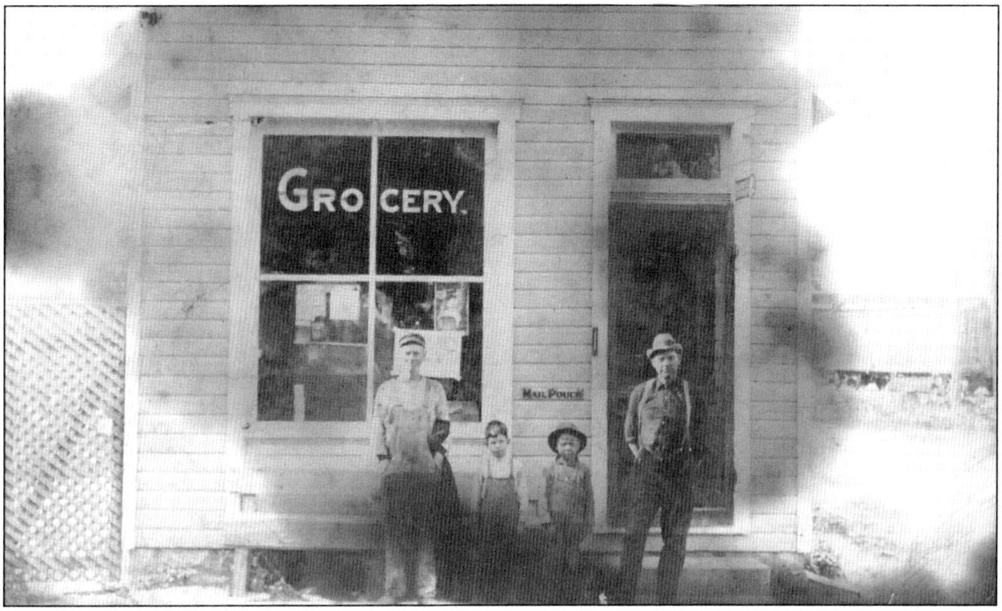

EAST END GROCERY, EAST MAIN STREET, *c.* 1910. A number of individuals had a hand in keeping this grocery, located at the northwest corner of Main Street and Maple Lane, in business for some 70 years, including William A. Cox, Thomas Randell, Charlie and Bessie (Randell) Evans, and Warren Armstrong. Seen here from left to right are Oliver Jackson Poe, four-year-old Harold Poe, Sn——Poe, and Oscar Ozment. Note the car sitting on the Pennsylvania Railroad line at right.

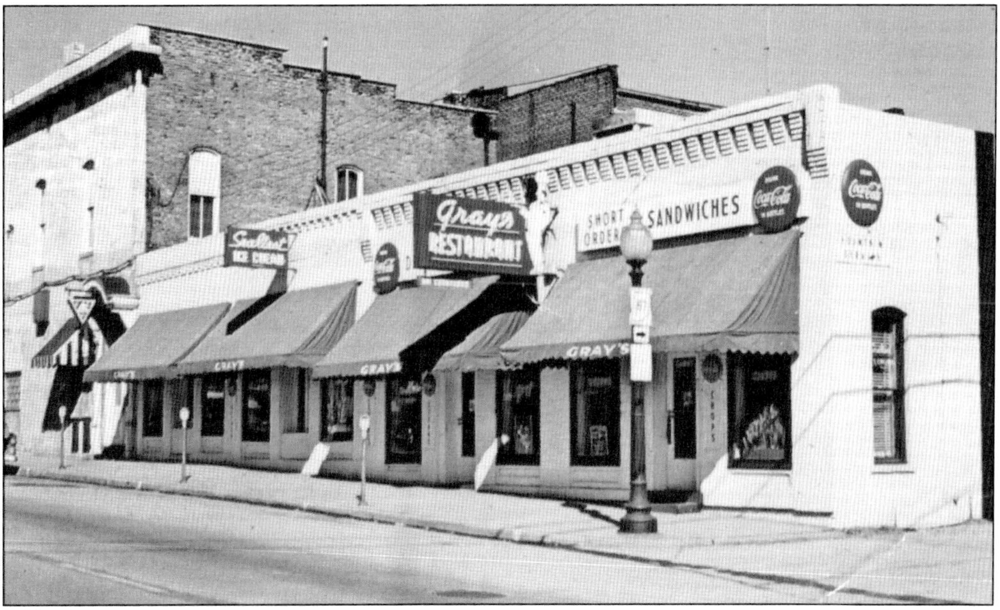

GRAY'S RESTAURANT, *c.* 1960. One of Indiana's treasured dining institutions, Gray's was opened on South Indiana Street by Forest Gray in 1944 as a one-room lunch counter. In September 1969, Forest's sons, Lawrence and Kenneth, moved Gray's into a new building on State Road 67, making it all the easier for devotees to dine on Gray's famous fried chicken, yeast rolls, and old-fashioned pies. Subsequent expansions kept pace with patrons' expanding waistlines.

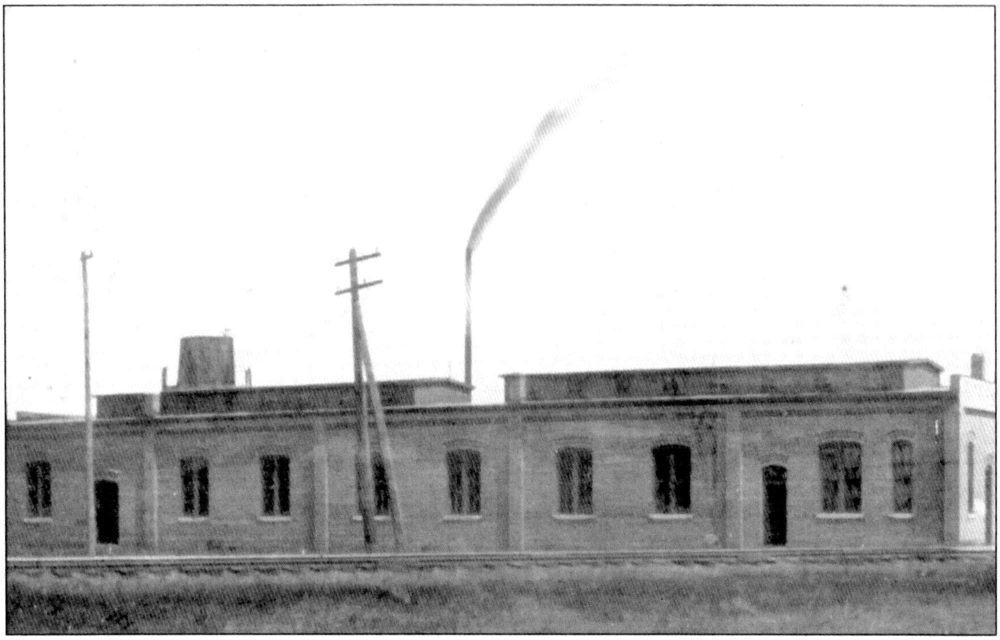

Indiana Brass and Iron Bed Company, 1914. Located at the corner of Maple Lane and East Washington Street, on the west side of the Pennsylvania Railroad, this factory was constructed in 1900. Operations were moved from Marion. Bed frames were manufactured of brass and recycled scrap iron from 1901 until 1916. For many years, the factory building was home to Johnson's Apple House.

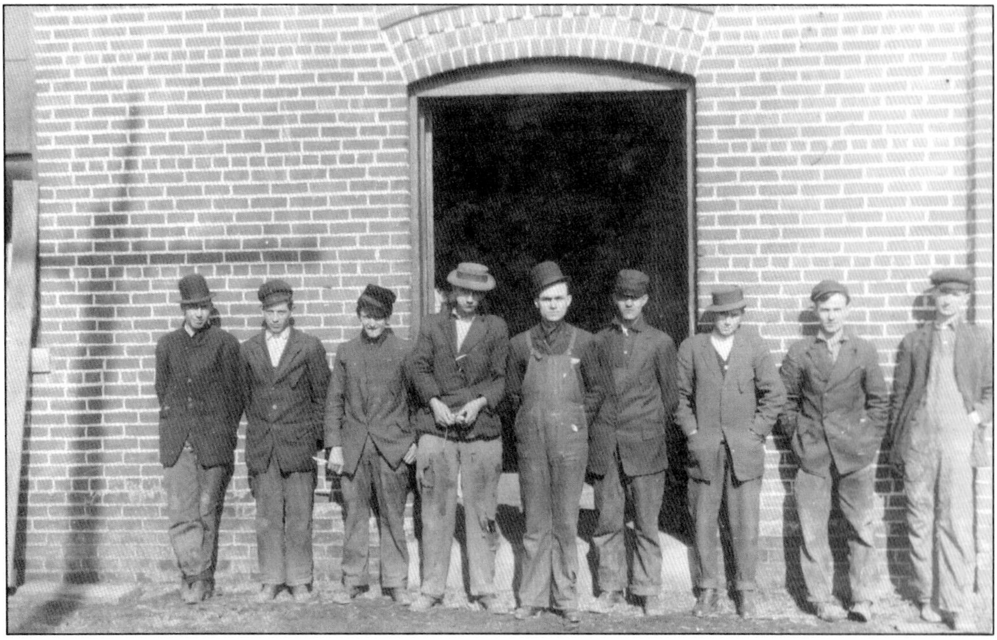

Bedstead Factory Workers, c. 1915. Pictured here from left to right are John Wilson, Ralph Self, Ed Ricks, Frank Randall, Walter Carroll, William Ferguson, Otis Davidson, Jim Johnson, and Brake Nelson. Nelson worked in the shipping department until the factory closed. The Indiana Brass and Iron Bed Company was owned by Simon B. Nussbaum of Marion.

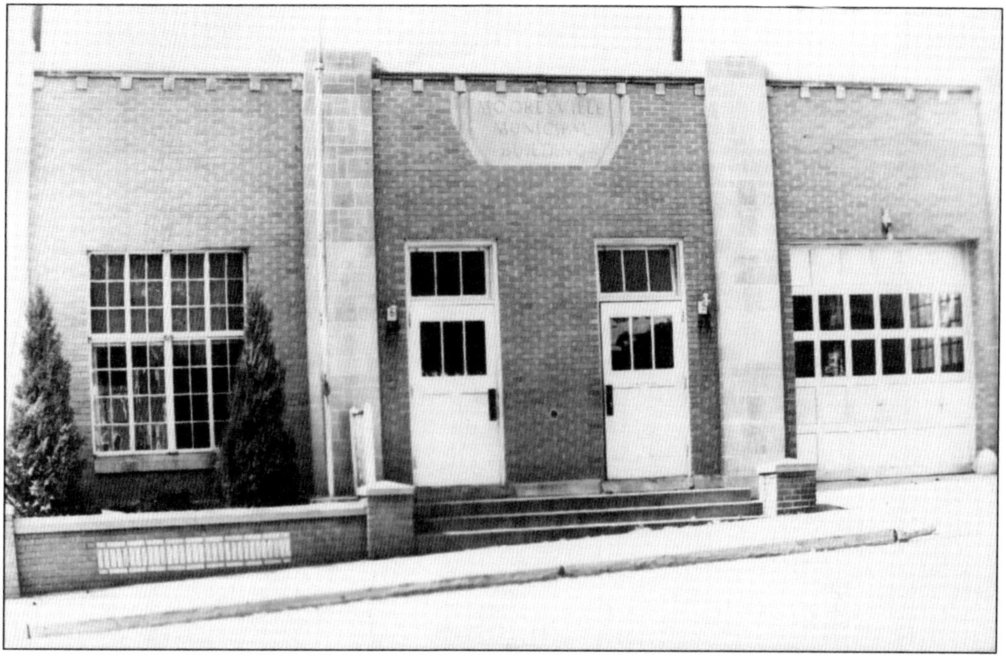

MUNICIPAL BUILDING, C. 1950. Jacob Mann and Sam Wade built this building in 1932 to house the town offices, fire department, and jail. The fire truck bay at right was converted into a police station shortly after this photograph was taken. A second story was added in 1980.

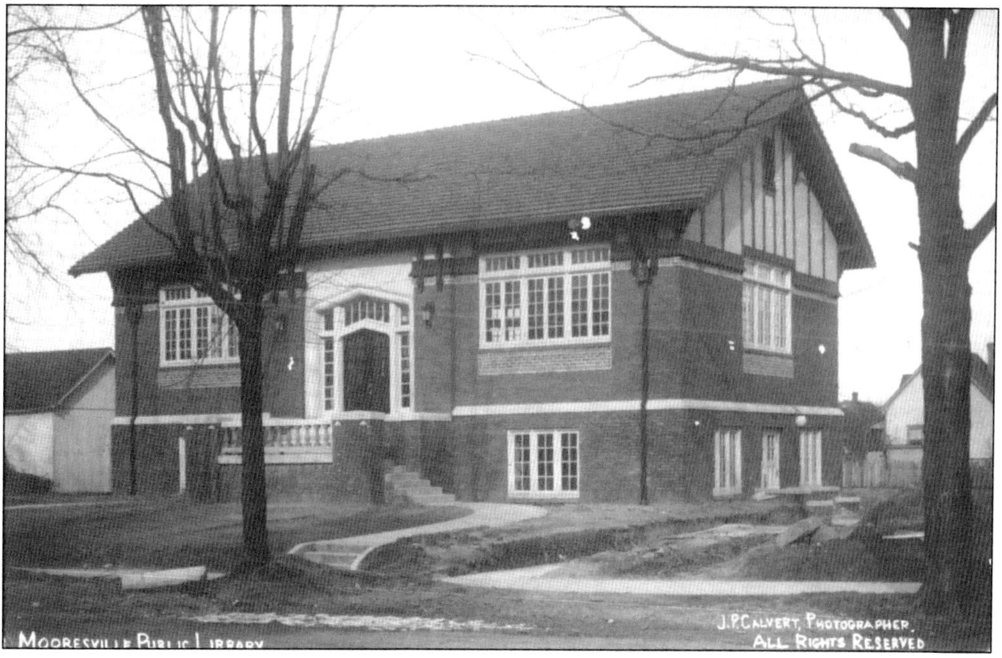

CARNEGIE LIBRARY, 1916. Mooresville's public library was made possible by a $10,000 gift from steel magnate and philanthropist Andrew Carnegie. Frank L. May, the sender of this card postmarked January 13, wrote, "I just thought I would send you a Picture of the new Library They have it all Finished now So you can see how it Looks I have never been inside of it yet, But I suppose it looks nice inside."

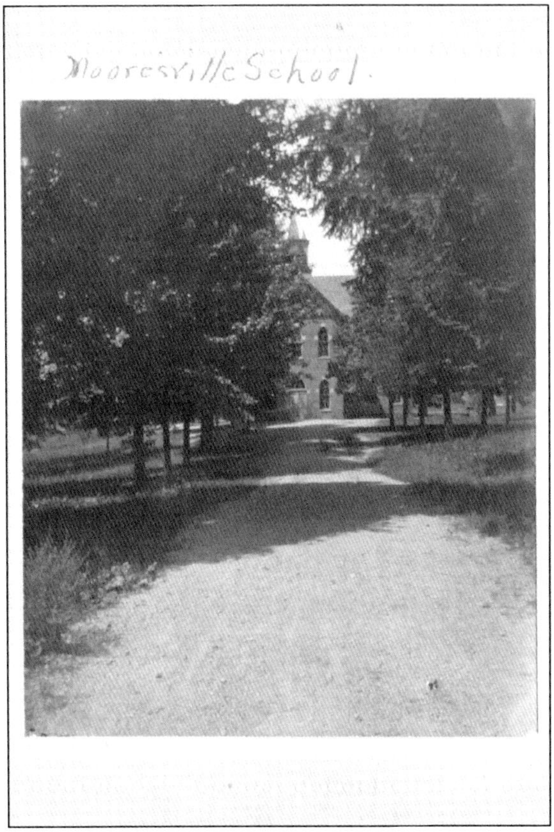

ACADEMY BUILDING/MOORESVILLE SCHOOL, 1903. The Friends had a significant impact on Mooresville's educational history. In 1861, they erected the original two-room, two-story Academy Building on North Monroe Street. It functioned as a subscription high school—the state's first—until 1867, when two west rooms were added to accommodate primary students.

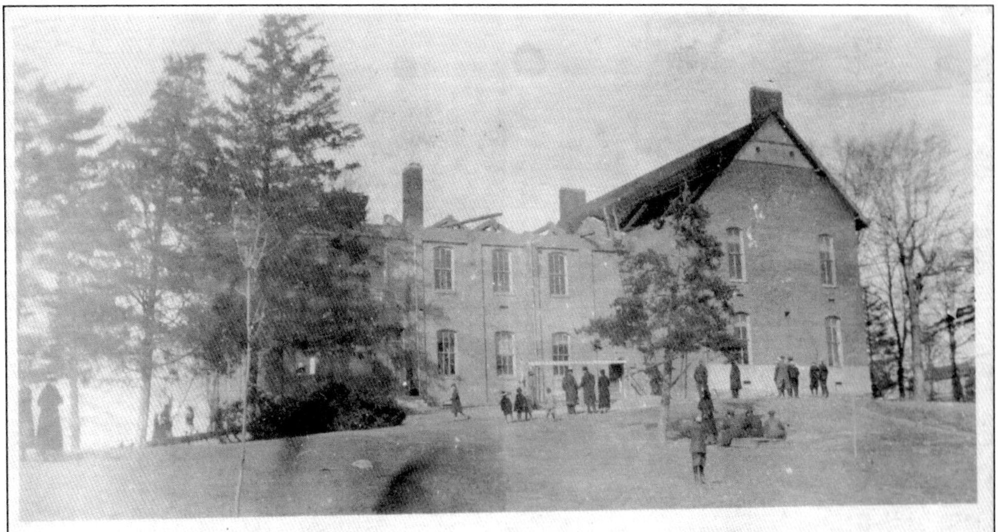

STORM DAMAGE, 1917 OR 1918. In 1870, the Friends deeded the Academy Building to the Town of Mooresville for use as a public school. A large T-plan wing was added across the front in 1883. When secondary students moved to the new high school building in 1908, the Academy Building became an elementary school. At the time of the storm whose damage is shown here, the sixth-grade class taught by Leorah Wall occupied the second floor.

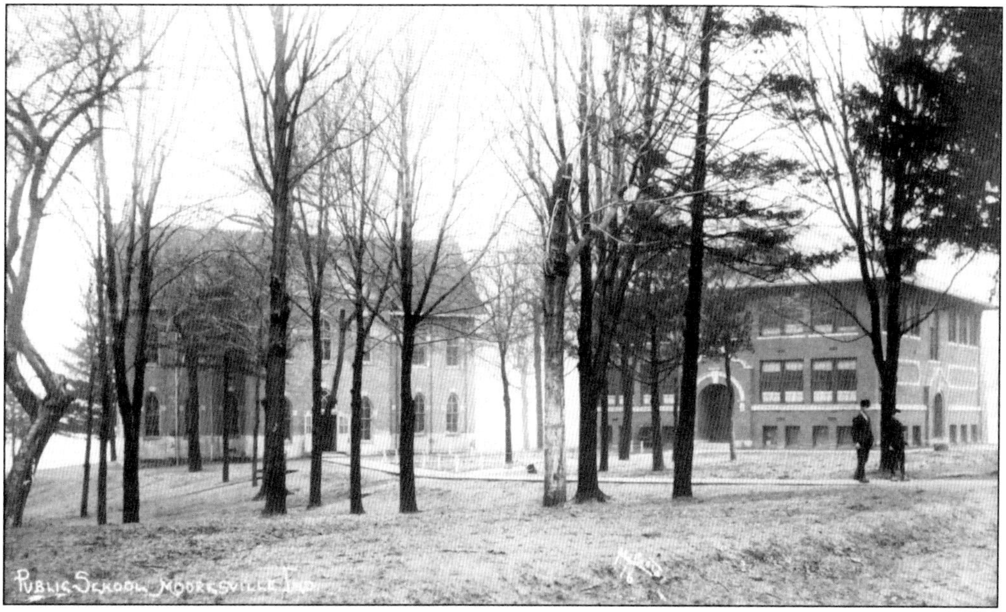

OLD AND NEW PUBLIC SCHOOLS, 1911. When students began the 1908–1909 school year in a thoroughly modern building featuring both secondary and primary classrooms, a library, and administrative offices, the Academy Building was abandoned. It remained a historical relic until 1966, when it was called back into service as an elementary school. Five years later, with the opening of the Neil Armstrong Elementary School, it was again discontinued—this time for good.

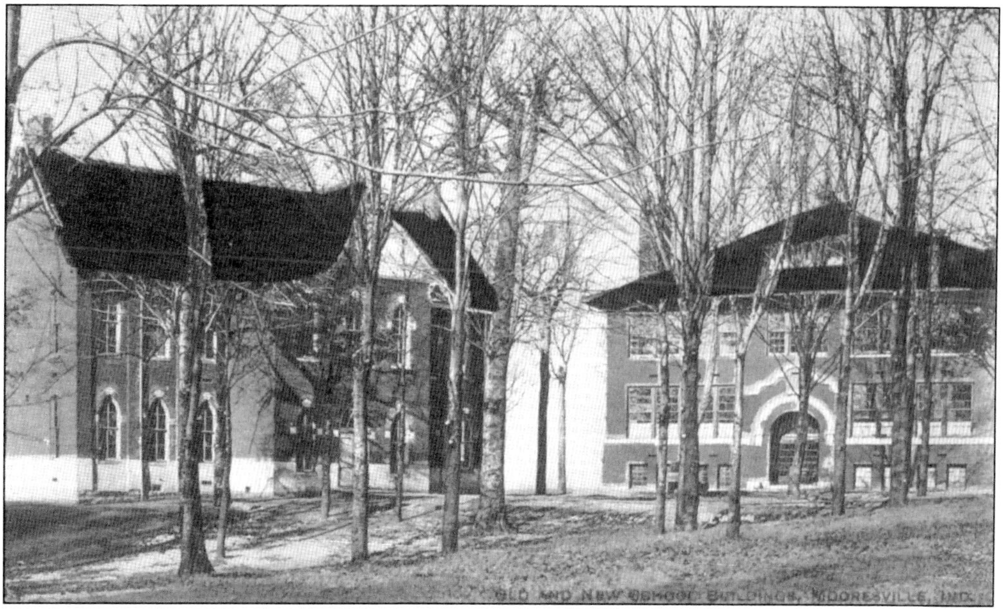

OLD AND NEW PUBLIC SCHOOLS, *c.* 1908. Here is a closer view. This postcard was published by Lyons' Bargain Store, owned by Billy Lyons. An advertisement in the 1909 Mooresville High School annual reads, "(Just what the name implies.) We have a little of everything. Ladies' and Gents' Furnishings, Dry Goods, China, Notions, etc., Magazines and Books, Post Cards: Home Views, Birthday and Seasonal. 'Once a customer—always.' "

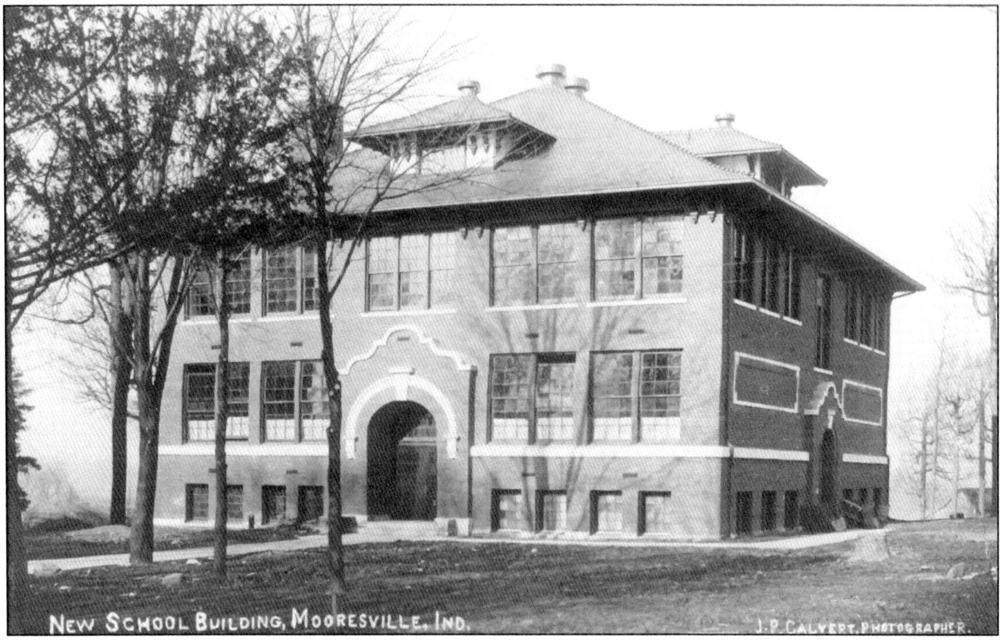

NEW SCHOOL BUILDING, *c.* 1915. Built by contractor Charles Ferguson at a cost of $26,000, the new school was supplemented with a basketball gymnasium (1921) and a separate heating plant (1924). First things first!

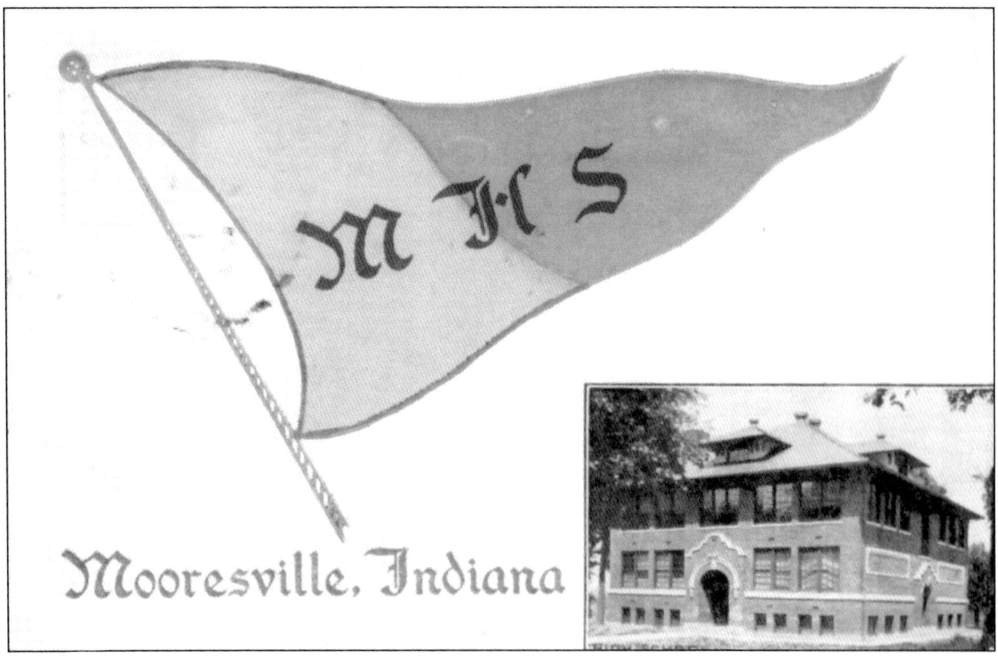

MOORESVILLE HIGH SCHOOL ON PENNANT CARD, 1909. The class of 1909 was the first to graduate from the new school. Ralph Cook was class president, Harvey Farmer was vice president, Florence Taylor was secretary, and Ida Park served as treasurer. Class colors were navy blue and old rose. "The only true way not to fail is to determine to succeed" was the class motto. The pale yellow Marshal Niel rose was the class flower.

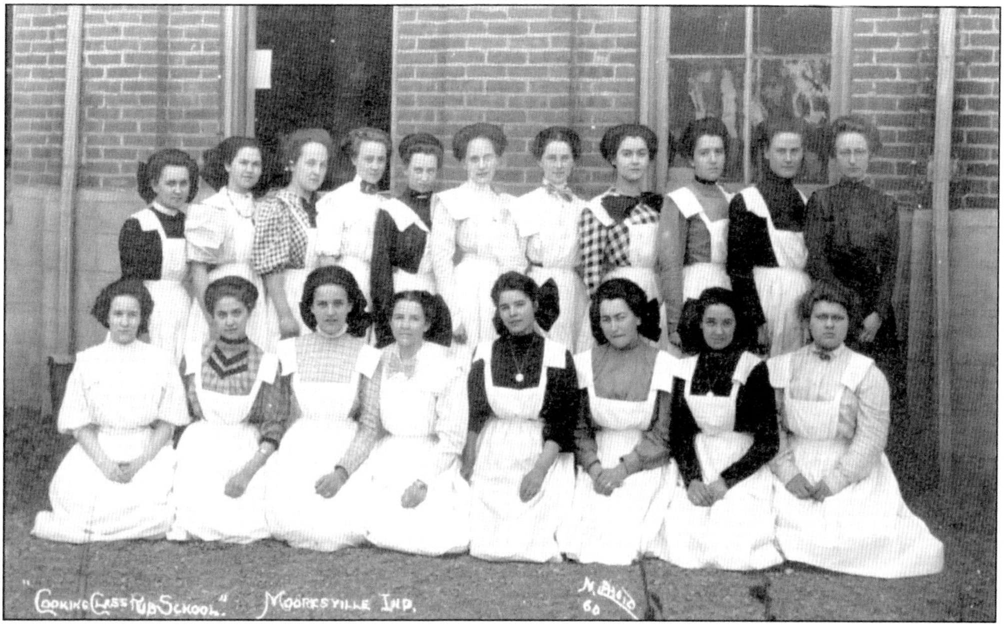

COOKING CLASS, 1909. The new public school was a thoroughly modern building with a modern course of study, including domestic science. "In a larger sense, the health and happiness of the world depend upon the woman of the home. . . . Why then should a woman not have the privilege of scientific training for her life work?" asked the student editors of the 1909 senior annual.

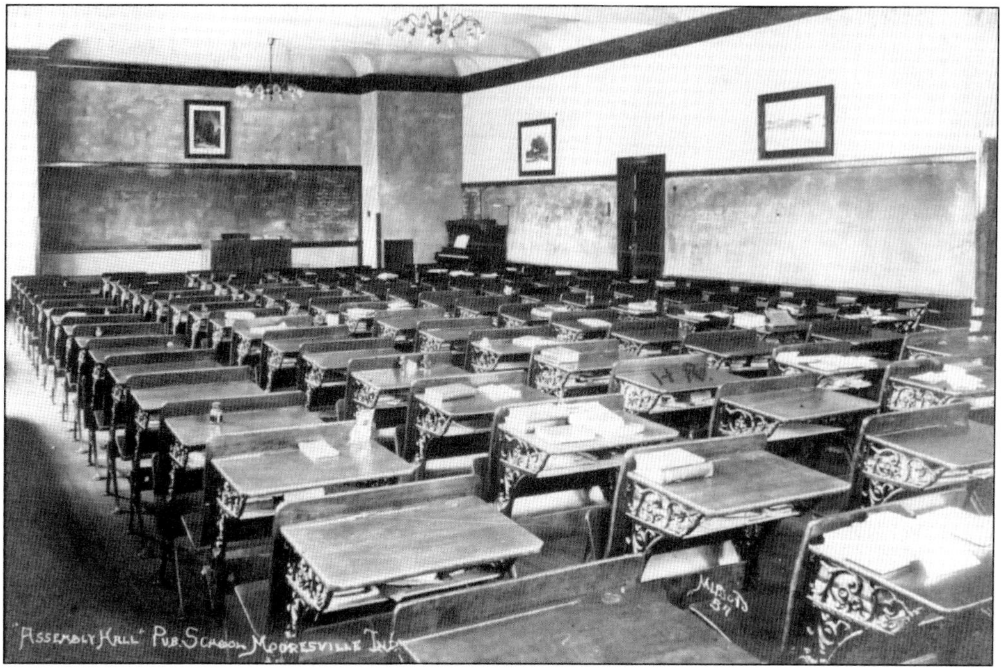

SECOND-FLOOR ASSEMBLY HALL, 1909. Note the initials on the desk that the sender of this card has occupied.

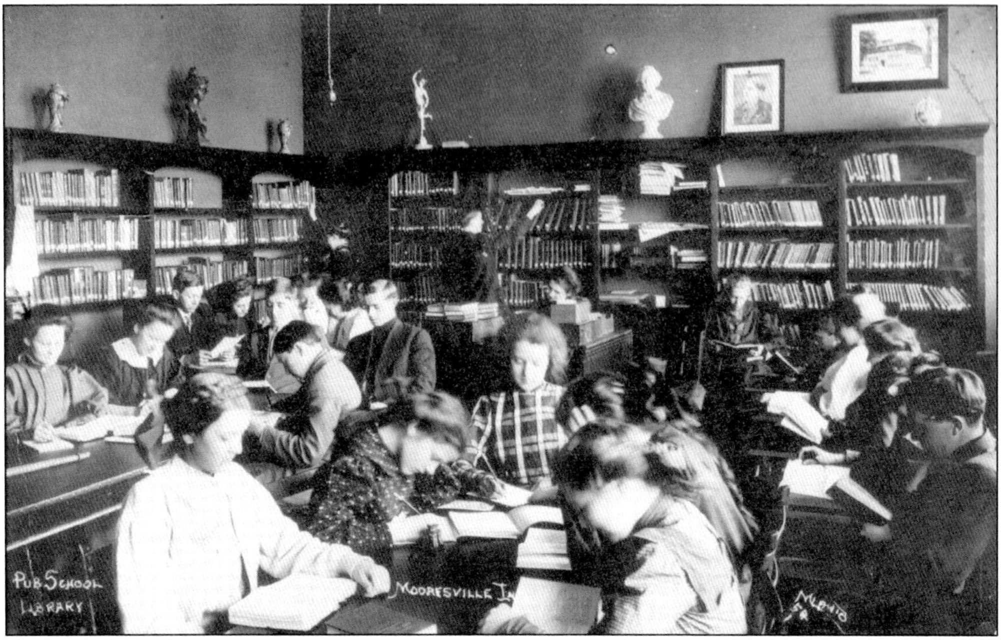

LIBRARY, 1909. "The high school library is a SELECTION, not a COLLECTION, of one thousand volumes of reference works in History, English, Latin, and Biography and books for general culture," boasted the 1909 annual. Students had free access four hours a day. The girl at far left with an arrow over her head is Mabel Richardson. At her left is Lizzie Sheets.

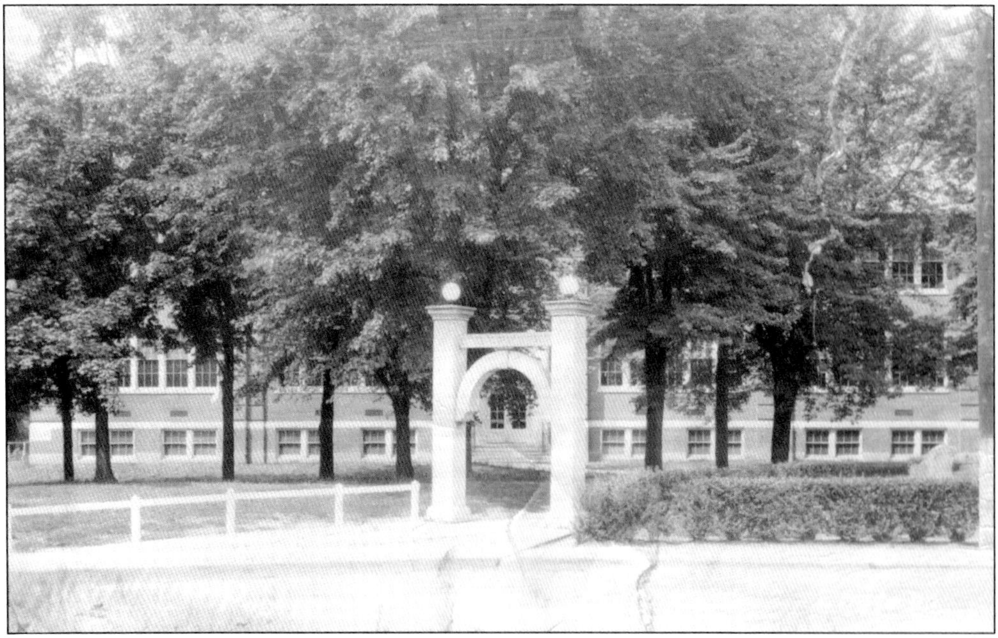

ENTER TO GROW IN WISDOM, c. 1940. A gift of the Mooresville High School class of 1912, this limestone gateway was so dilapidated by 1965 that the school board voted to tear it down. Surviving members of the classes of 1912, 1913, and 1914 raised funds and succeeded in restoring it. Today, as in this postcard, the arch perfectly frames the paired entrance doors of Newby Memorial Elementary School.

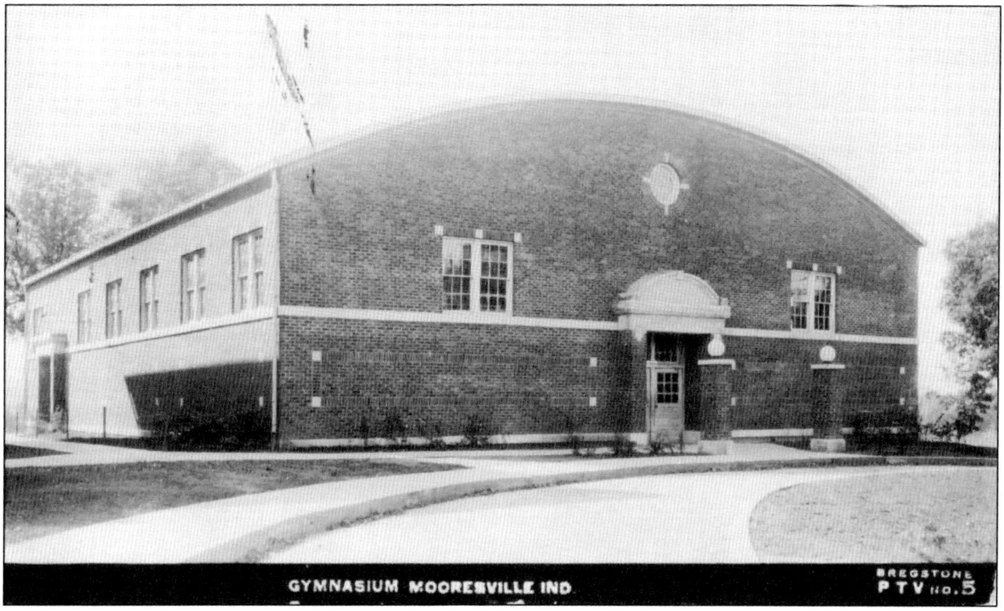

MOORESVILLE GYMNASIUM, *C.* 1921. Prior to the December 31, 1920, dedication of this basketball gymnasium—Morgan County's first—high school games had been played on the second floor of G. A. Keller's hardware store, shown on page 23. This photograph was taken by H. H. Bregstone of St. Louis, Missouri.

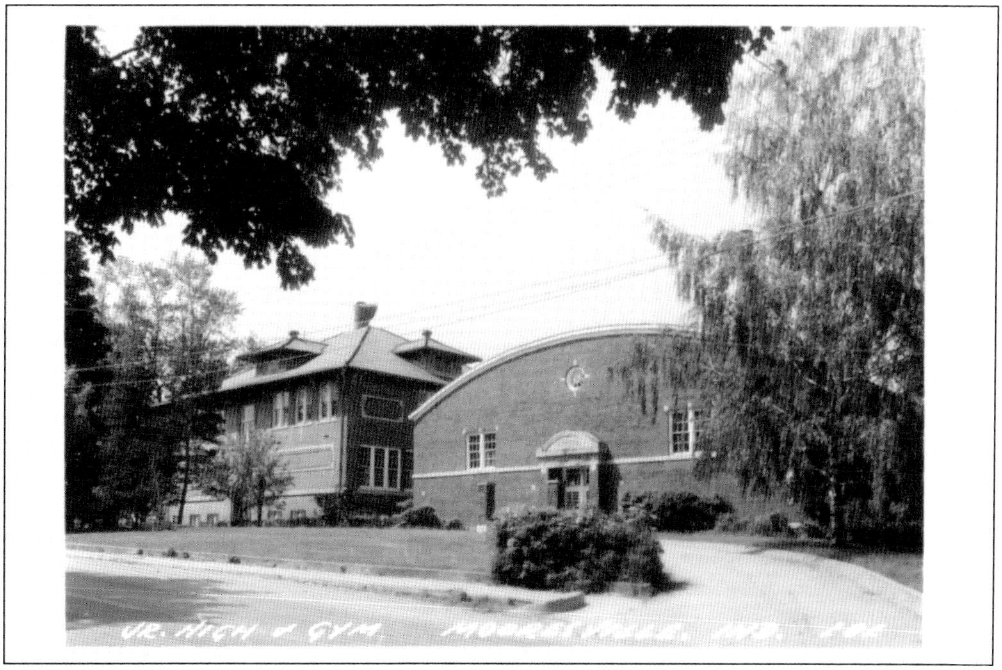

JUNIOR HIGH AND GYMNASIUM, *C.* 1960. Following the completion of the new Mooresville consolidated high school building on North Indiana Street in 1960, the old high school became Mooresville Junior High. It was vacated when Paul Hadley Junior High School was completed five years later, and in 1971, it was razed and the site cleared. The historic gymnasium has remained in almost continuous use by Mooresville's junior basketball leagues.

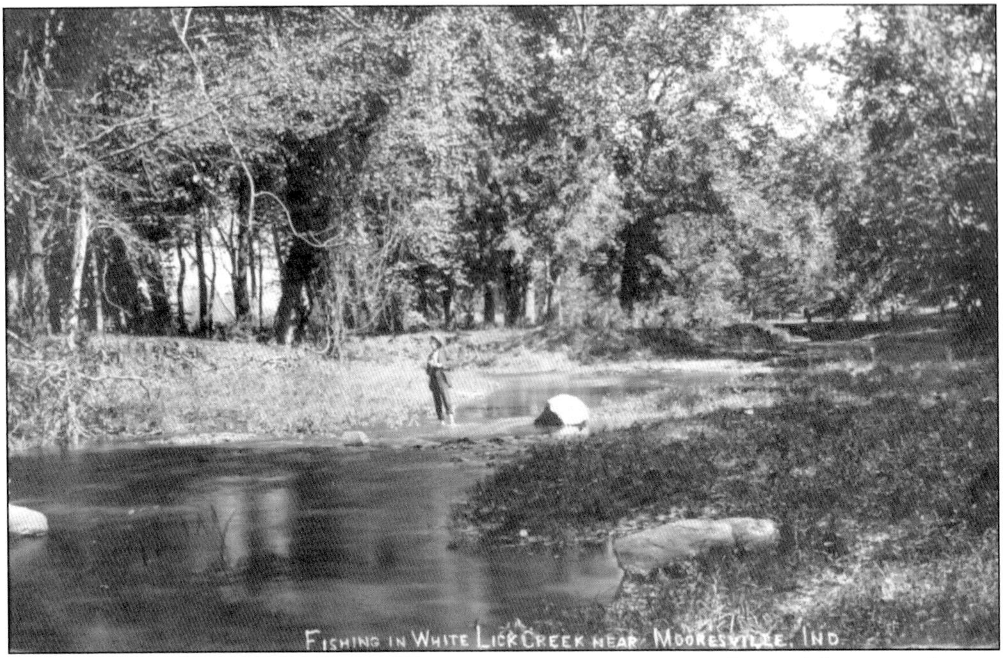

FISHING IN WHITE LICK CREEK, 1914. A solitary fisherman is the focus of this pastoral scene captured by J. P. Calvert many years ago.

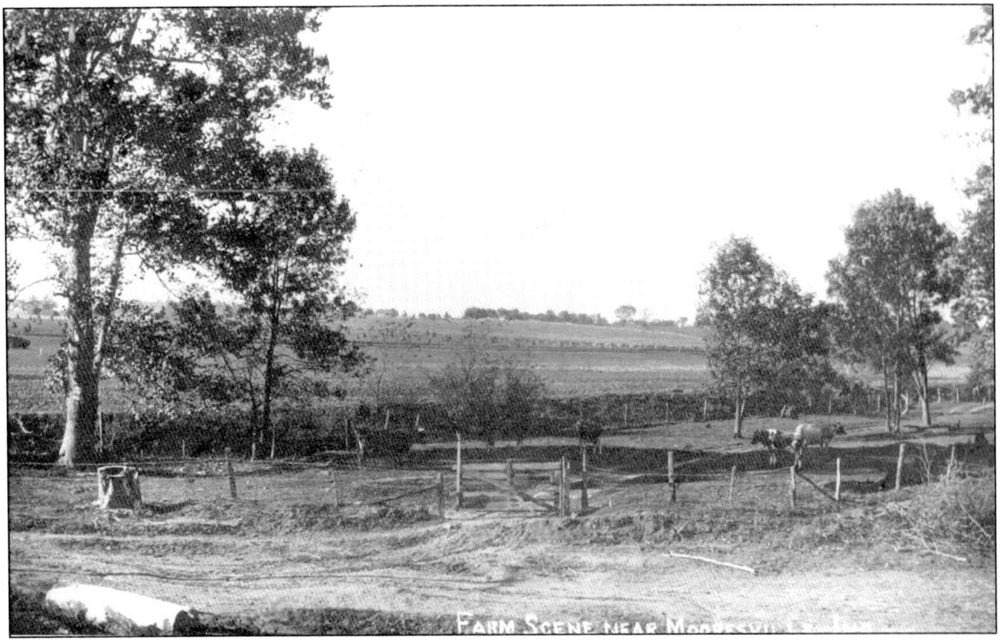

FARM SCENE NEAR MOORESVILLE, 1910. "Isn't this a natural looking place?" the sender of this card wrote to Prudence Dawson of Franklin. "I am getting along very well considering the weather. Have put up hay a day and a half this week."

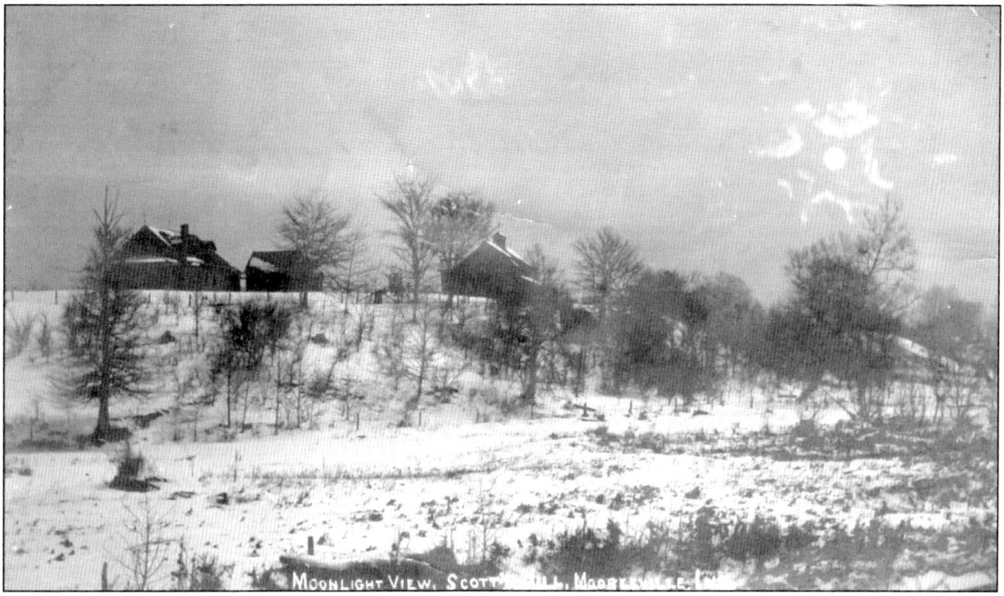

Moonlight View, Scott's Hill, 1909. J. P. Calvert's enhancement of the full moon's glow adds a whimsical charm to this winter scene. Scott's Hill is located on the west side of Mooresville north of High Street and east of White Lick Creek.

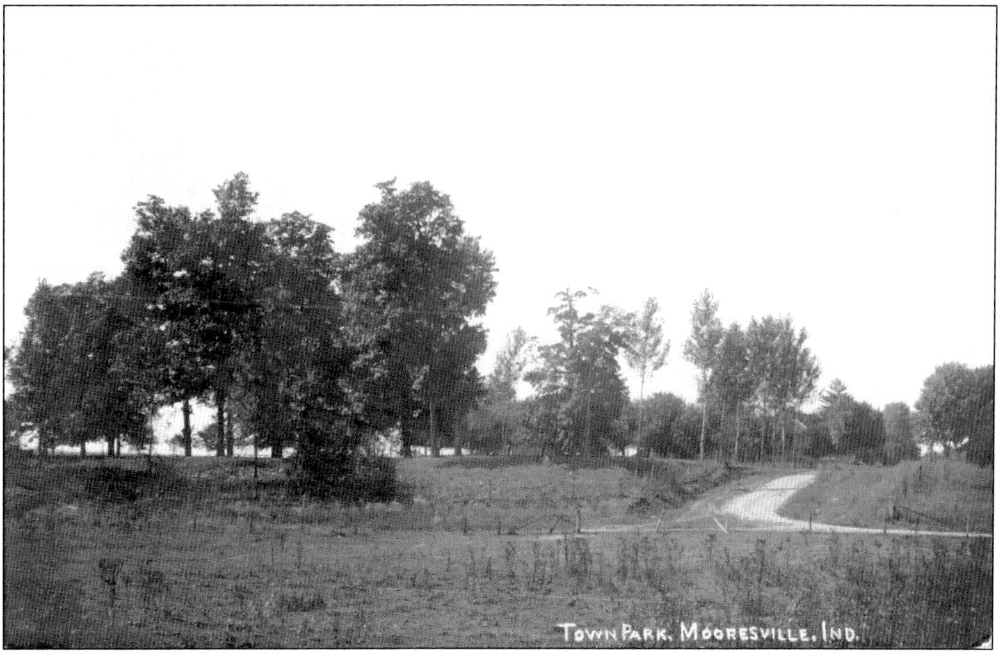

Town Park, 1909. Mooresville founder Samuel Moore donated the site of the original town park in 1877, specifying its use for public recreation. "I forbid baseball, bandyball, town ball, or any such game as would mar the enjoyment of women and children. I forbid horse racing or the training of horses," he wrote. As Moore intended, the park was long the site of the annual Old Settler's picnic, begun in 1870.

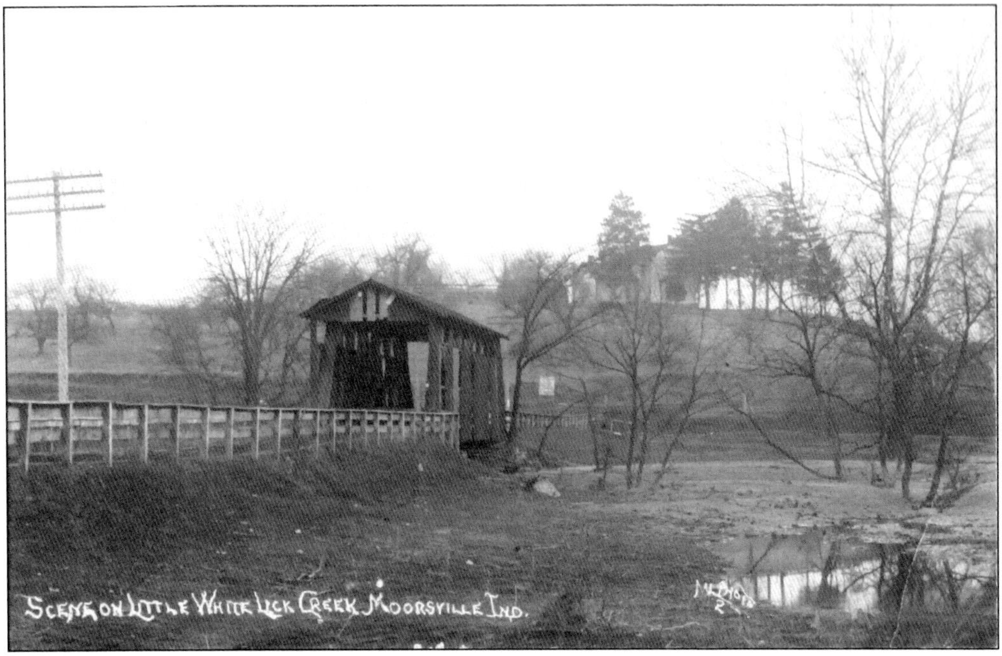

LITTLE RED BRIDGE, 1911. Spanning Little White Lick Creek east of the old town park on the Waverly Road (now State Road 144), this covered bridge, with missing and unpainted side boards, was showing clear signs of its age when M. L. Photo Company captured this scene. The view is looking southeast to Day's Hill, named for the homestead of Richard and Hannah Day, pioneers whose house is visible through the trees.

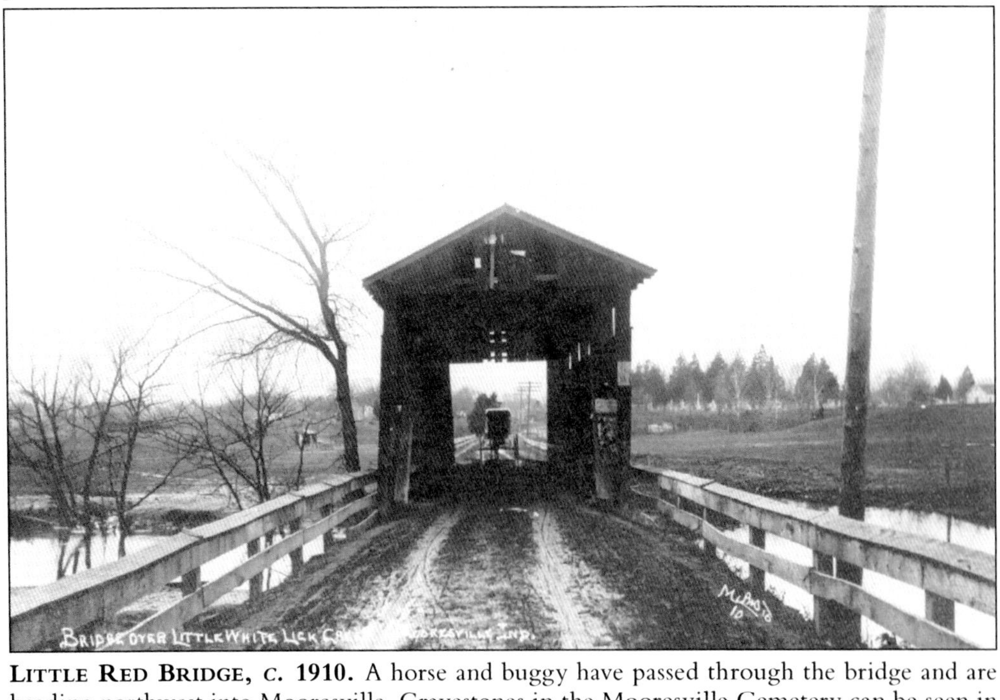

LITTLE RED BRIDGE, *C.* 1910. A horse and buggy have passed through the bridge and are heading northwest into Mooresville. Gravestones in the Mooresville Cemetery can be seen in the distance.

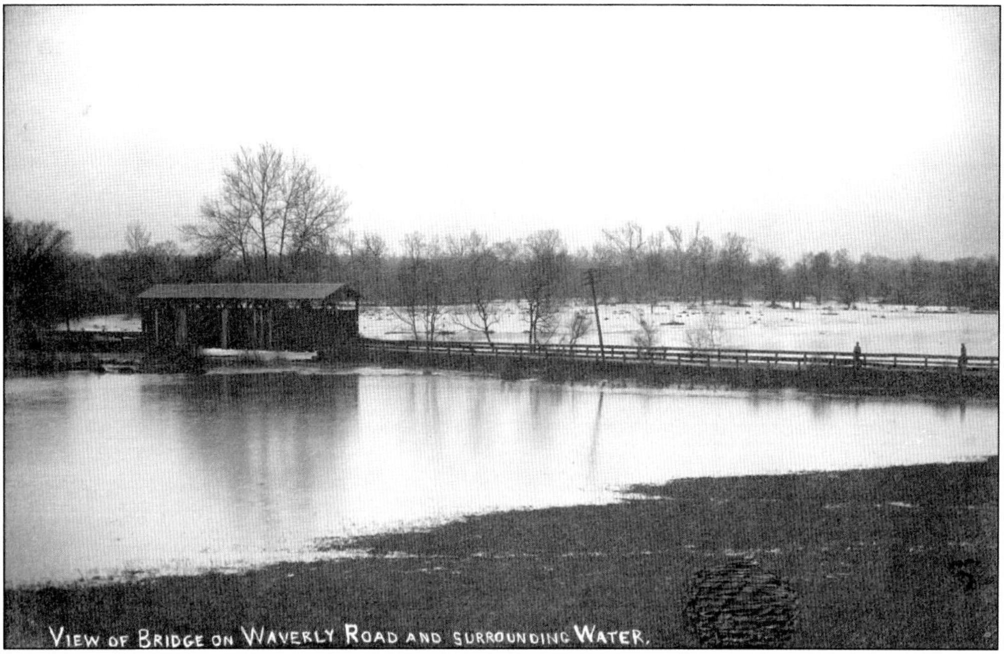

LITTLE RED BRIDGE, 1913. On March 25, 1913, unprecedented rainfall caused severe flooding throughout Morgan County. This photograph was taken by J. P. Calvert.

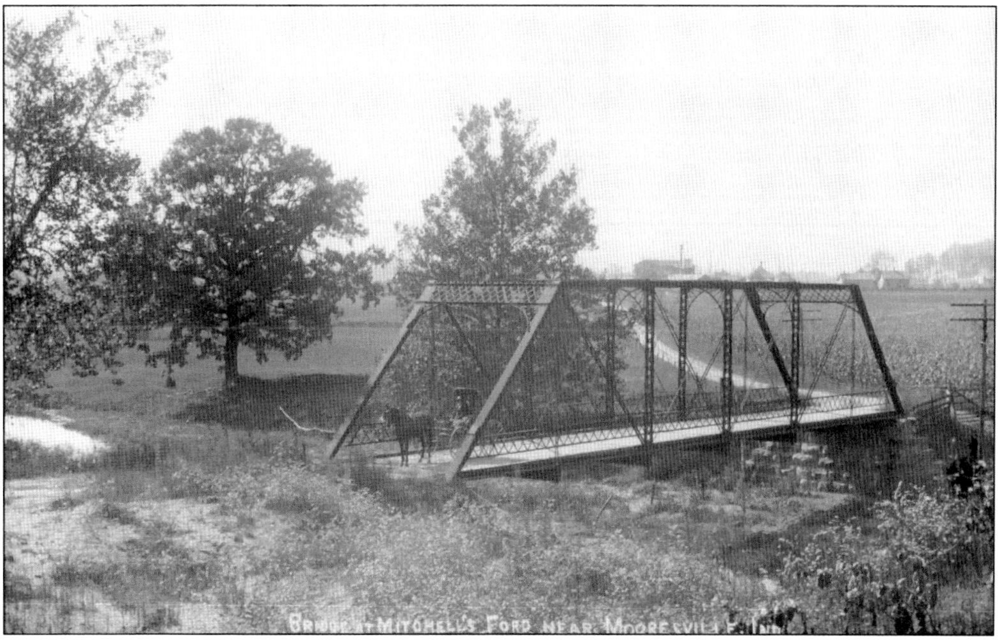

BRIDGE AT MITCHELL'S FORD, C. 1908. Carrying Bridge Street over Little White Lick Creek, this Pratt through truss metal bridge was located on the Giles B. Mitchell homestead. Identified by the pattern of its vertical and diagonal members locked in tension, the Pratt truss was repeatedly selected by the Morgan County commissioners in a period of extensive bridge building between approximately 1880 and 1900.

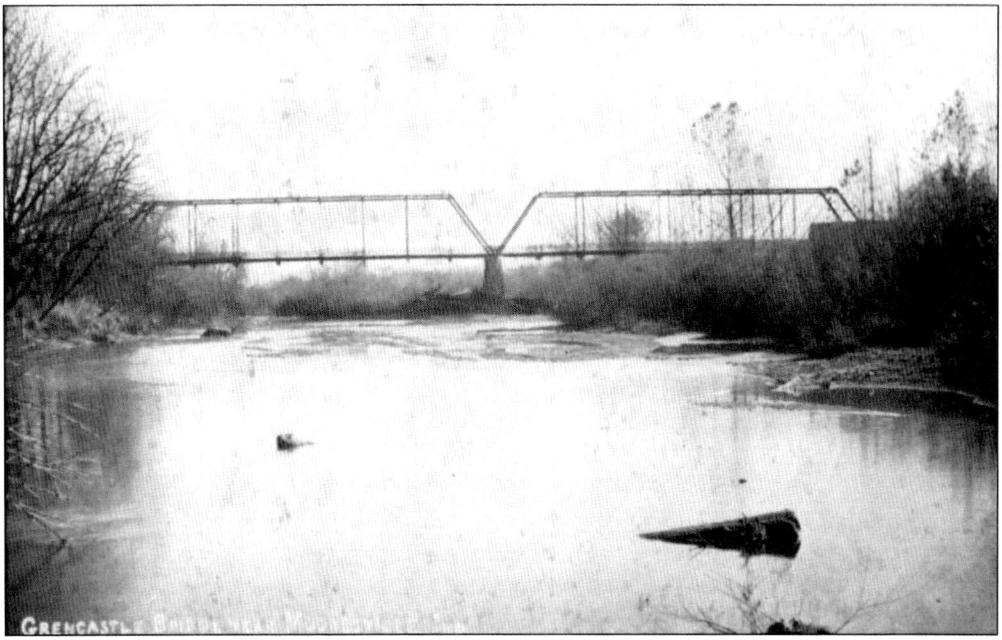

GREENCASTLE BRIDGE, *C.* 1910. Erected on Greencastle Road over White Lick Creek in 1884, this bridge is comprised of two Pratt through trusses. In September 1950, a semitruck carrying frozen fish plunged through the wood decking. The bridge was repaired. Then in December 1956, a car collided with the east span causing its collapse. The entire structure was replaced by a concrete bridge in 1958.

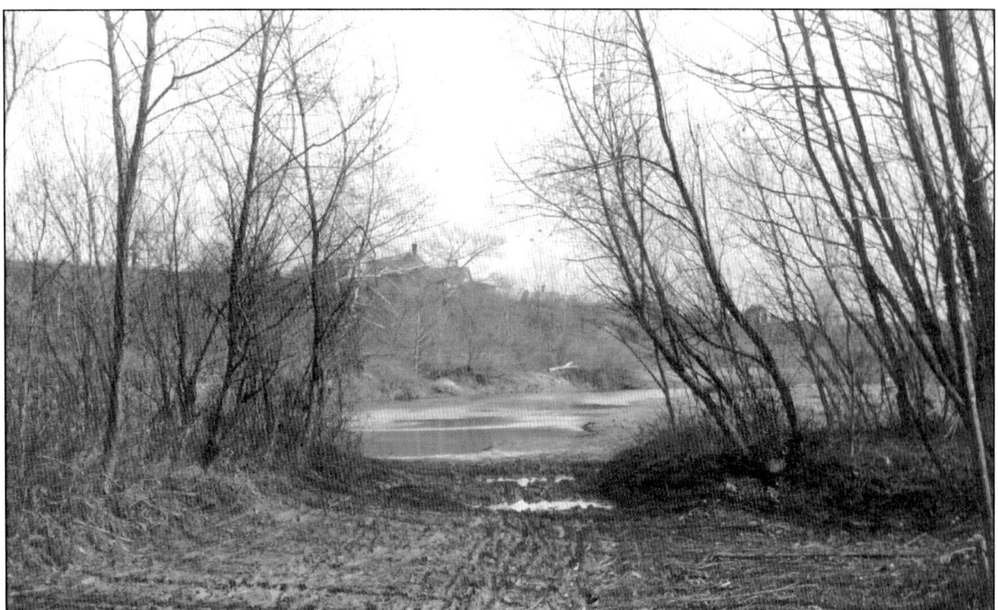

FORD BELOW MONROVIA PIKE BRIDGE, 1909. Wheel tracks can be seen in the mud at this White Lick Creek crossing used by farmers and other travelers who opted to bypass the bridge west of Mooresville on what is now State Road 42.

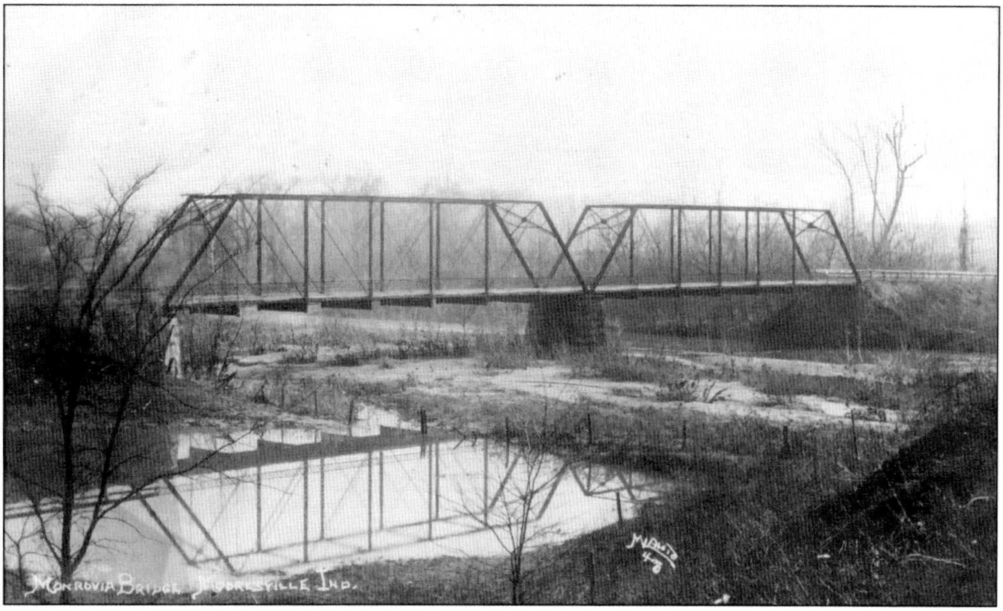

BRIDGE OVER WHITE LICK CREEK ON THE ROAD TO MONROVIA, 1911. This two-span Pratt bridge was fabricated in 1891 by the Wrought Iron Bridge Company of Canton, Ohio. Pieces were shipped to the train depot in Mooresville and then transported to the site. Employees assembled them, Erector Set–like, completing the bridge by the late-October deadline. The bridge remained in use until it was replaced in 1964–1965. Its replacement was in turn replaced in 2006.

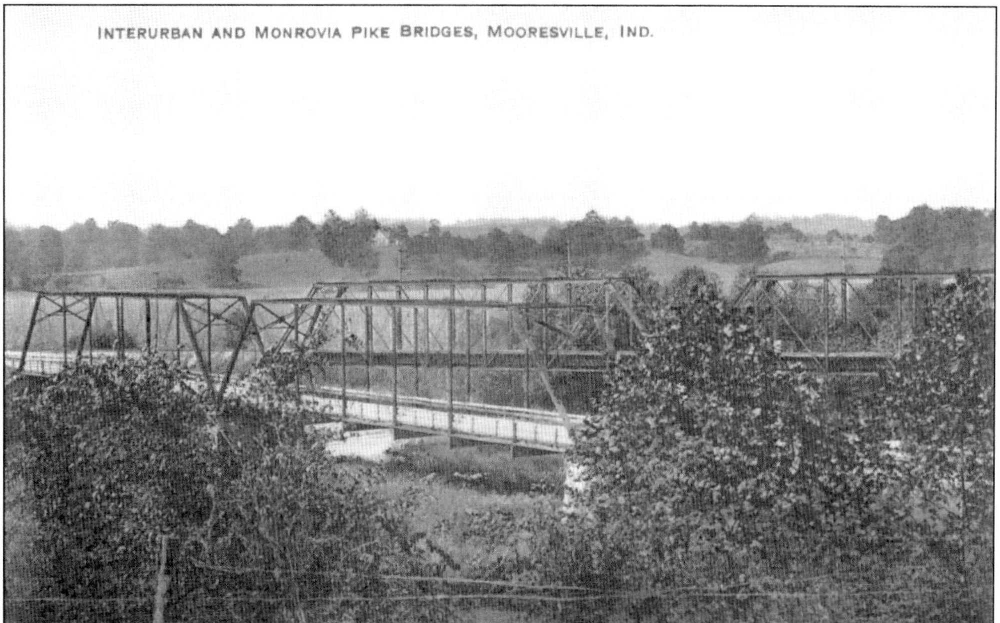

INTERURBAN AND MONROVIA BRIDGES, *C.* 1915. In 1901, a bridge carrying the line of the THI&ET was constructed at a 45-degree angle to the Monrovia Bridge. The line ran south from the state capitol to its midpoint—a power station on Harrison Street—before continuing on to its termination in Martinsville.

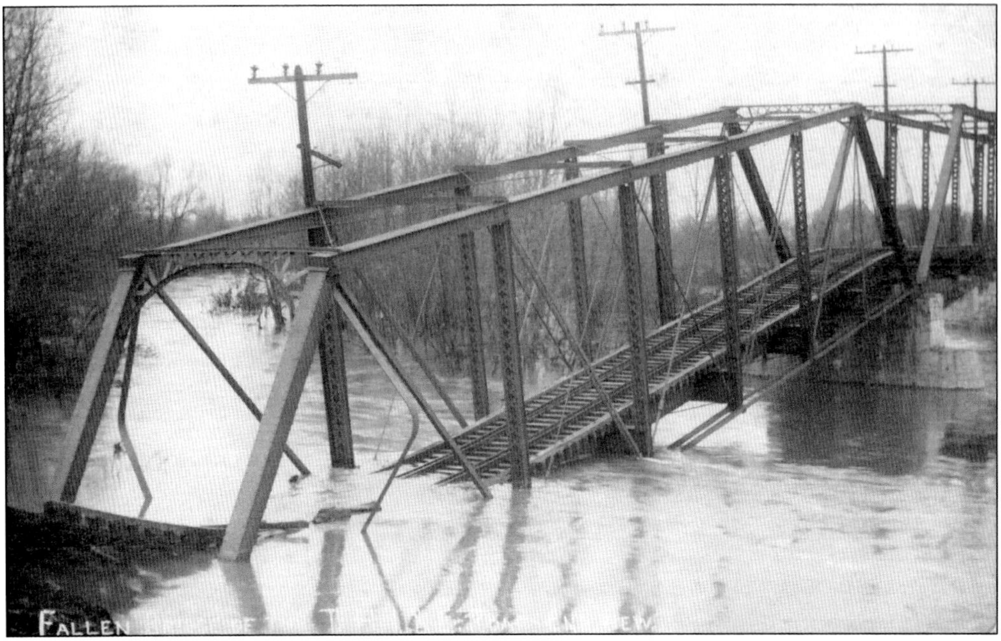

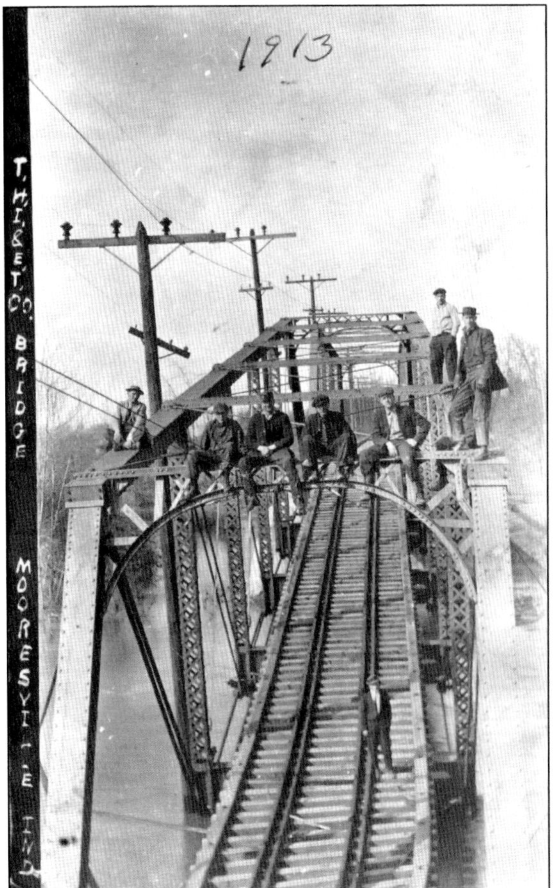

Fallen THI&ET Bridge, 1913. A penciled message on the reverse side of postcard above reads, "This is a picture of the street car bridge below the power house. Calvert took it Wednesday it look, just that way when we went to see it." The bridge collapsed during the 1913 flood.

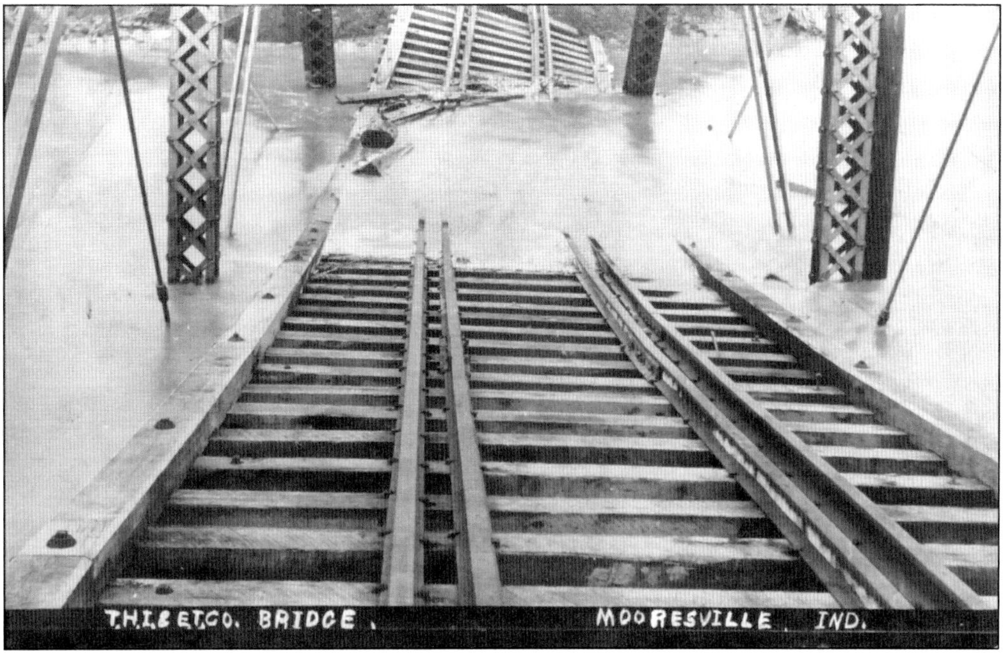

FLOOD-DAMAGED THI&ET BRIDGE, 1913. The bridge, tracks, and service were restored within months of the flood.

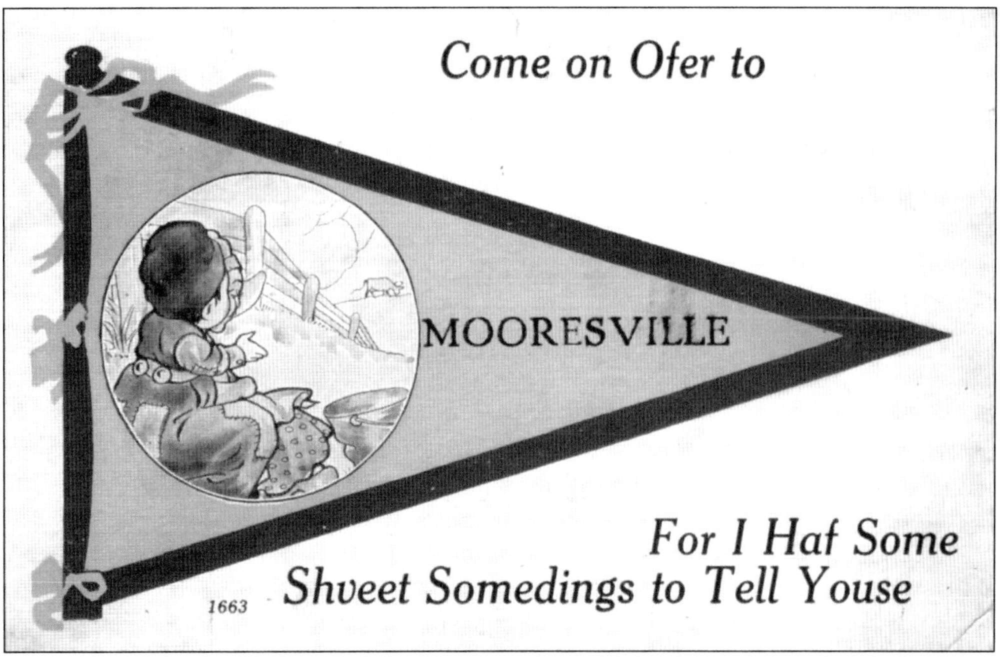

COMIC PENNANT CARD, 1913. Portrayed in profile, wearing traditional costume, and apparently speaking heavily accented English, this Dutch couple is reminiscent of Bertha Corbett Melcher's illustrations of Sunbonnet Babies, which inspired the Sunbonnet Sue quilt pattern popular around 1905–1930.

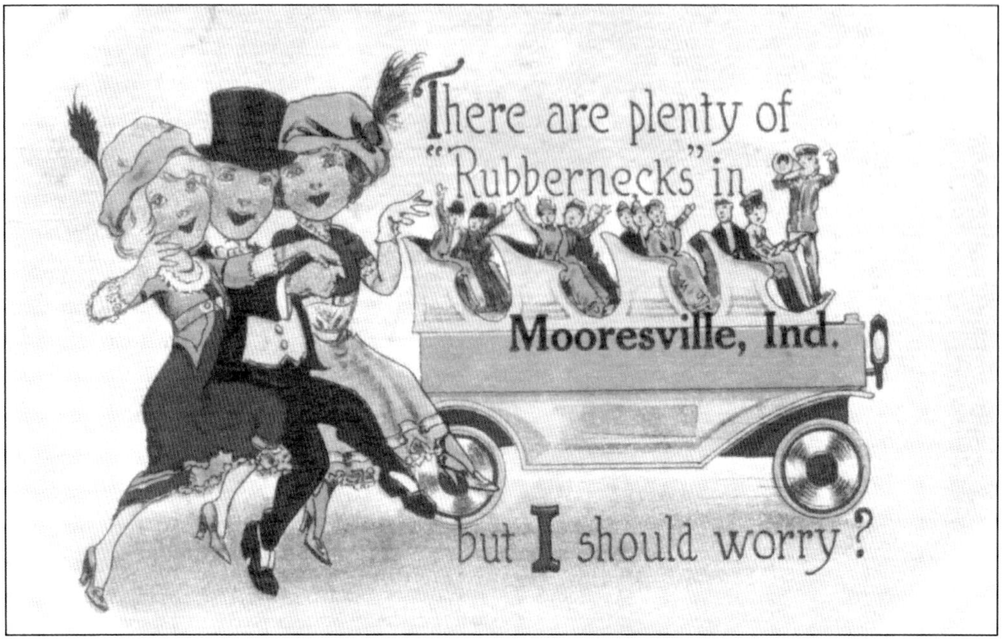

GENERIC COMIC CARD, 1914. From the innocence of Sunbonnet Babies, to the sexual innuendoes of the flapper age, to the increasing popularity of the newfangled motorcar, postcard themes of the second decade of the 20th century covered the gamut of American popular culture.

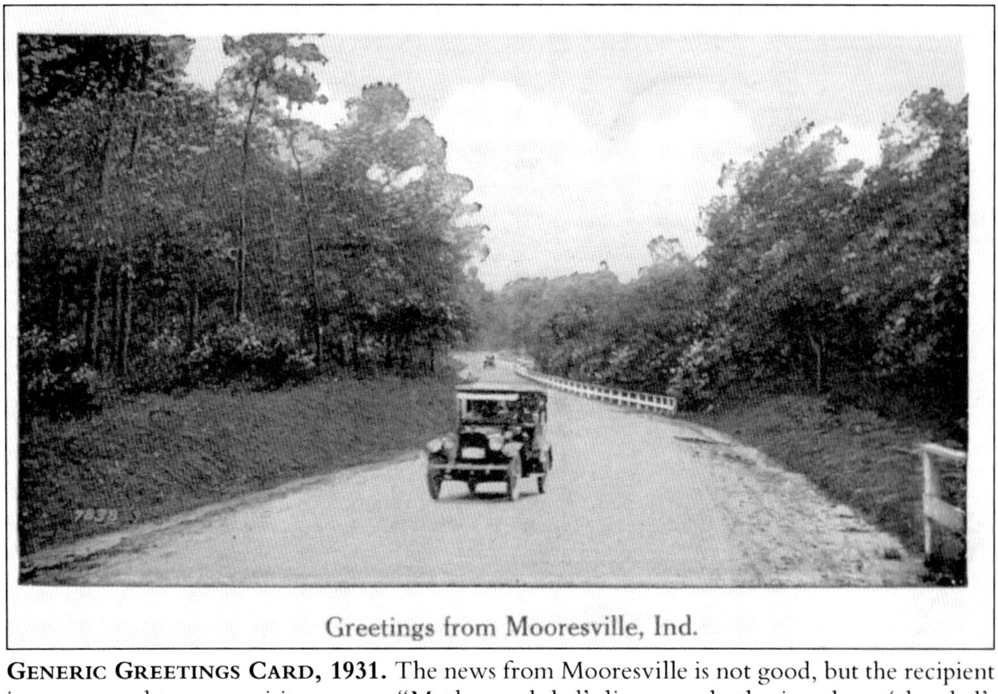

GENERIC GREETINGS CARD, 1931. The news from Mooresville is not good, but the recipient is encouraged to pay a visit anyway. "Mother and dad's livers are bothering them (also dad's collitis). I have a blister on my heel and can't walk good. Come out soon." The writer, Mother, and Dad are staying in rooms 15 and 16 at Dr. Jot Comer's sanitarium.

Three

Morgantown, Mahalasville, Paragon, and Waverly

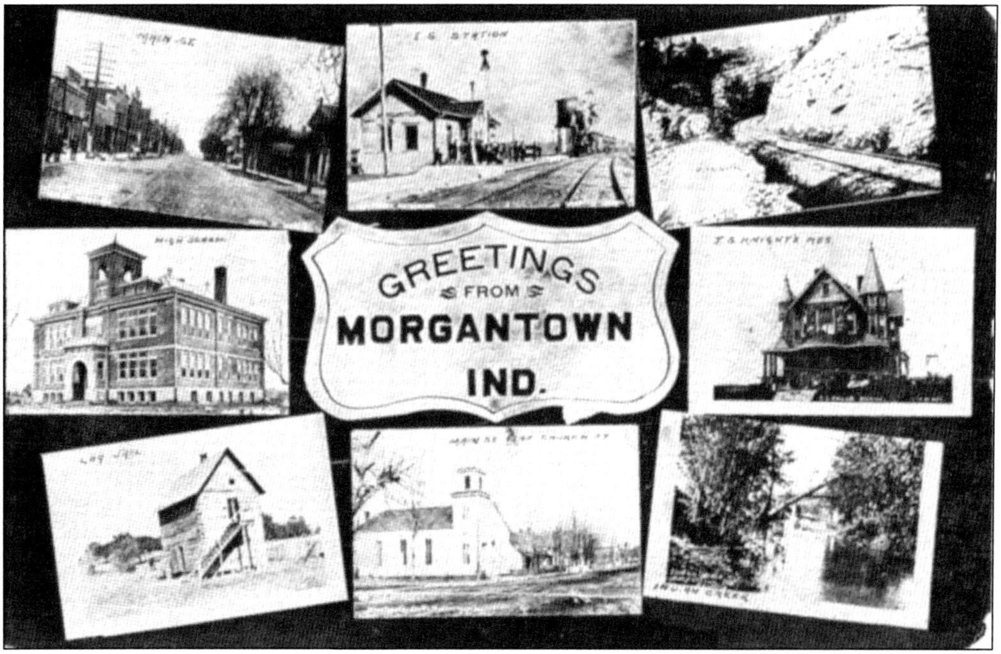

Morgantown Multiview, *c.* 1910. This postcard is a product of the B. H. Grimes Company of Frankfort, Indiana. Clockwise from the upper left, the scenes are Main Street looking west from Cross Street; the Indianapolis Southern (later the Illinois Central) depot; the Indianapolis Southern railroad tunnel at Unionville (oops!); James S. Knight's house, now known as the Rock House; Indian Creek; the Methodist church and the north side of Main Street; a log jail in Nashville (another oops!); and Morgantown High School.

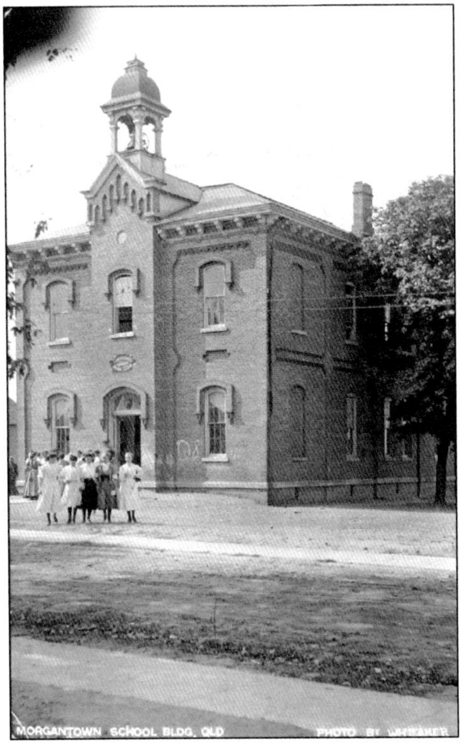

OLD MORGANTOWN SCHOOL, 1908. Built on Marion Street in 1870, this four-room school building was dubbed Arnold University after the Jackson Township trustee then in office. The school housed grades 1 through 12, with the first four-year high school class graduating in 1901. The unidentified owner of this card—presumably one of the girls shown—wrote on the reverse, "Where I graduated and was then torn down ha ha." A new building on Elm Street replaced this school in 1909.

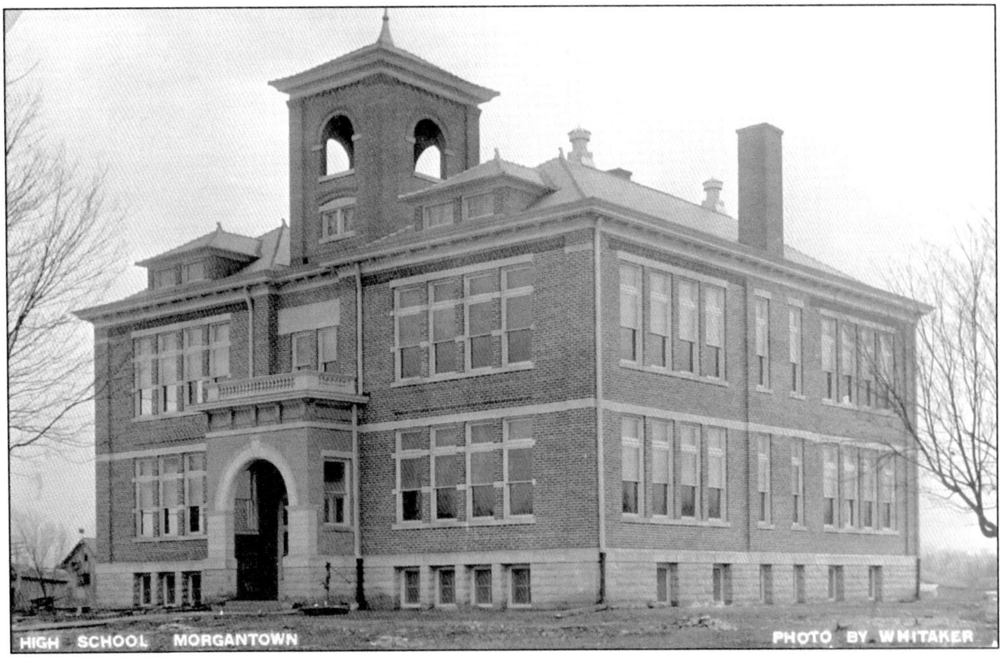

NEW MORGANTOWN HIGH SCHOOL, 1909. Following the last graduating class in 1967, this building became Morgantown Elementary School. It closed in 1986 and was torn down six years later. Susie F., the sender of this card, wrote to Mr. and Mrs. William Obenshain of Baltimore, Maryland, "I sending you picture of new school House. Don't you think it is a fine building—almost wish I was going to school again."

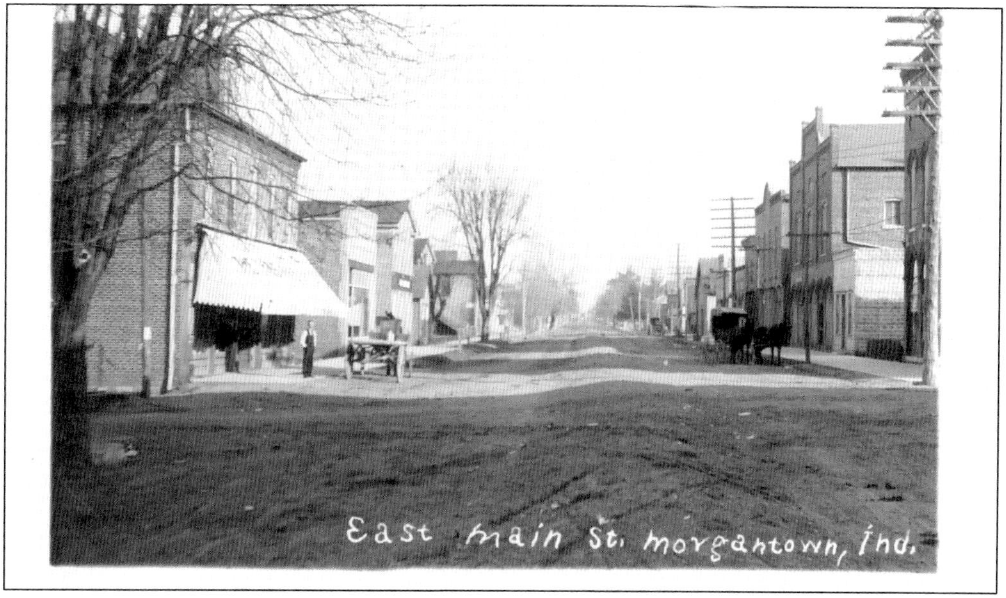

WASHINGTON STREET, LOOKING EAST FROM MARION STREET, 1909. At left is the Farmers Cooperative Store (now the bank building), the First National Bank of Morgantown, built in 1905, and the pre-Civil War-era Obenshain Hotel. At right, on the south side of the street, are the two-story Masonic and IOOF lodges. The slightly shorter building behind the telephone pole—note the absence of lines—is Mitchell Hardware, now Morgantown Hardware.

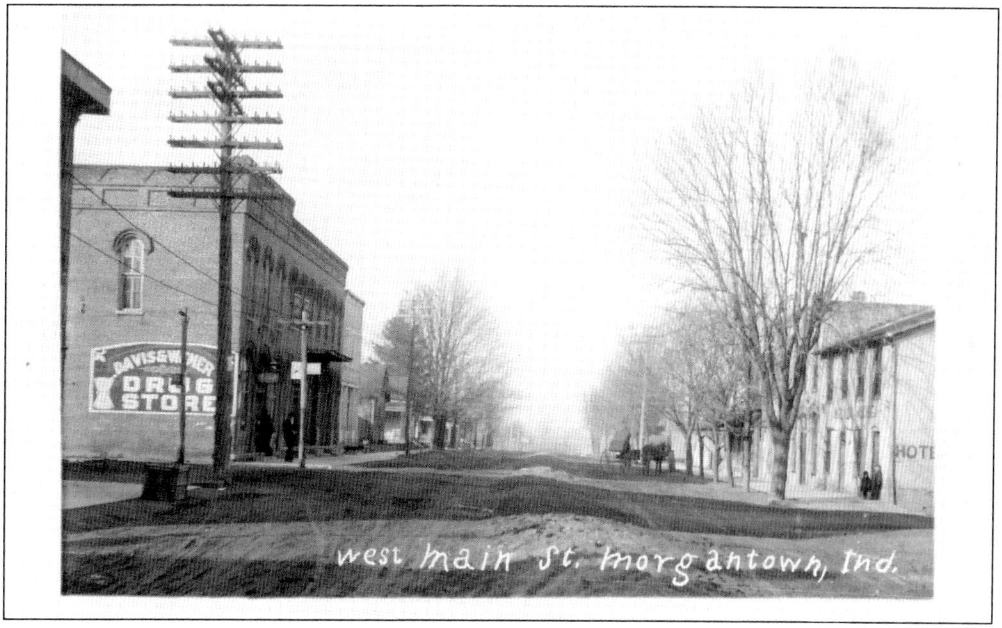

WASHINGTON STREET, LOOKING WEST FROM MARION STREET, C. 1910. A traveler heading west to Martinsville would have passed on the left the Davis and Wemer drugstore, the post office, a pool room, and the Morgantown Truth newspaper office. On the right stood the large Walker House hotel, a barbershop, and meat market. Only the drugstore remains standing—and only the shorter portion of it at that.

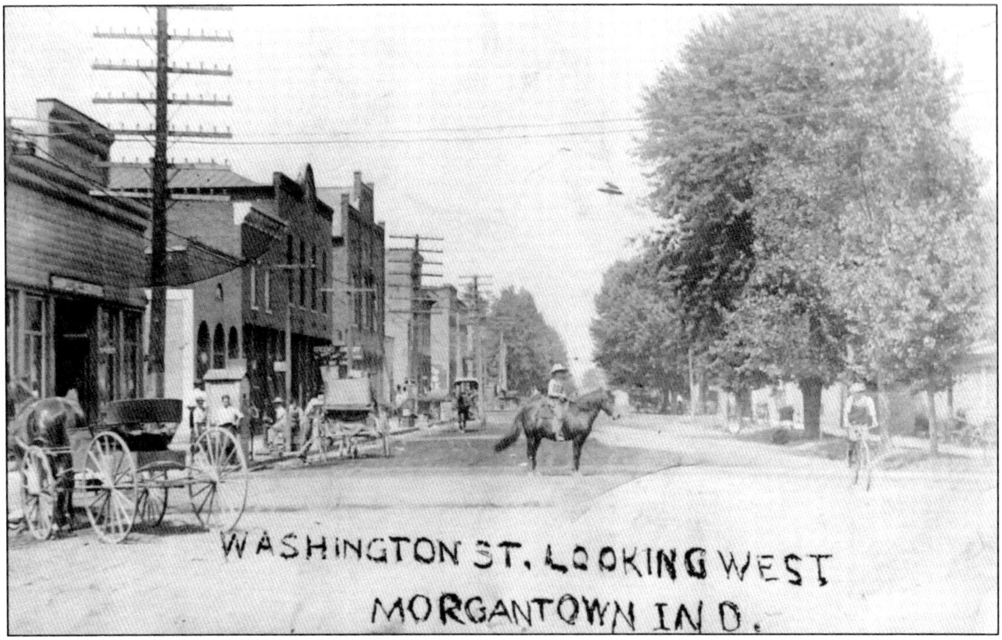

WASHINGTON STREET, LOOKING WEST FROM CROSS STREET, C. 1909. At left is Woods and Whitaker grocery, followed by Louis Kuhn's ice-cream parlor, Mitchell Hardware (now Morgantown Hardware), the IOOF hall, the Masonic lodge, a barbershop, Karst dry goods store, and Davis and Wemer drugstore.

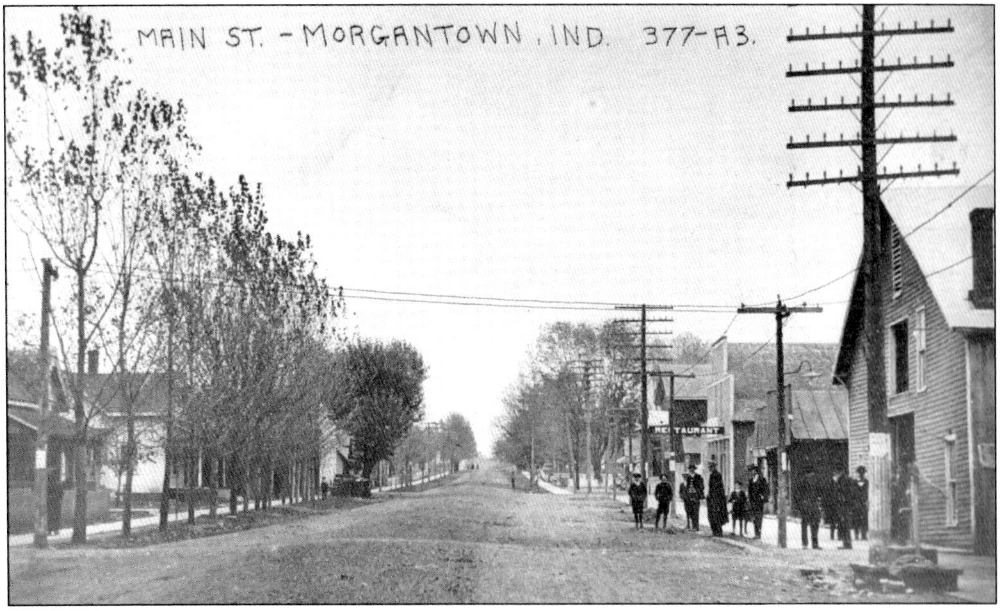

VIEW OF WASHINGTON STREET, LOOKING EAST FROM CROSS STREET, C. 1907. This photograph was taken a short time prior to a 1908 fire that destroyed the buildings shown on the right. In the foreground is Cap Lawrence's livery barn. In 1914, Joe Woods and Morris Canatsey opened a Dodge and Plymouth dealership on the same corner. As cars replaced horses, the hand pump used for watering horses, shown in the right foreground, was replaced by service stations.

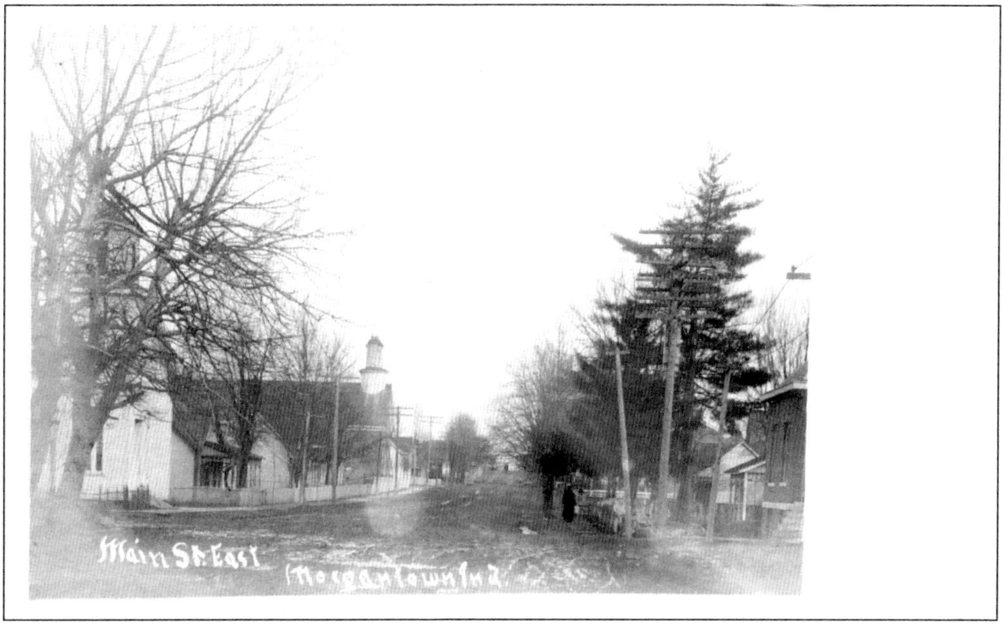

WASHINGTON STREET, LOOKING EAST FROM CHURCH STREET, *c.* 1910. The Methodist church, built in 1858, is seen through the tree branches at near left. It was extensively remodeled and given a brick veneer in 1928. Farther east is the Christian church, completed in 1871 at a cost of $3,000. The steeple makes it easily recognizable. The brick telephone exchange appears at the near right.

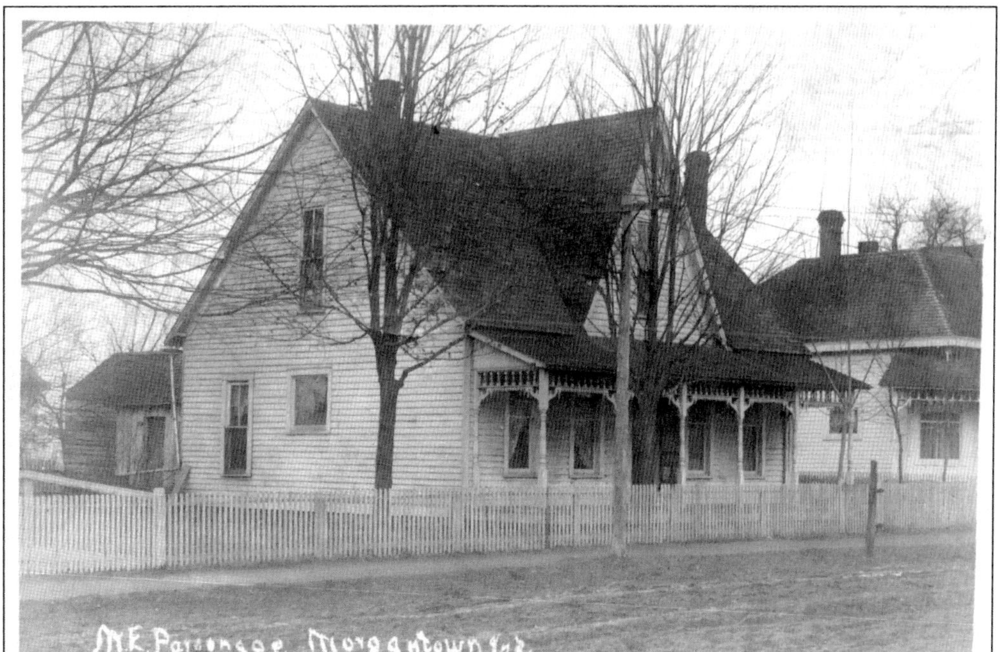

METHODIST PARSONAGE, 1907. Located a few doors east of the Methodist church, this Gothic Revival–style house served as the first parsonage. It was replaced by the existing house at 80 East Washington Street about 1910. The house shown at right was purchased by Dr. Ira and Rosalie Willan in 1924. They added the brick veneer it wears yet today.

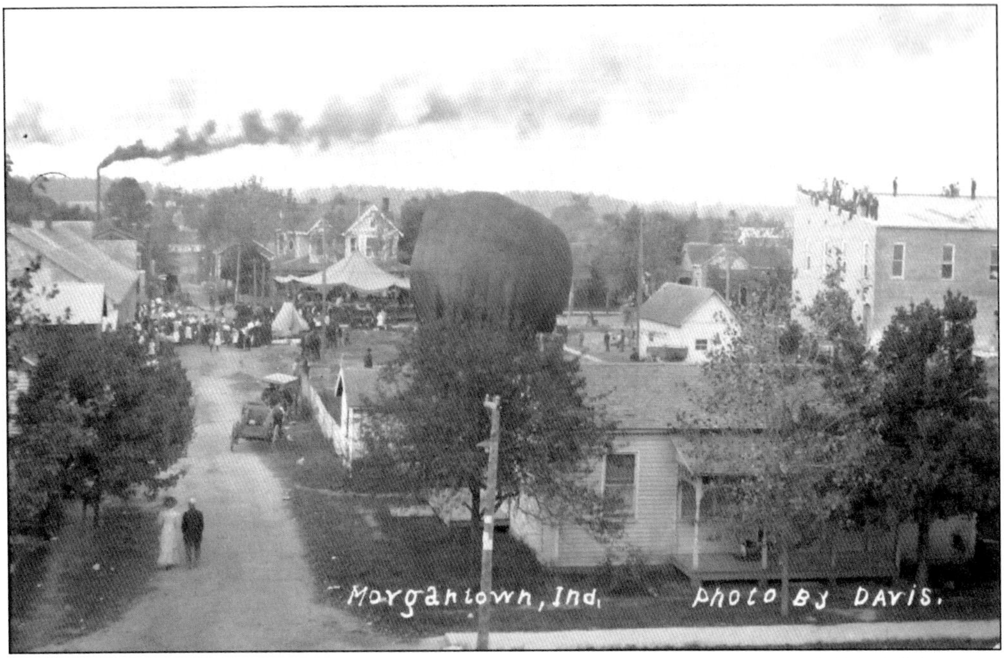

Street Fair with Balloon, Washington and Cross Streets, 1909. This event occurred in late summer 1909, a year in which balloonists, known as aeronauts, captured the popular imagination. In this photograph, spectators sit on the roof of the new Redmen Hall, the first building completed after the fire of 1908 devastated the block. The smokestack in the background is the electric light plant.

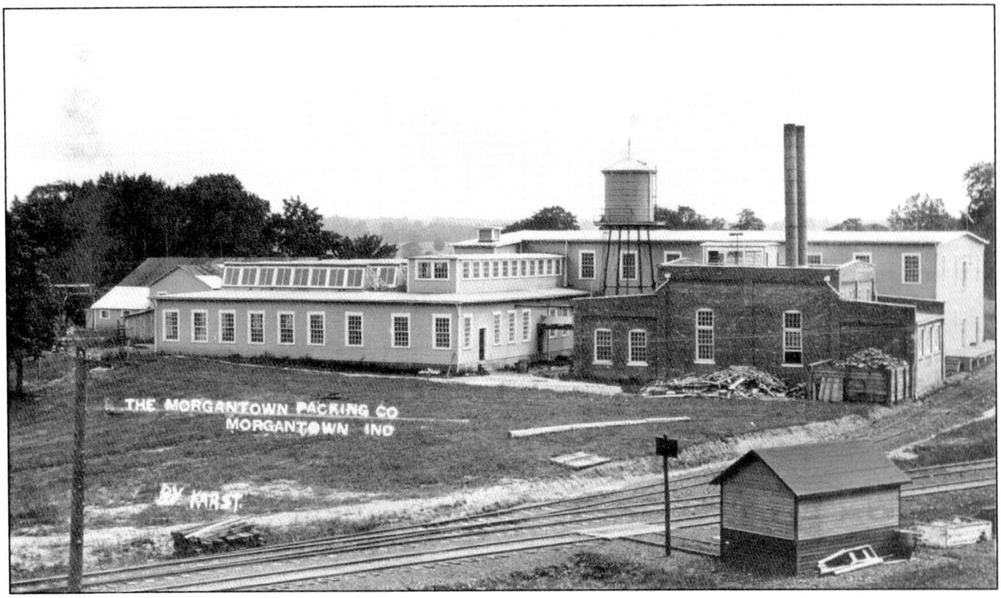

Morgantown Packing Company, 1912. "This will give you some idea of our canning factory," the sender of this card writes. "We have a Saw tooth Roof and a North Light, fine drainage and a fine breeze. We have sent aunt Pet another view so you can all see what our factory is like from the different sides. They are awfully busy canning now." The factory operated from about 1912 to 1950.

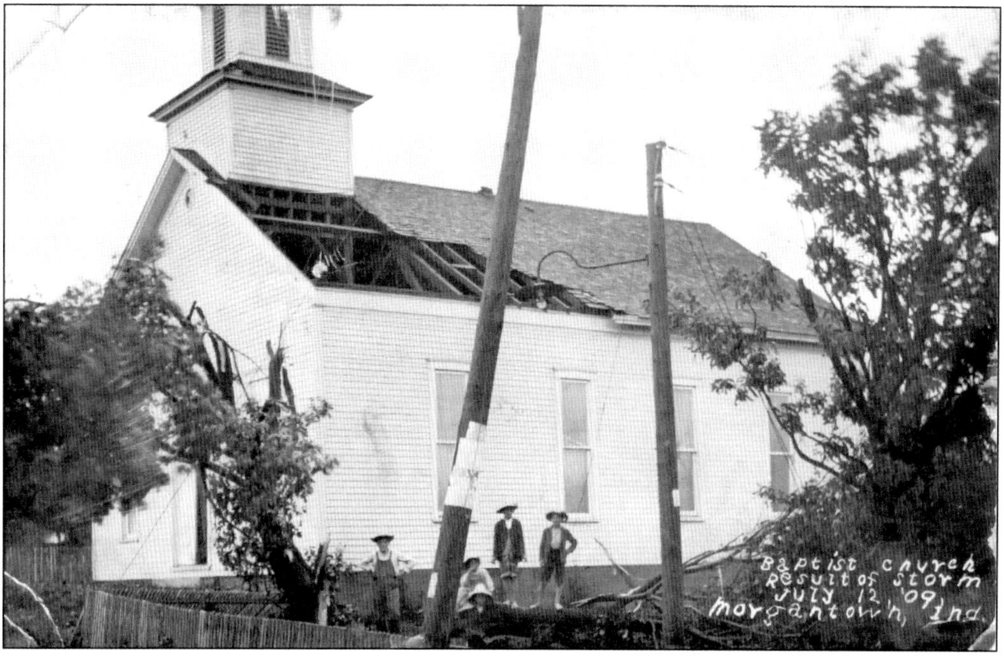

MORGANTOWN BAPTIST CHURCH, 1909. On July 12, a twisterlike storm tore off a portion of the roof of the Baptist church at the northeast corner of Mulberry and Marion Streets, causing damage estimated at $300. Built in 1875, the church has been remodeled many times. In 1927, it was raised and a basement was constructed. Today it is a popular restaurant and dance hall.

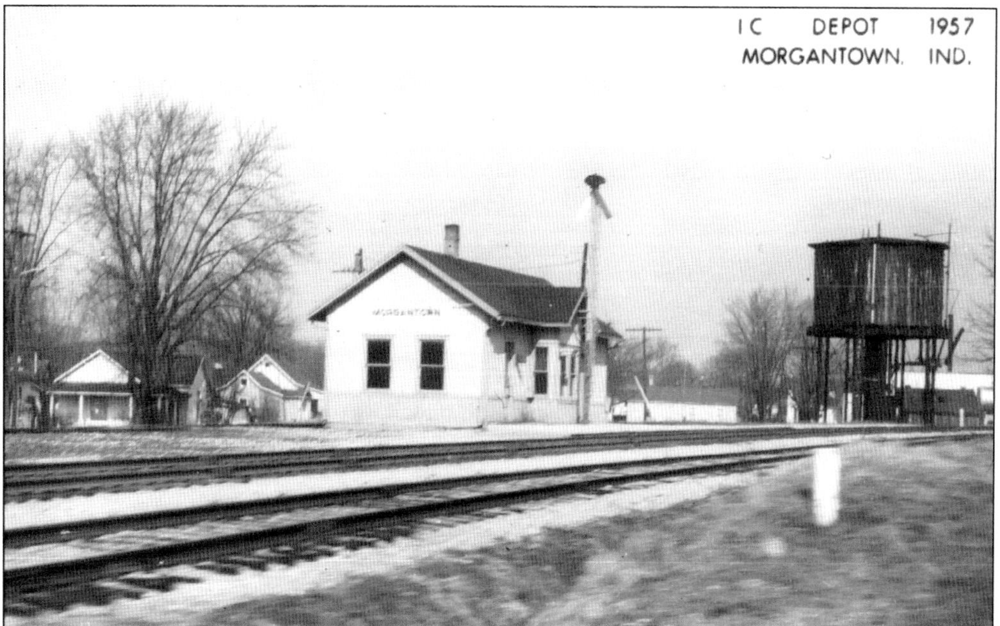

ILLINOIS CENTRAL DEPOT, 1957. A retired railroad worker who traveled across Indiana photographing old depots captured this view of the Illinois Central depot and roofless water tank not long before both were demolished.

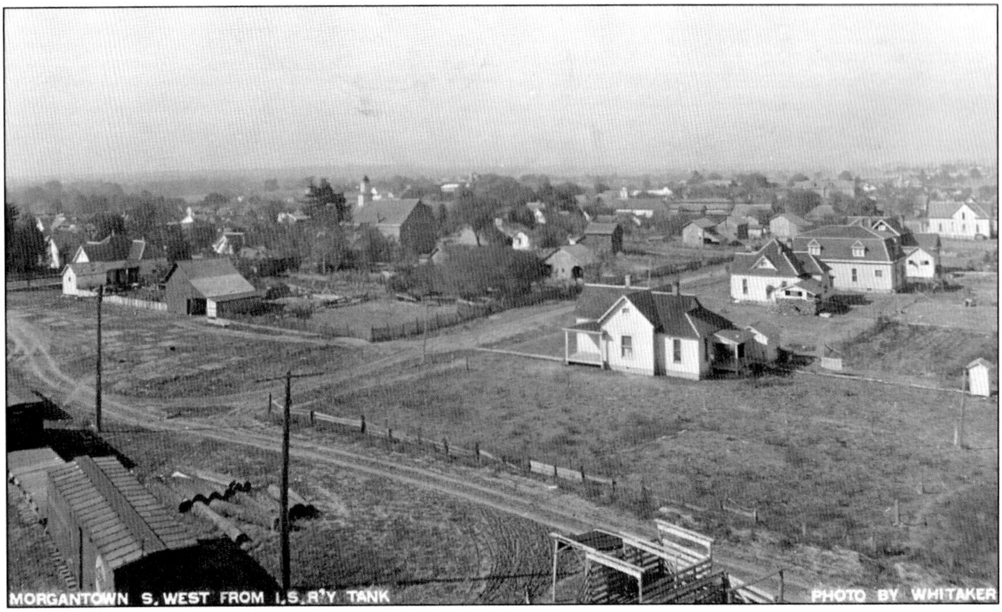

LOOKING SOUTHWEST FROM INDIANAPOLIS SOUTHERN WATER TANK, *c.* 1909. Photographer Whitaker, about whom nothing more than a last name is known, must have been a bit of a daredevil. From the top of the water tank, the Christian church steeple can be picked out. Note the agricultural use of rear yards with their large gardens and barns.

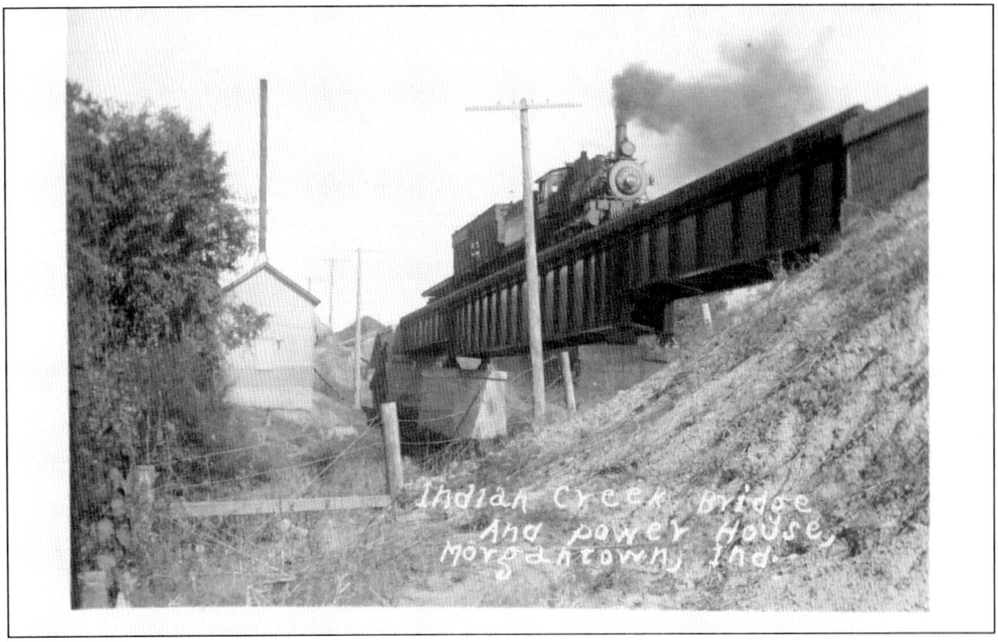

INDIAN CREEK BRIDGE AND POWERHOUSE, ILLINOIS CENTRAL RAILROAD, 1911. Two trains a day carried freight, mail, and passengers between Morgantown and Indianapolis and Effingham, Illinois. Charlie Teeters of Morgantown operated the coal-fired powerhouse for many years. It drew water from the creek and pumped it to the storage tank at the depot. This photograph is by Granville E. Davis.

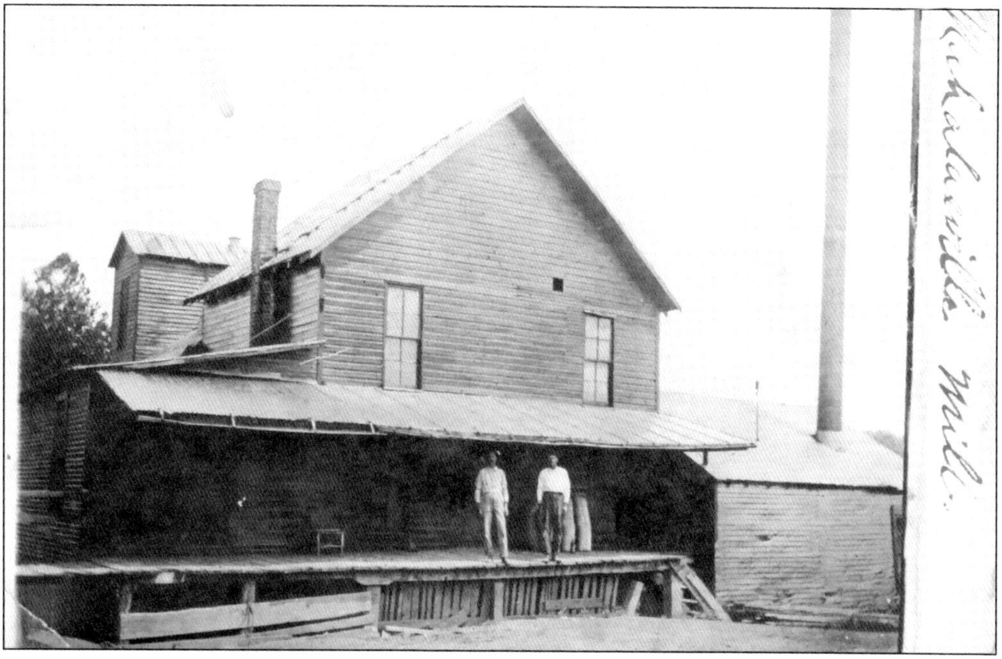

MAHALASVILLE MILL, 1909. Located on Indian Creek, this gristmill was built in the 1840s by John Coonfield. It went through a number of owners and/or operators, including these two men, miller Billy Grubbs and mill manager Charlie Frounfelter. The mill was destroyed by fire in the mid-1940s.

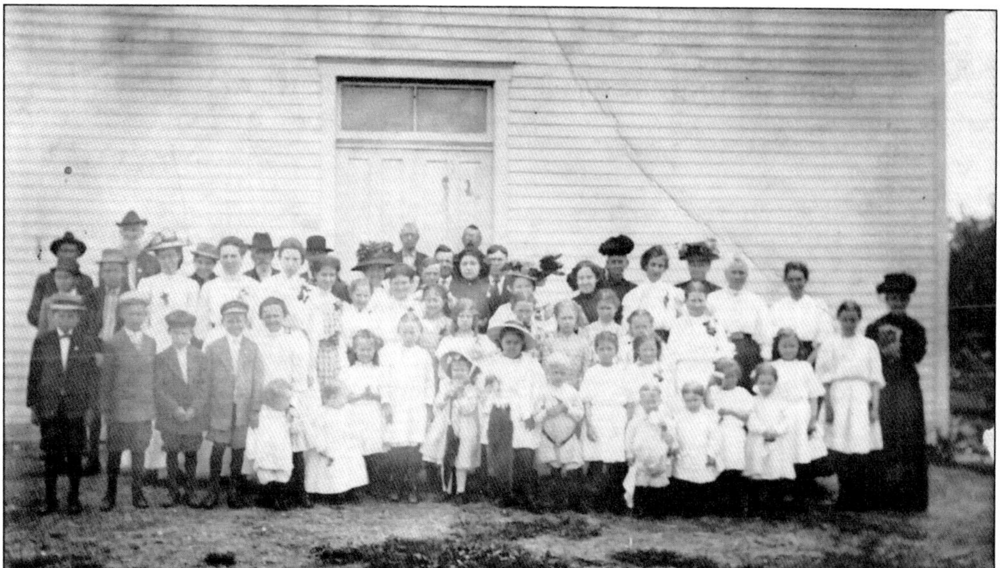

SUNDAY SCHOOL CLASS, MAHALASVILLE METHODIST EPISCOPAL CHURCH, *c.* 1910. Located next to the town cemetery on Voyles Road, the Methodist church was an important community center from about 1885 to 1945. A rift between Republican and Democrat members in 1888–1889 led to the organization of a Methodist Protestant congregation. The only identified persons in this photograph are Sylvia Thacker Smith (first row, fifth from left) and Christine Platt McElroy (third row, black-haired girl at center).

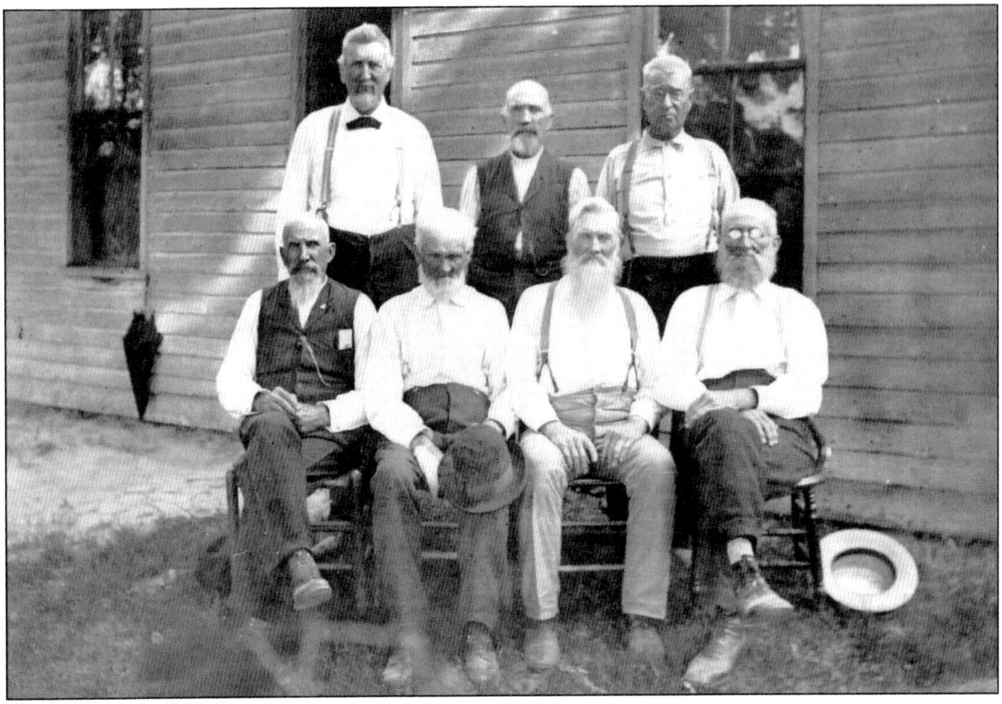

Civil War Veterans, Mahalasville, c. 1914. As part of a community Decoration Day celebration, these survivors of the Civil War posed for the photographer. The backdrop may be the Mahalasville Baptist Church. They are, from left to right, (first row) Tom Townsend, Jesse Smith Cain, Mose Coffey, and Joe Clendenen; (second row) John Tutterow, John Wells, and John Renigar.

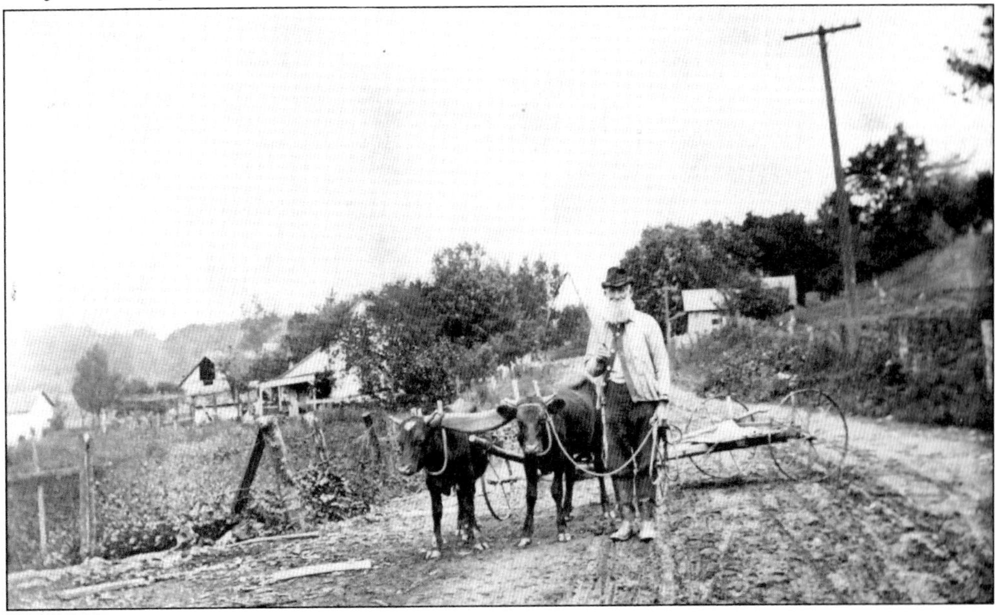

Joe Clendenen, c. 1910. Having walked his team of young oxen a mile up hill from Mahalasville, this farmer, Civil War veteran, and respected community member pauses before turning onto Townsend Road.

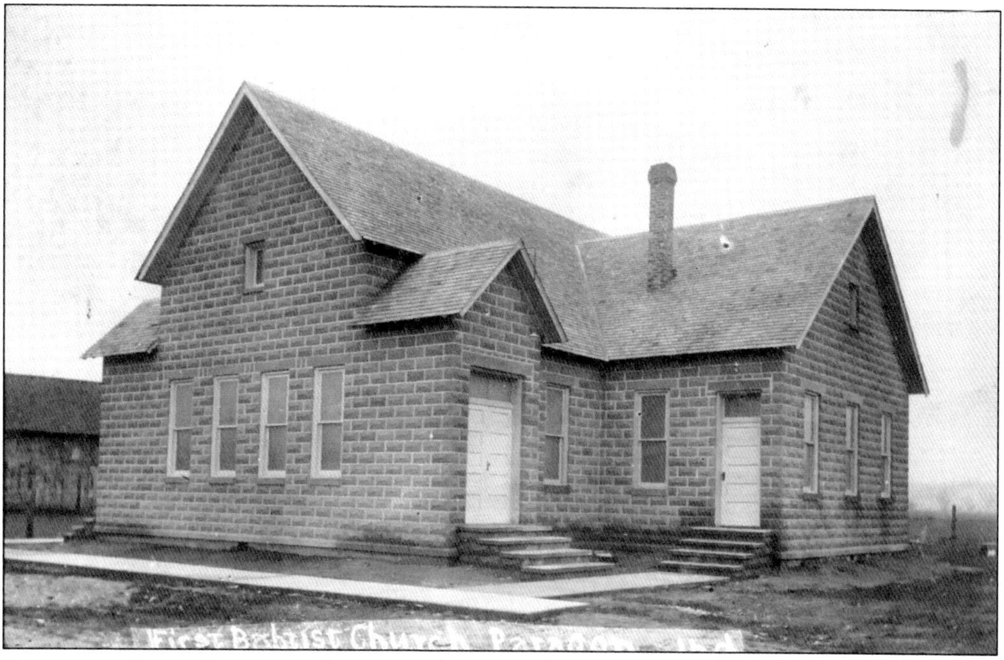

Paragon First Baptist Church, 1914. Dedicated on November 2, 1913, the Baptist church was a faith-filled effort by a very young congregation established just a year earlier. Later enhancements to the block building include stained-glass windows and a bell tower that replaced the entrance shown at center. The church is in use yet today.

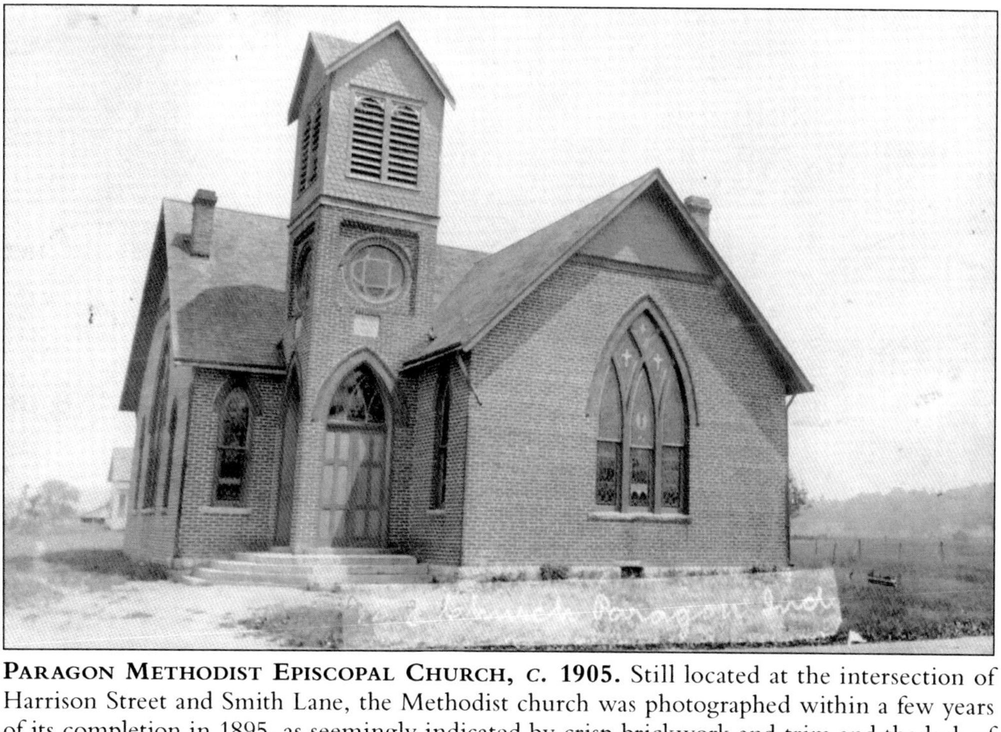

Paragon Methodist Episcopal Church, c. 1905. Still located at the intersection of Harrison Street and Smith Lane, the Methodist church was photographed within a few years of its completion in 1895, as seemingly indicated by crisp brickwork and trim and the lack of foundation plantings and trees.

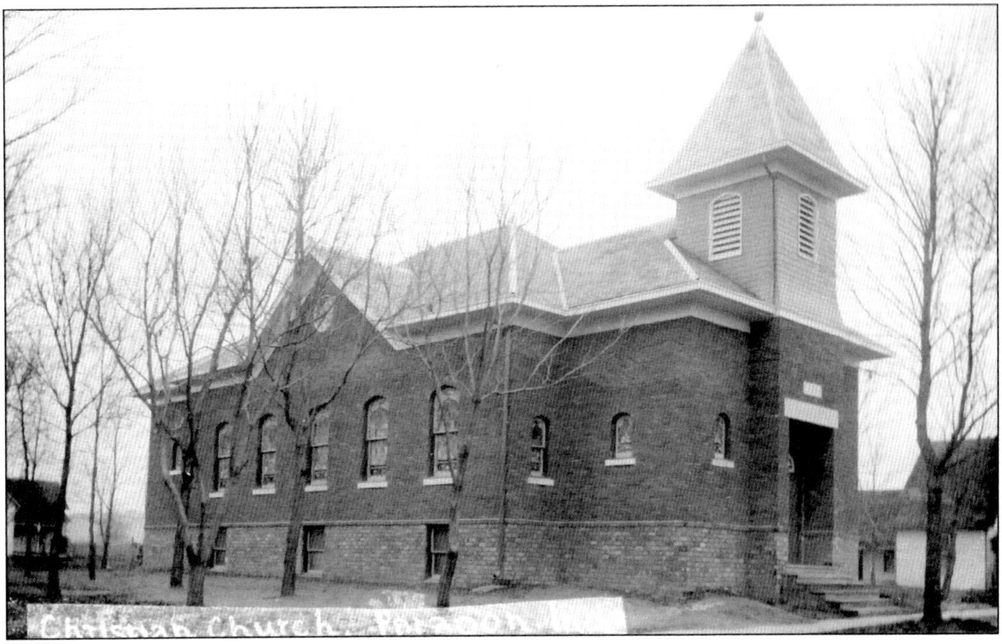

PARAGON CHRISTIAN CHURCH, *C.* 1915. The Christian congregation was organized in 1852. The first church—a frame building—was built in 1858, moved to the present site in 1890, and rededicated a year later. In 1912, the church was entirely remodeled and clad with brick. In 1913, the building was raised and a basement added. The church continues to serve its congregation.

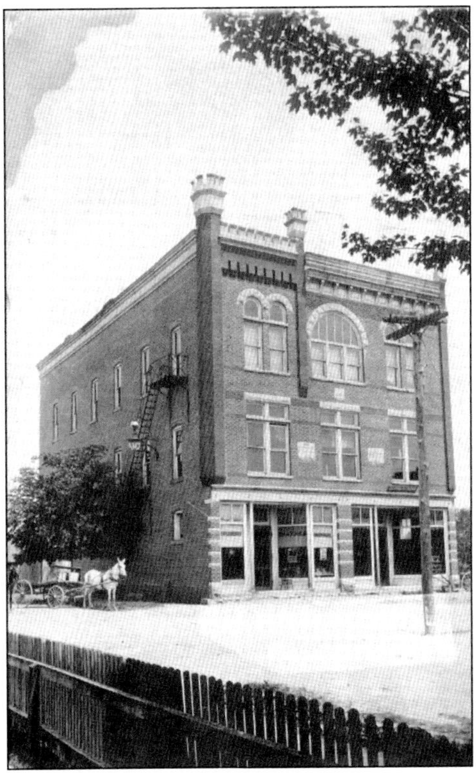

IOOF/KNIGHTS OF PYTHIAS HALL, 1908. The third floor of this striking Romanesque Revival building, built 1898–1899, contained two rooms, each serving as the lodge of the different fraternal orders. In October 1936, a sketch of Paragon's Main Street by noted Hoosier artist Frederick Polley appeared in the *Indianapolis Star.* Polley wrote that he was inspired by "the octagonal corner rising above the main building and ending in a turetlike finial."

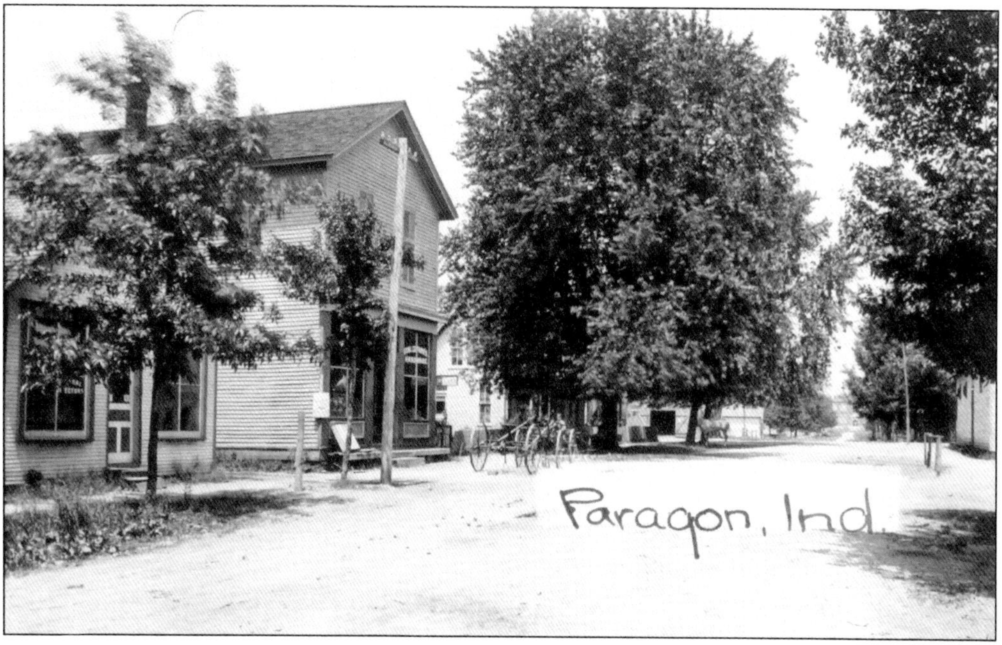

WEST SIDE OF MAIN STREET, LOOKING NORTH, 1908. At the near left is the undertaking and furniture business operated by brothers Paul and Earl Beggeman. Paul Beggeman had a nearly 50-year career as a funeral director in Paragon. Next is Coble and Farr's hardware store. Samuel F. Coble, who passed away in 1929, was a former teacher and a prominent merchant and banker. Paragon School can be seen in the distance, at the end of Main Street.

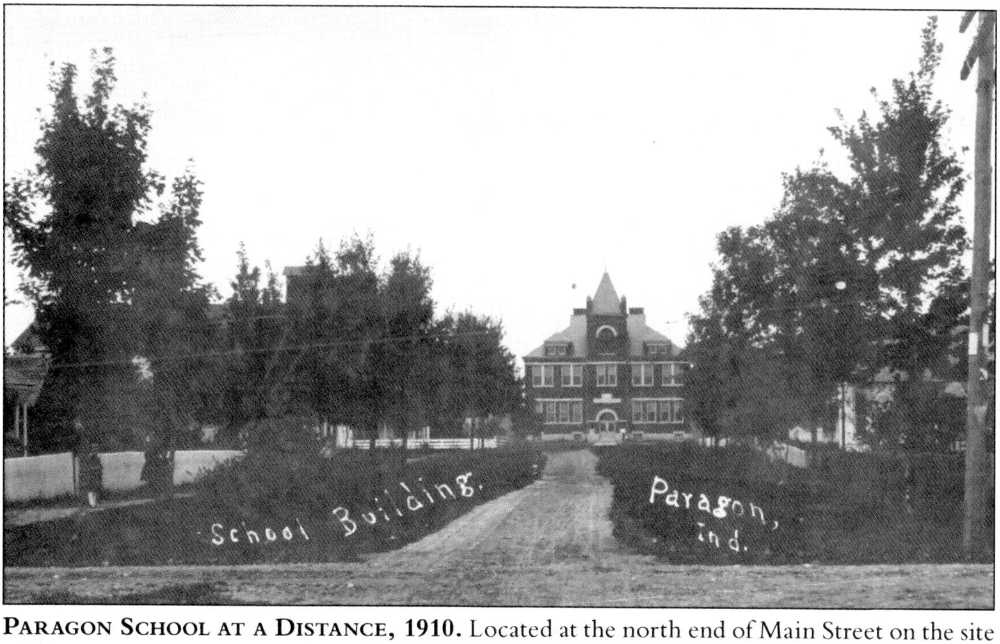

PARAGON SCHOOL AT A DISTANCE, 1910. Located at the north end of Main Street on the site of the current town park, the school received a classroom and gymnasium addition in 1923. In 1956, the high school was discontinued and students went to Martinsville. Until it was replaced by the current school in 1971, this massive old building served as Paragon Elementary School. It was dismantled gradually until 1981 when it was finally demolished.

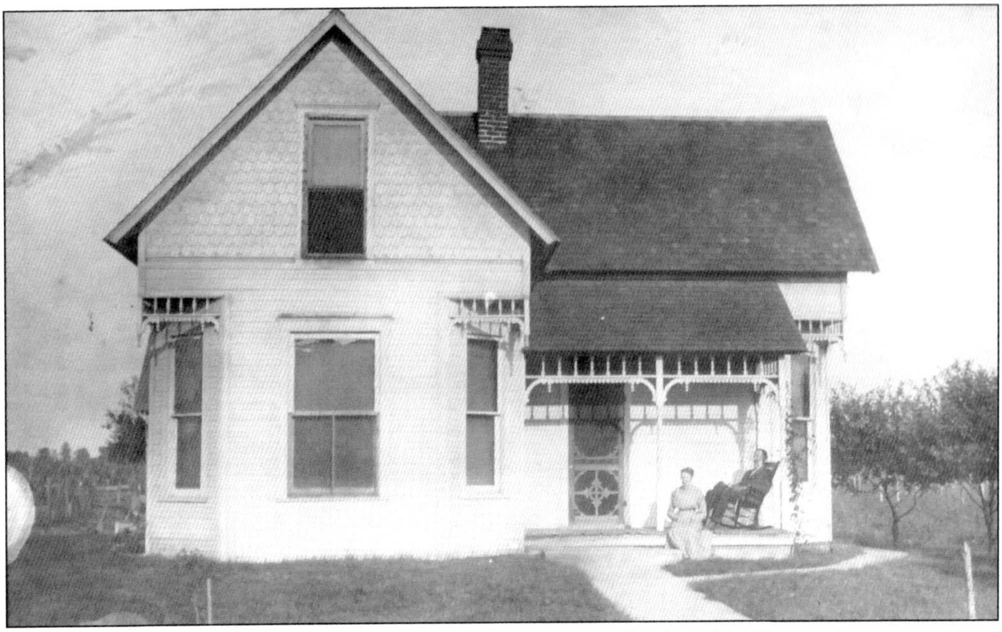

HENRY AND MARY BURKHART HOUSE, PARAGON, *C.* 1908. This Queen Anne cottage at 299 North Smith Lane appears to have been built for the Burkharts, shown here, following their retirement from farming northeast of Paragon. The Burkharts left Morgan County about 1910 for California, where their son Ambrose was employed as a postmaster. They never returned.

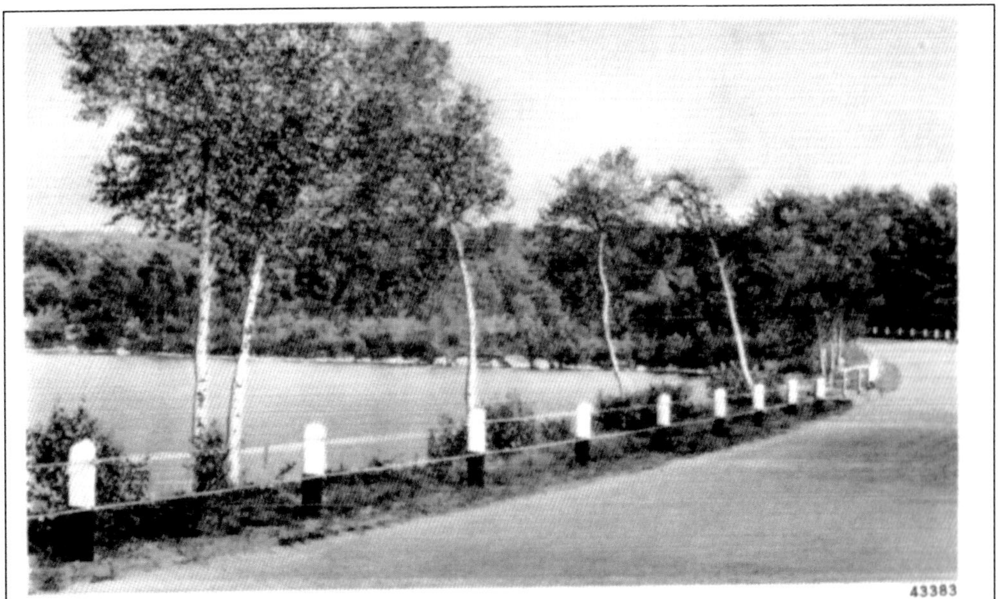

GENERIC GREETINGS CARD, FRIENDLY NEIGHBOR'S CAFE, *C.* 1946. Clarence and June Alexander operated this café on State Road 67 from about 1946 to 1953. The Alexanders' daughter, Phyllis Newton, remembers that the 1949 Indianapolis 500 was aired on Clarence's new television, the first and only live broadcast of the race in Indiana. "The cafe was so full of people. They ordered one food item at a time so they could sit there all day and watch the race."

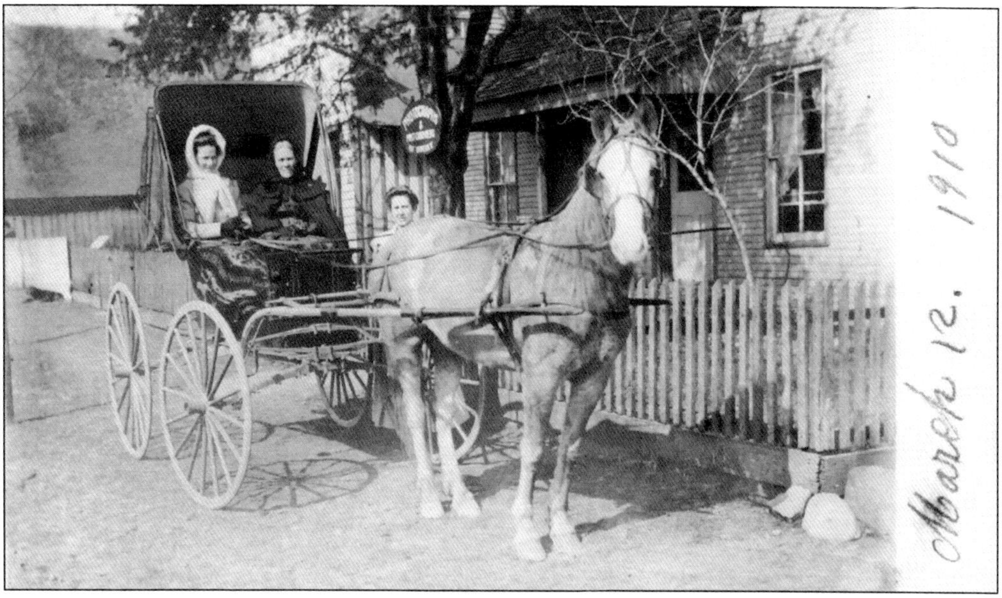

JOSEPH COUNSILMAN HOME AND SHOP, WAVERLY, 1910. The photographer of this unlikely collection of Waverly postcards was Joseph Counsilman, the father of famed Indiana University swim coach James "Doc" Counsilman. In the buggy before his home and shop—a sign advertises "Photographs & Post Card Views of Waverly"—are his mother, Anna (right), and one of his sisters (left). Joseph's wife Carrie stands beside the buggy. Anna's handwriting records the date the photograph was taken.

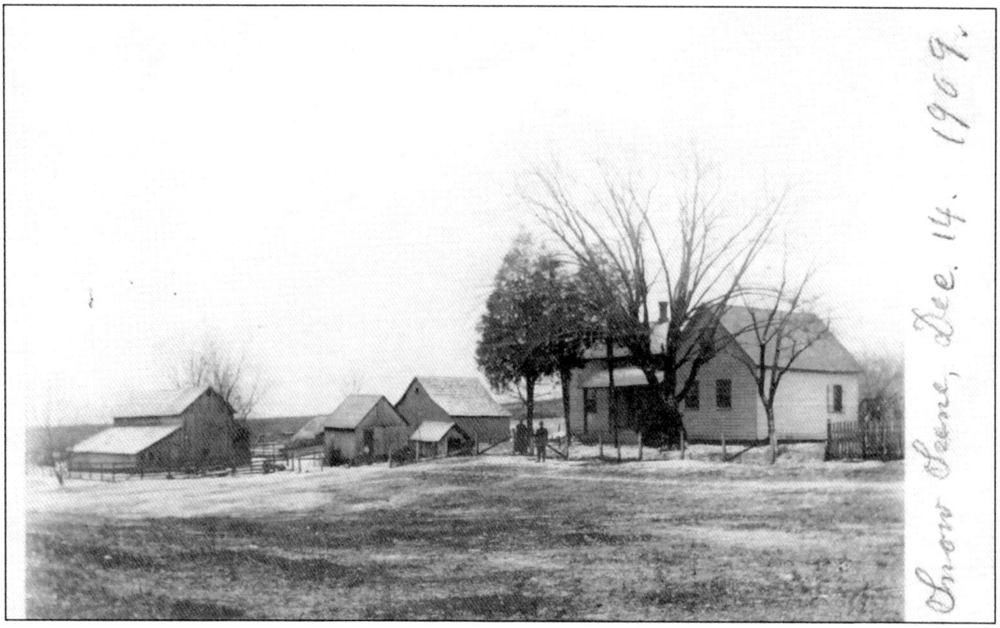

COUNSILMAN FARM, DECEMBER 14, 1909. "I don't know if you know this place or not," Anna Counsilman wrote in jest to her married daughter Anna, who grew up on the Waverly home place but lived at Smith Valley with her husband and son. Today the Counsilman farmstead is occupied in part by the Harrison Township–Waverly Volunteer Fire Department, and the house itself is covered with blue vinyl siding.

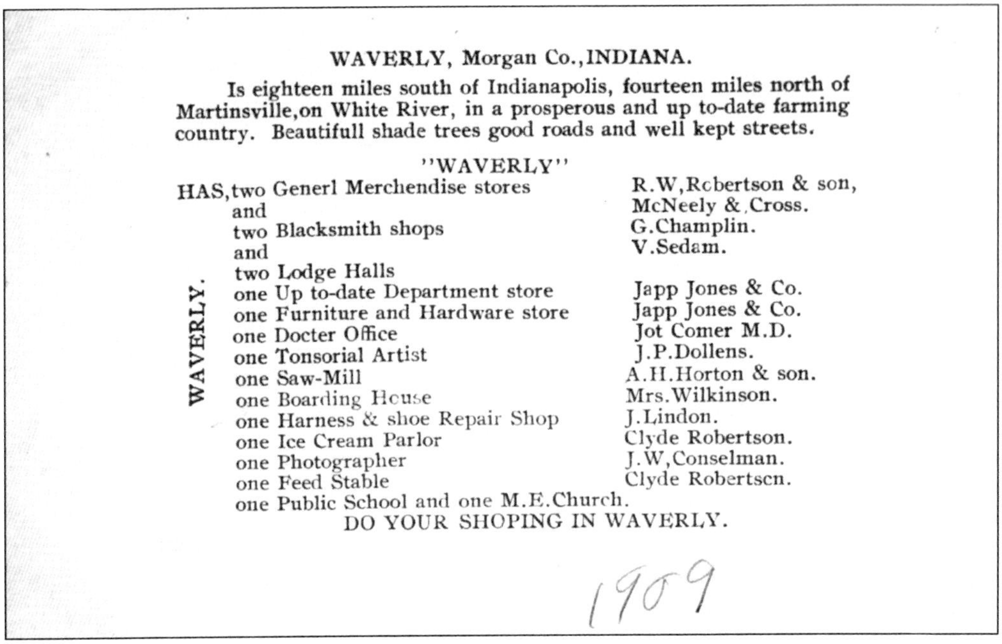

WAVERLY, Morgan Co.,INDIANA.

Is eighteen miles south of Indianapolis, fourteen miles north of Martinsville,on White River, in a prosperous and up to-date farming country. Beautifull shade trees good roads and well kept streets.

"WAVERLY"

WAVERLY.

HAS,two Generl Merchendise stores	R.W,Robertson & son,
and	McNeely & Cross.
two Blacksmith shops	G.Champlin.
and	V.Sedam.
two Lodge Halls	
one Up to-date Department store	Japp Jones & Co.
one Furniture and Hardware store	Japp Jones & Co.
one Docter Office	Jot Comer M.D.
one Tonsorial Artist	J.P.Dollens.
one Saw-Mill	A.H.Horton & son.
one Boarding House	Mrs.Wilkinson.
one Harness & shoe Repair Shop	J.Lindon.
one Ice Cream Parlor	Clyde Robertson.
one Photographer	J.W,Conselman.
one Feed Stable	Clyde Robertson.

one Public School and one M.E.Church.

DO YOUR SHOPING IN WAVERLY.

1909

DO YOUR SHOPPING IN WAVERLY, 1909. This inventory of Waverly businesses and their proprietors provides an invaluable glimpse of the village during its heyday. Among those listed are Dr. Jot Comer, who would become owner of a Mooresville sanitarium and hospital, and photographer Joseph Counsilman, whose last name appears with the original German spelling.

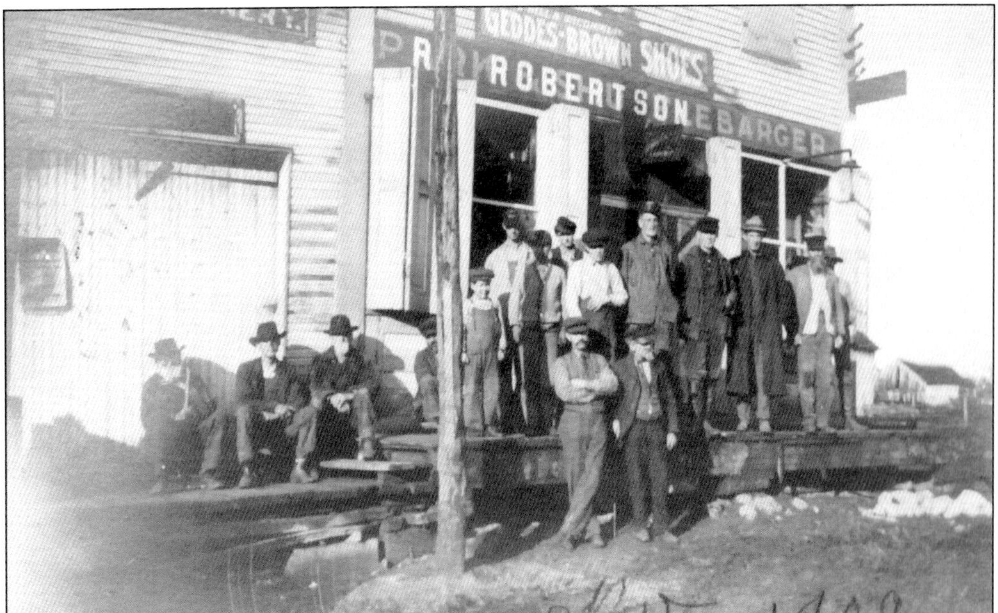

R. W. ROBERTSON AND SON, WAVERLY, 1909. The names of Park and Shufflebarger, the previous proprietors of this general store, can still be seen painted on the storefront. The front porch and plank sidewalk appear to have provided a perfect spot for loafers and others with a little too much time on their hands.

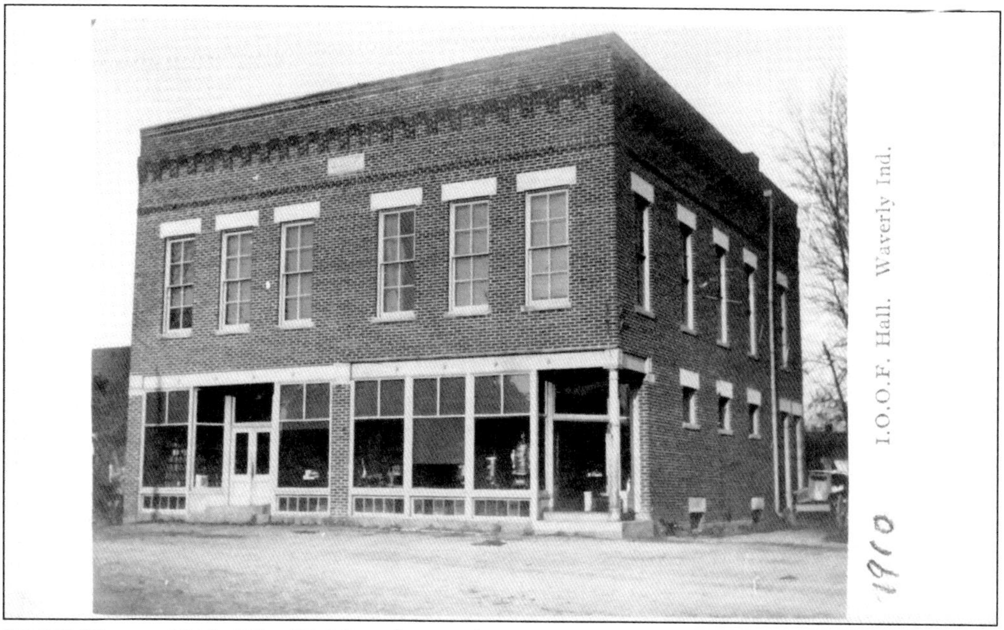

IOOF HALL, 1910. The IOOF, a fraternal organization, occupied the second floor of this building located on the northeast corner of Main Street and Water Street (now Whetzel Street). Its first floor offered commercial space to a variety of merchants. The building was destroyed by fire about 1918.

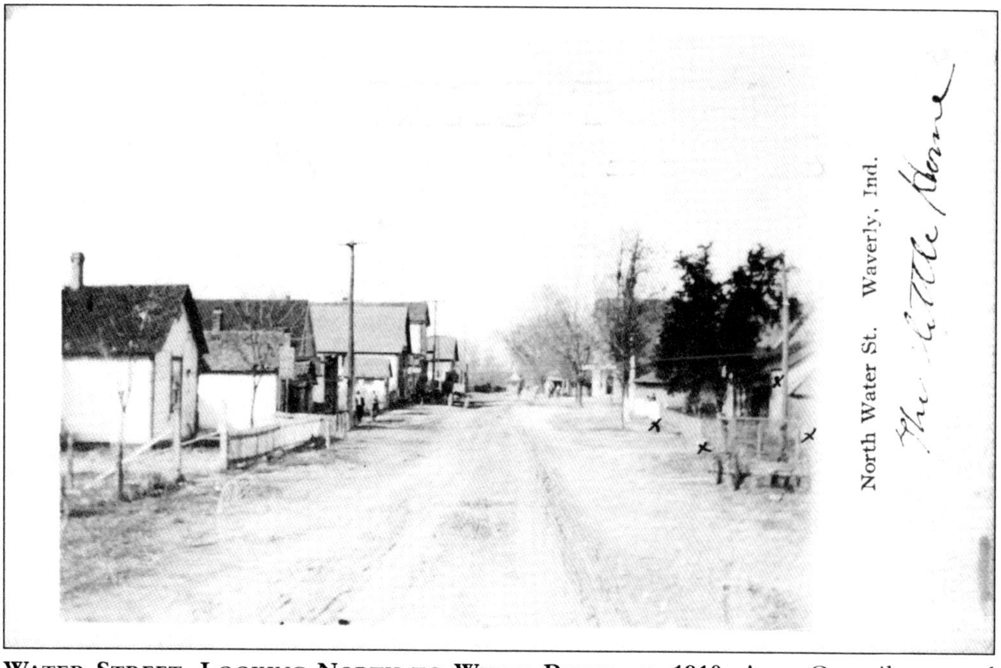

WATER STREET, LOOKING NORTH TO WHITE RIVER, *C.* 1910. Anna Counsilman used *X*s to mark the location of "Little House," the home and photography shop of her son Joseph. Little House, and many of the modest frame cottages pictured here, remains standing on Water Street (now Whetzel Street). A traveler continuing north would have reached the old Waverly covered bridge.

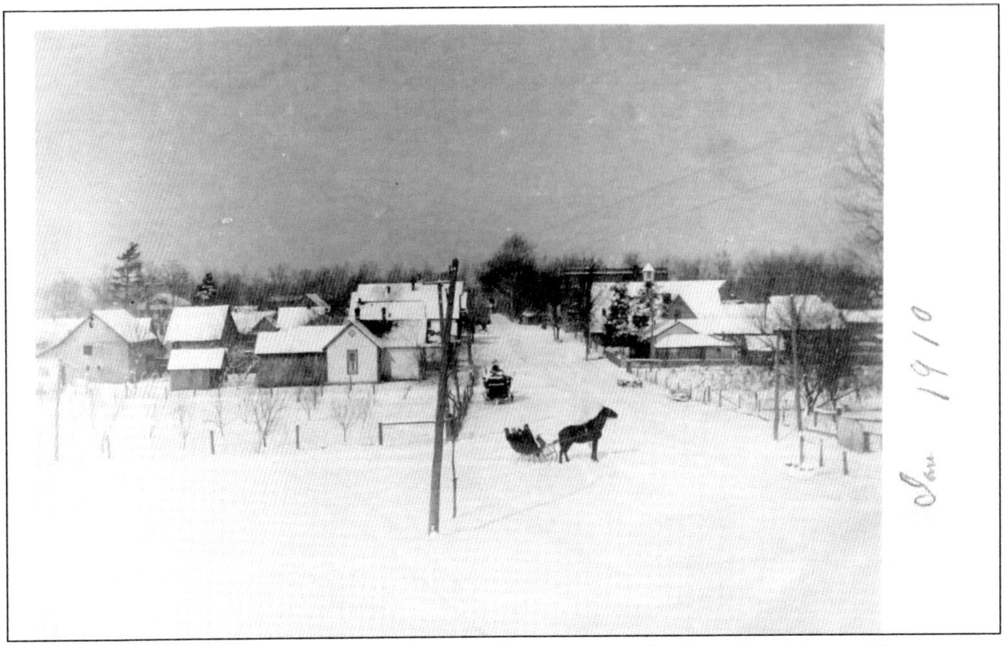

SLEIGHING IN WAVERLY, 1910. Joseph Counsilman captured a Grandma Moses–like scene on snow-covered streets in January 1910. The two-story brick IOOF lodge hall can be seen in the distance on the right side of the street. Little House is enclosed by a fence at right center.

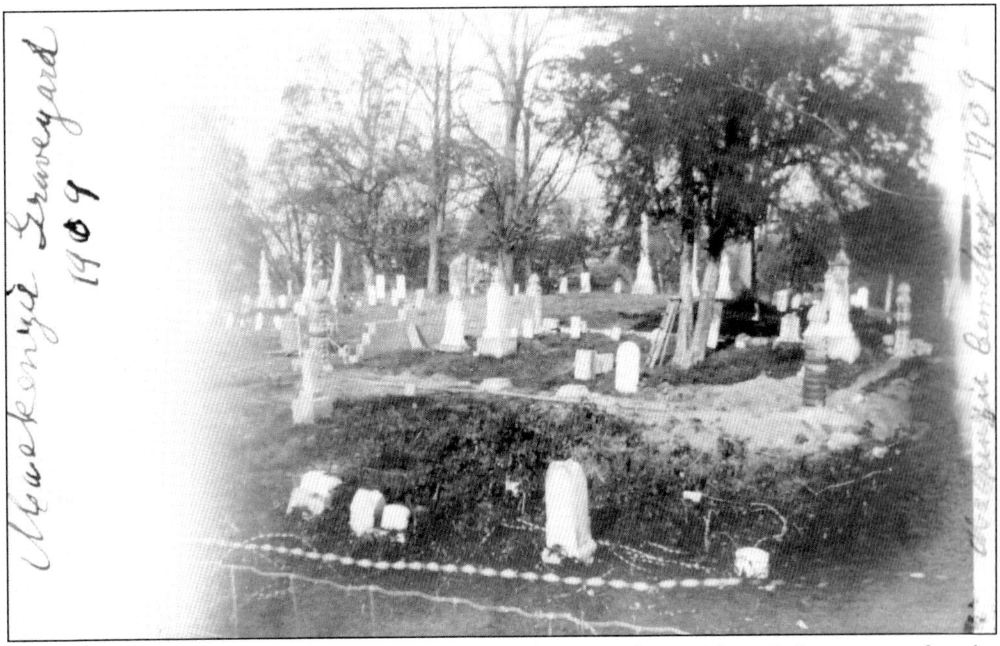

MACKENZIE CEMETERY, 1909. Also known as the Waverly or Whetzel Cemetery, after the family of pioneer trailblazer Jacob Whetzel, this cemetery is located southwest of Waverly on Old State Road 37. The earliest burial dates to 1821.

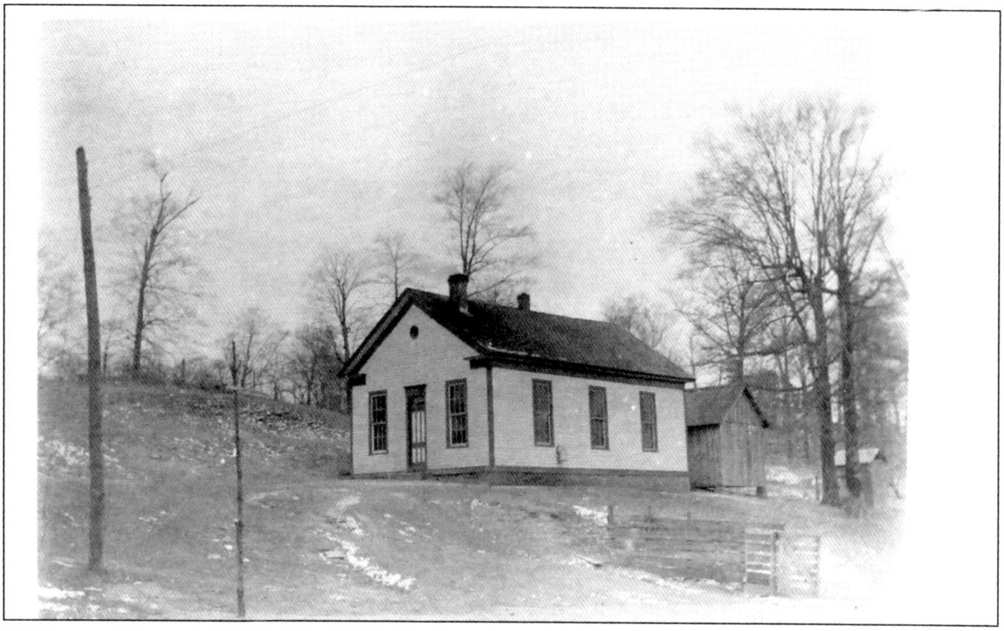

WAVERLY SCHOOLHOUSE, C. 1910. At the edge of the river bottoms and west of the cemetery stood this little frame schoolhouse, built about 1850. It was replaced in 1916 by a two-room brick building that consolidated the three Harrison Township rural schools. On the back of this card, Alice Magenheimer Sheetz, a niece of Joseph Counsilman, wrote in 1951, "School at Waverly where I went 70 yrs. ago and 60 yrs. ago."

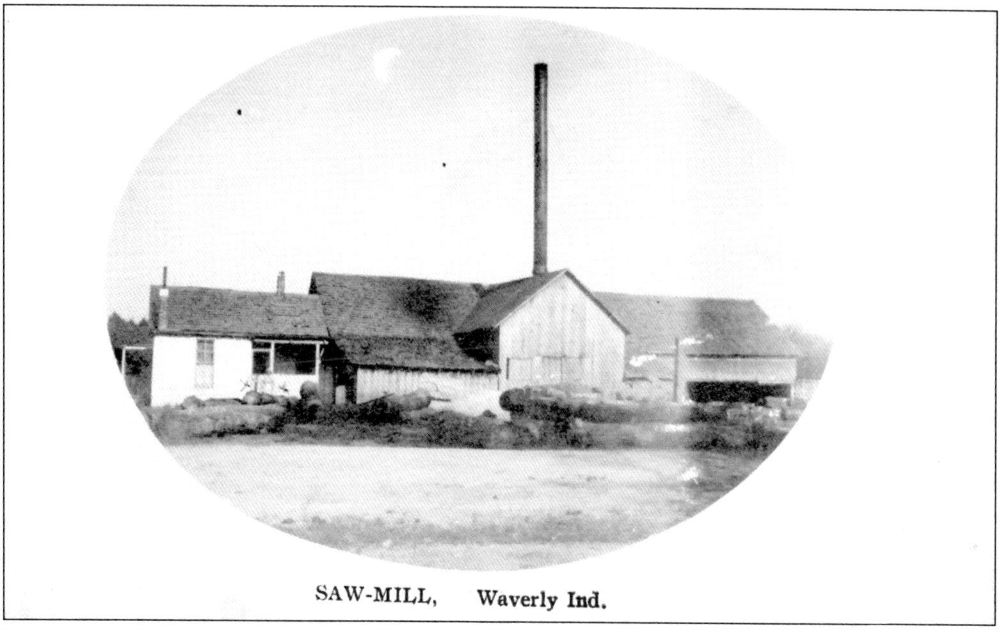

HORTON'S OLD SAWMILL, C. 1910. Alford Horton operated this sawmill at the south end of the Waverly bridge. His son Ervin and brother James were head sawyers. A note written in pencil on the back of this card reads, "Link and I went to house keeping in the little house on the left. Maude Wheeler was living there at the time this picture was taken, she can be seen standing between [the *X*s]." The writer's identity is unknown.

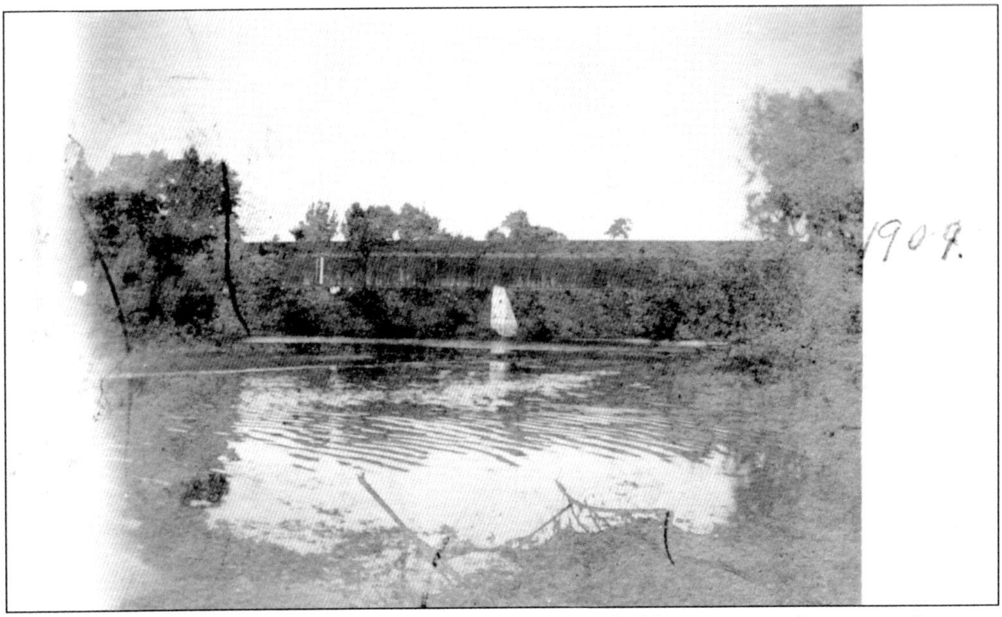

Waverly Covered Bridge, 1909. This three-span bridge supported on two piers was constructed by Robert Smith in 1873. Smith was a Morgan County commissioner who promised a good and strong bridge. It proved to be so sturdy that it did not shake even under the heaviest of loads.

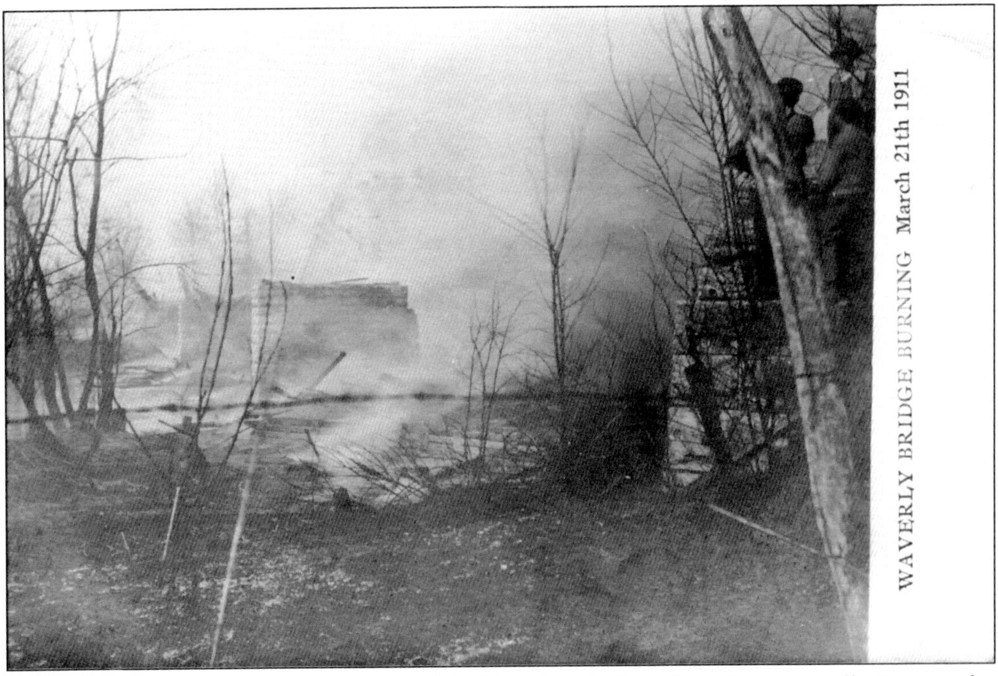

Waverly Bridge Burning, March 21, 1911. Sparks from burning cornstalks in a nearby field were thought to be the cause of a fire that destroyed the Waverly covered bridge. Its loss was a great inconvenience to Waverly residents, who relied on a ferry until a replacement concrete bridge opened later that year. When this bridge closed in 1969, following a partial collapse a few years earlier, Waverly lost its river crossing for good.

Four

Centerton, Brooklyn, and Bethany Park

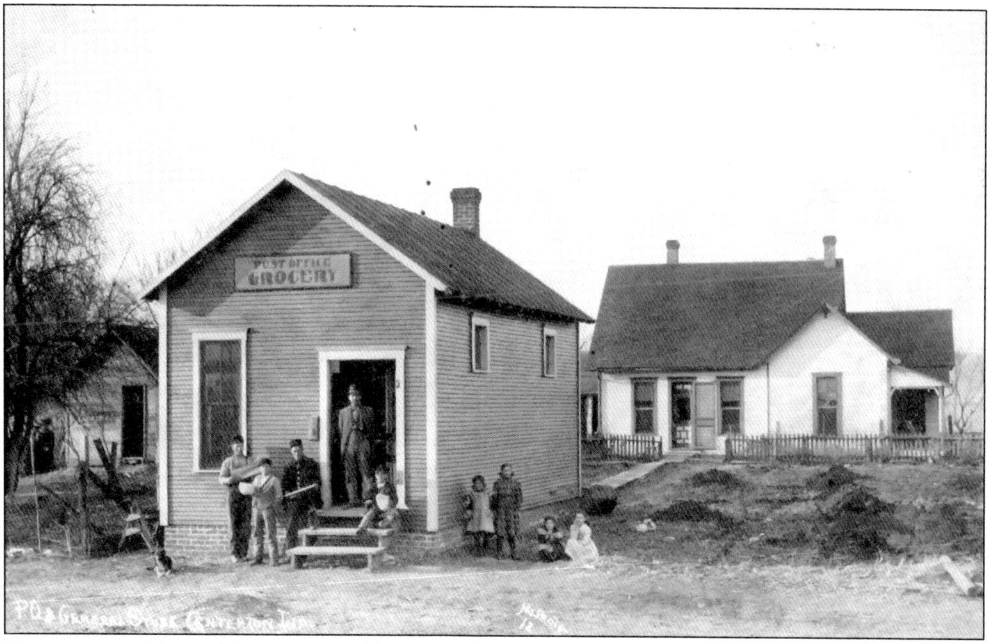

Centerton Post Office and General Store, c. 1910. The proprietor of this store was Joshua Rothrock, presumably the man standing in the doorway. The little girls standing at right may be some of his four daughters, and the house behind the store is likely the family home.

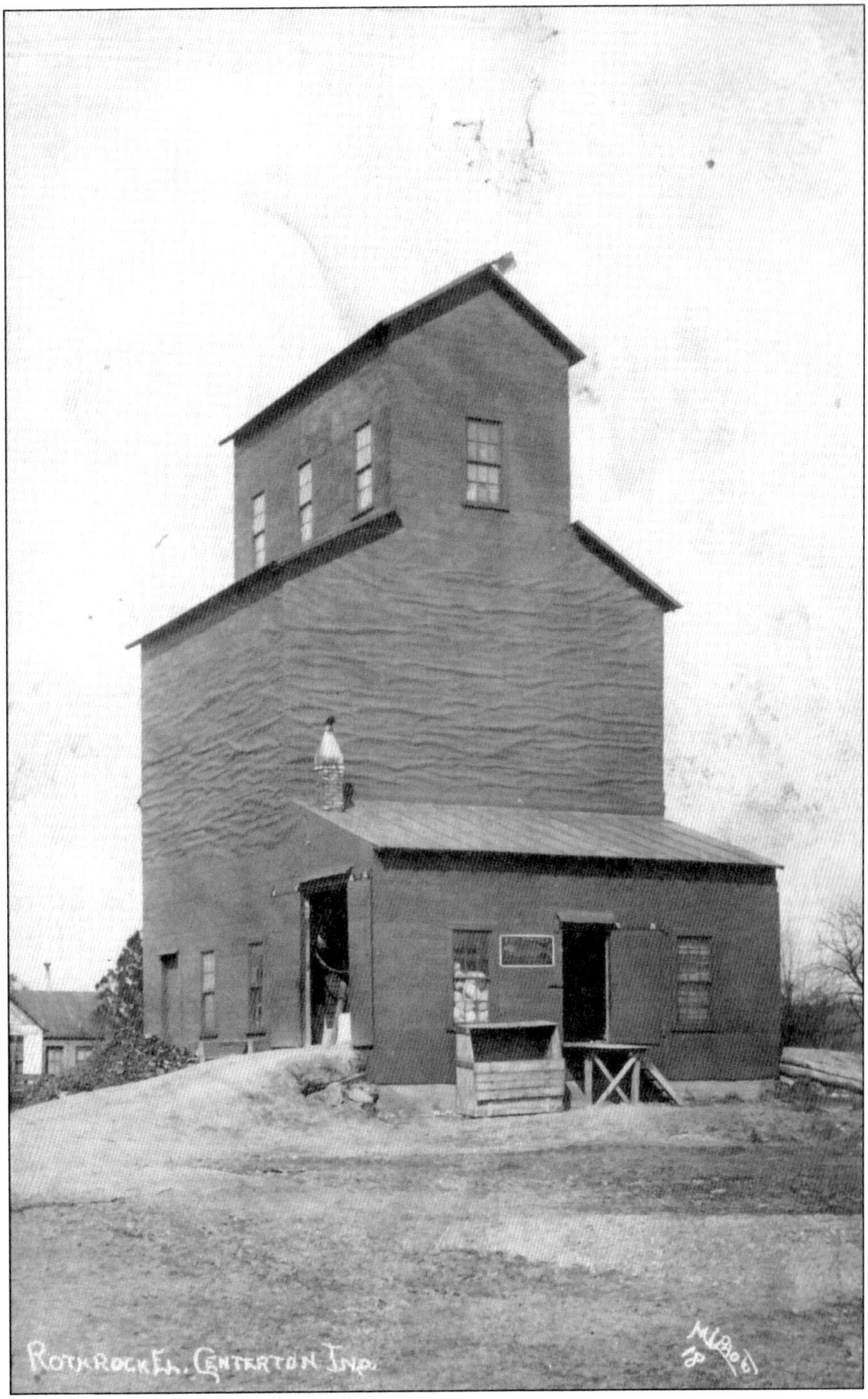

ROTHROCK ELEVATOR, 1912. On August 12, 1913, a mid-afternoon crowd gathered in Centerton to gawk at a 35-car pileup on the Vandalia line of the Pennsylvania Railroad. Those who lingered until dusk witnessed a second tragedy: the conflagration of the Rothrock Elevator. Sparks from the wreck may have ignited the blaze. Completely destroyed were the elevator, 1,500 bushels of corn, 4,500 bushels of wheat, and a large quantity of feed, seed, and other supplies.

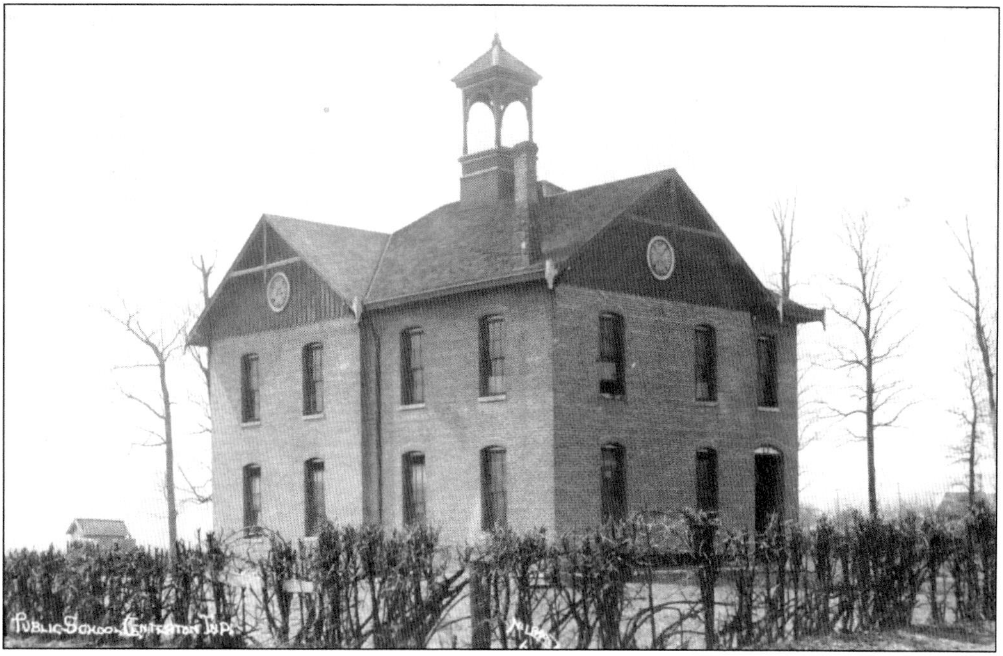

CENTERTON SCHOOL, 1911. Built in 1883, this was the second school building erected in Centerton. It was destroyed by lightning in the summer of 1917. Children attended classes in a nearby church until a third school was built. A famous graduate of the third building is legendary basketball coach John R. Wooden. In 1950, the third school was also destroyed by fire. The current Centerton Elementary School—the fourth at Centerton—was built in 1956.

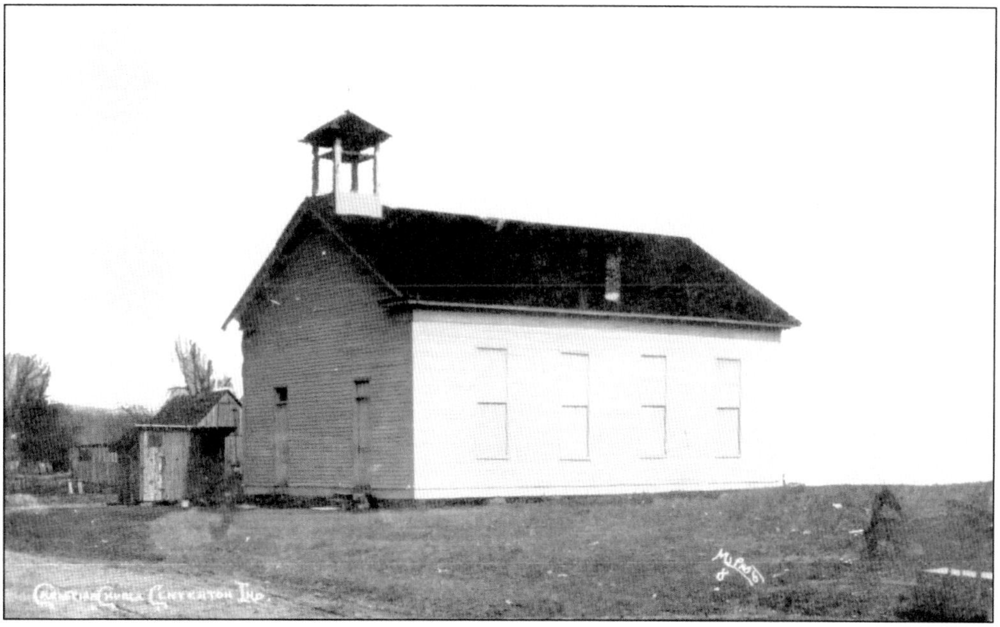

CENTERTON CHRISTIAN CHURCH, 1911. Built as Zion Chapel, a Methodist church, this frame building was moved from a nearby farm to Centerton about 1880. It was shared by the Christians and Methodists until 1890 when the latter congregation dissolved. The building was torn down in 1957 after its bell and other furnishings were removed to a new church building.

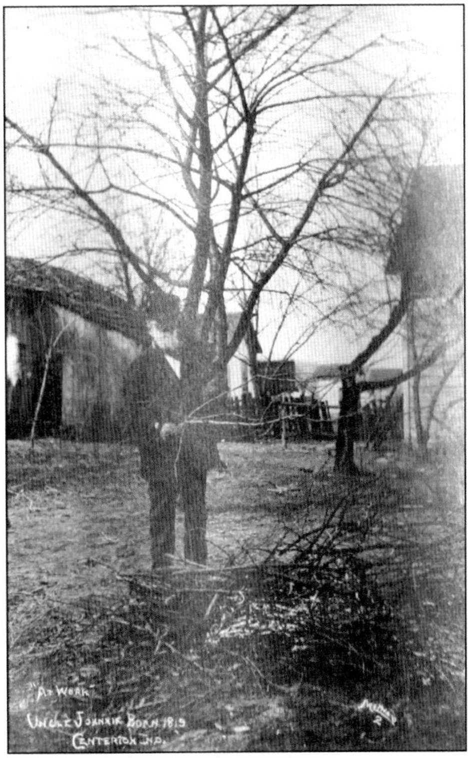

UNCLE JOHNNIE AT WORK, *c.* 1910. The near-centenarian captured at work stacking twigs and brush seems to be John Williams, who the 1910 federal census identifies as a widower and retired farmer living with his unmarried daughter, Vilena. He was born on May 11, 1819, and is buried in Williams Cemetery at Henderson Ford Road and State Road 37.

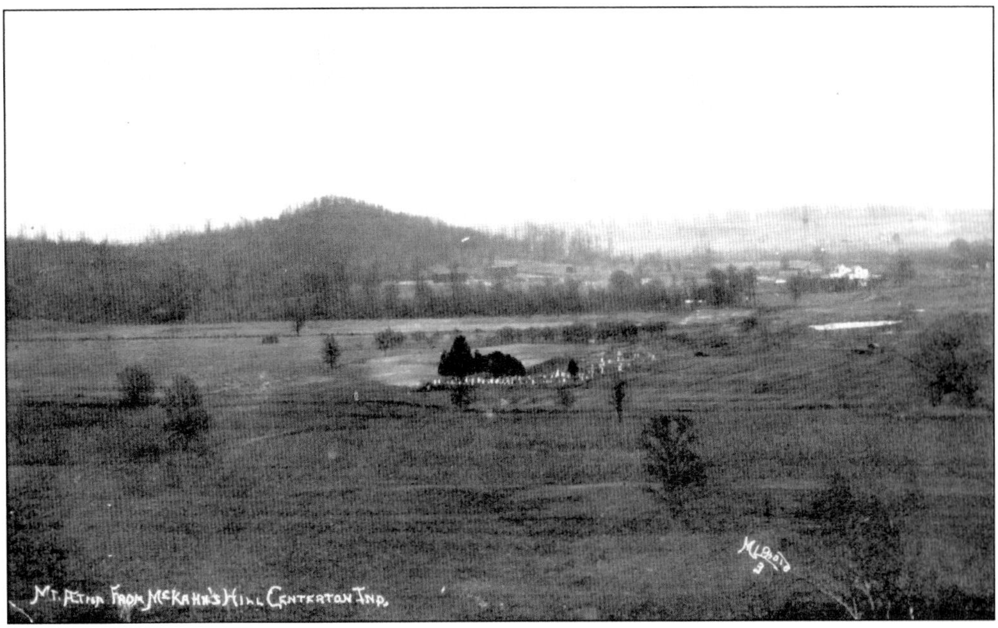

MOUNT AETNA FROM MCKAHAN'S HILL, *c.* 1910. Once the second-highest elevation in Indiana, Mount Aetna, located between Brooklyn and Centerton, is now merely a bump. Its valuable blue shale was mined for the manufacture of clay tile and brick. Marble and limestone grave markers in Centerton Cemetery appear at the center of the photograph. Today Goat Hollow Road runs along the top of McKahan's Hill, named for landowner William McKahan.

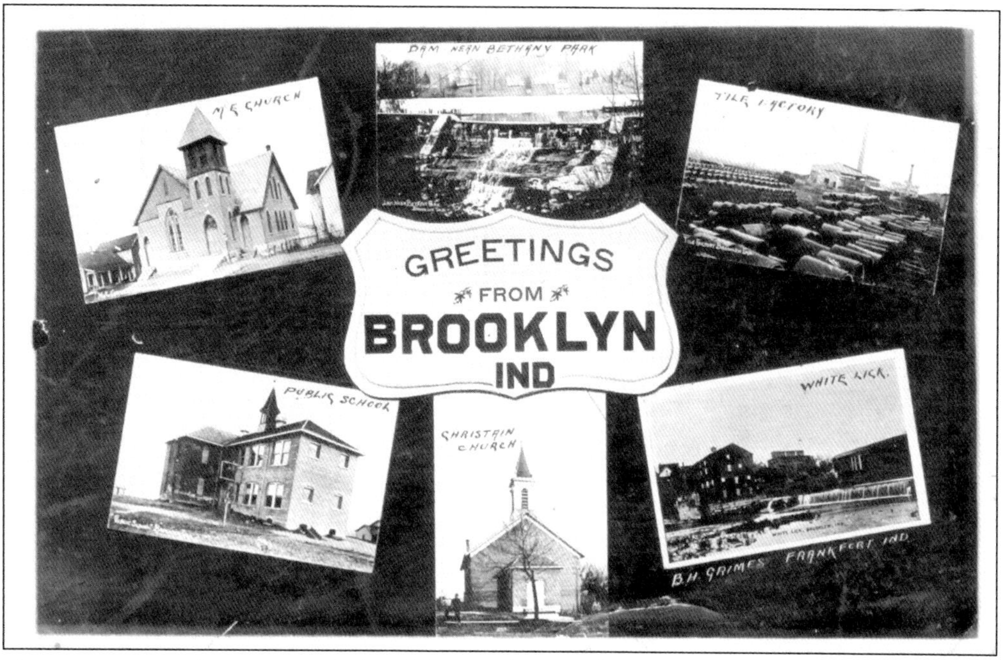

Greetings from Brooklyn, 1911. This real-photo, multiview card includes images (clockwise) of the Methodist church, built in 1870; the dam at Bethany Park, southwest of Brooklyn; Indiana Drain Tile Company; the mill, dam, and covered bridge over White Lick Creek; the Christian church; and the Brooklyn School. The publisher was the B. H. Grimes Company of Frankfort.

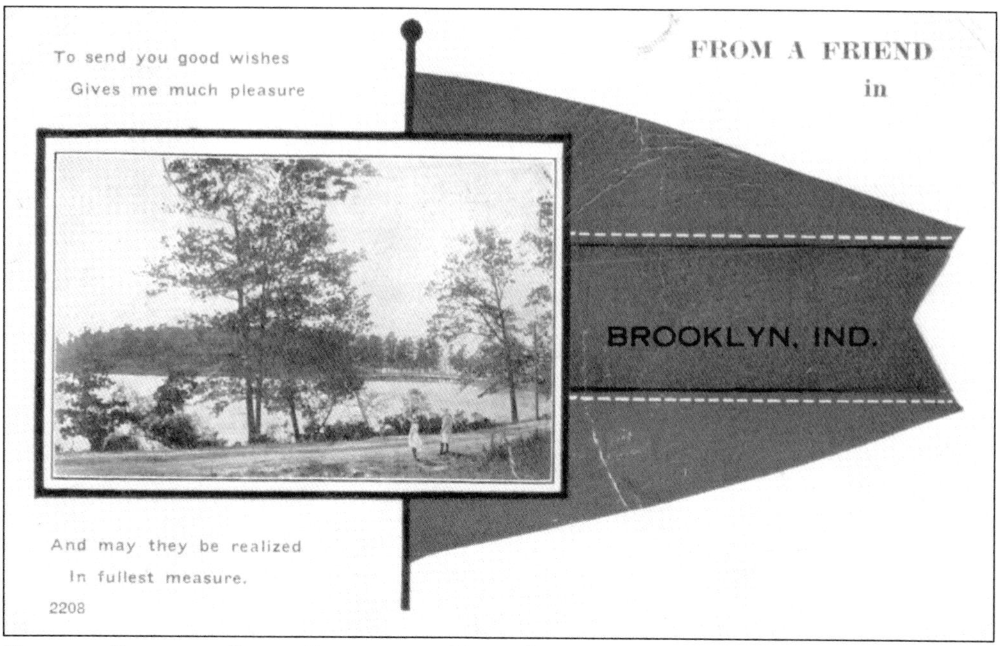

Generic Pennant Card, Brooklyn, 1911. The publisher could localize this generic image by adding the name of any town anywhere.

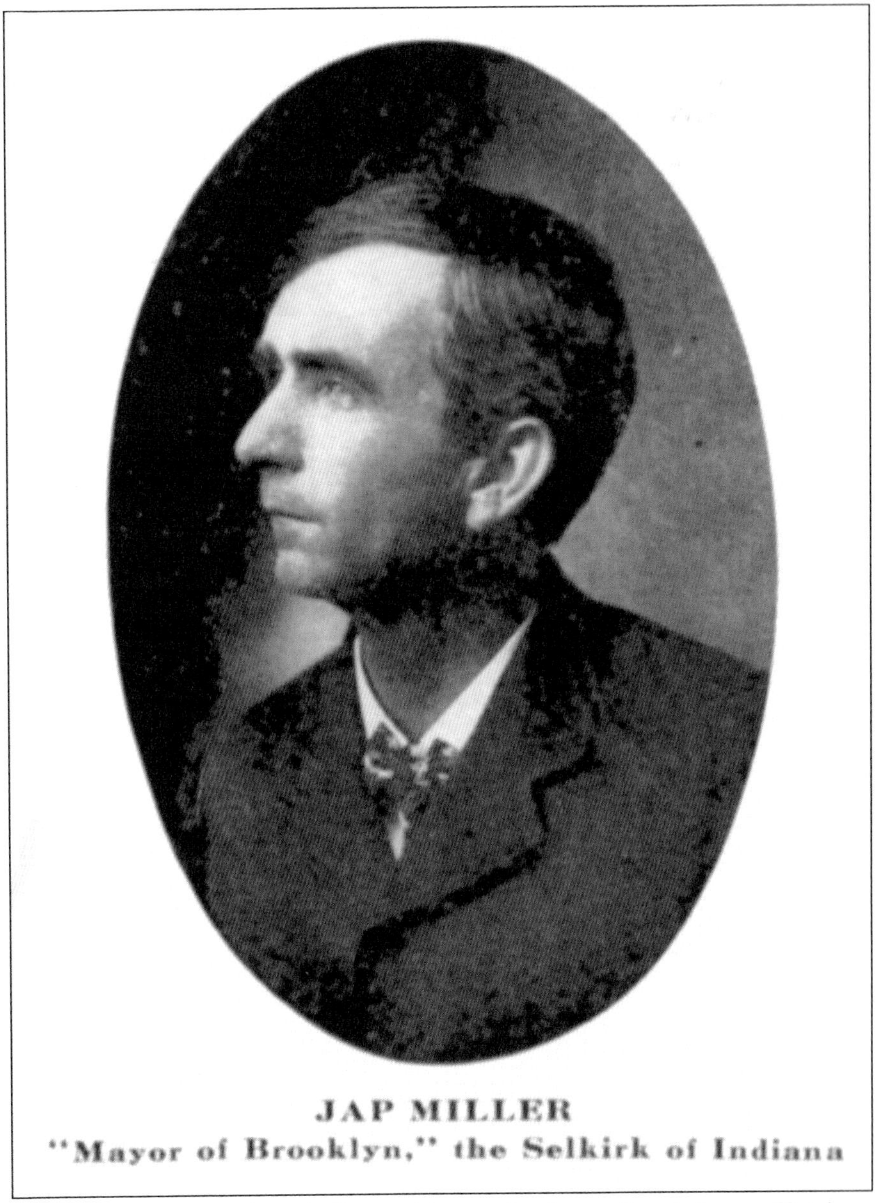

JAP MILLER, 1908. A merchant in "everything under the sun" and the unofficial mayor of Brooklyn, Jap Miller was immortalized by his close friend James Whitcomb Riley in a poem that shared his name. Miller was also the muse for vaudeville comedian Ezra Kendall, who modeled main characters Sandy Loam (*Top Soil*, 1909) and Joe Miller (*The Vinegar Buyer*, 1903) after him. On this postcard, the "Mayor of Brooklyn" penned to his niece Laura Blanche Miller, "Just want you to know old Brooklyn had as good looking man as any old town of its size in the state." An excerpt of Riley's poem goes, "W'y, that-air blame Jap Miller, with his keen sircastic fun, / Has got more friends than ary candidate 'at ever run! / Do n't matter what *his* views is, when he states the same to you, / They allus coincide with your'n, the same as two and two: / You *can't* take issue with him—er, at least, they haint no sense / In startin' in to down him, so you better not commence.— / The best way's jes' to listen, like your humble servant does, / And jes' concede Jap Miller is the best man ever wuz!"

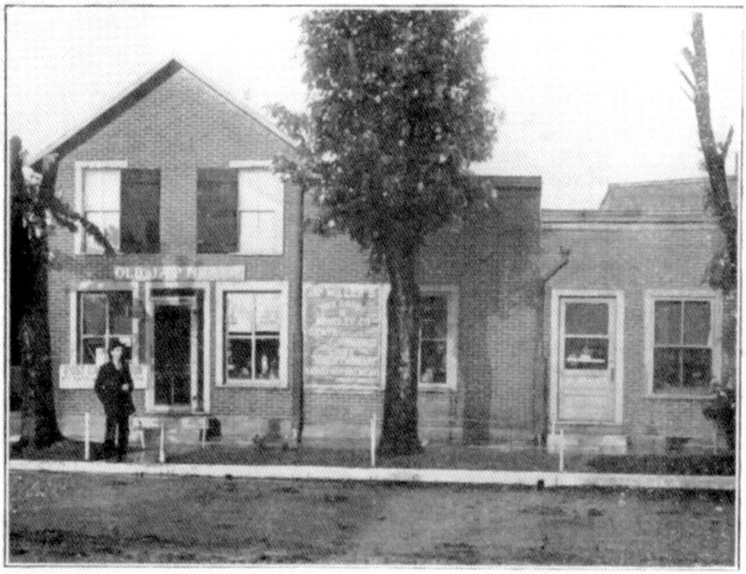

Jap Miller's Famous Store — The Indiana News Co., Publishers

JAP MILLER'S FAMOUS STORE, 1908. Jap Miller relocated his store from Martinsville to Brooklyn about 1897. In a message to his niece Laura Blanche Miller, of Morristown, Jap writes, "Mr. Riley was down last week. Brooklyn is not only a good town but a hot one now."

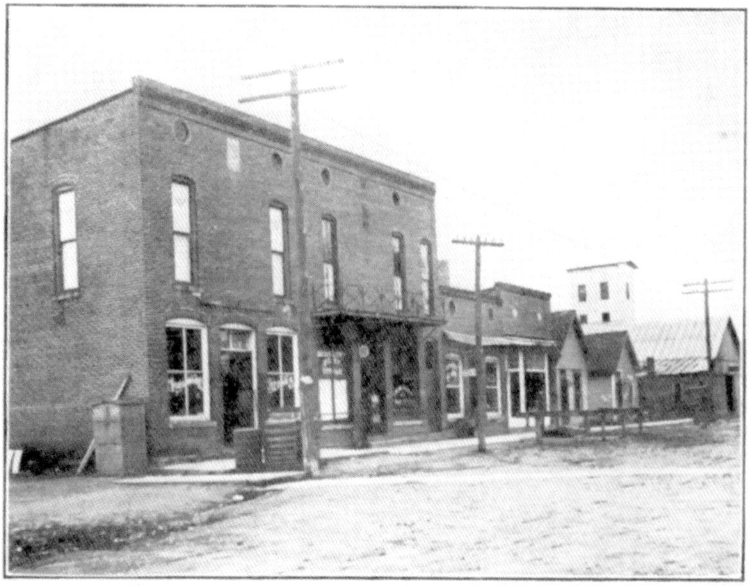

Main Street, Brooklyn, Ind.

WEST SIDE OF MAIN STREET, C. 1908. Built about 1880, the two-story brick commercial building in the foreground was home to William Smith's hardware store (left) and the Brooklyn Post Office (white windows). The elevator operated by Hughes Lumber and Grain Company appears at right.

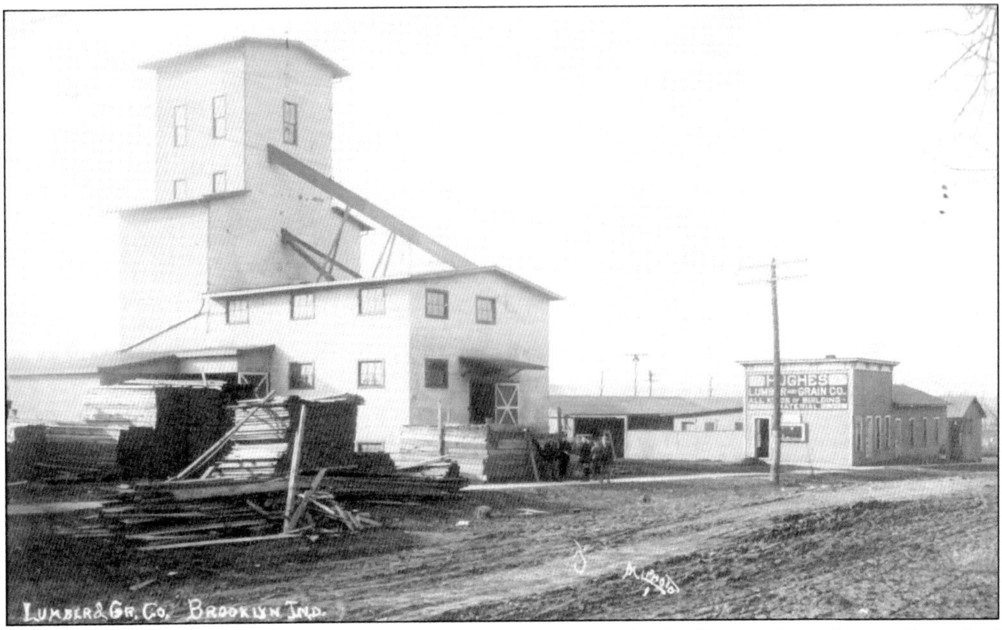

HUGHES LUMBER AND GRAIN COMPANY, BROOKLYN, 1915. Located on the north end of Main Street adjacent to the Pennsylvania Railroad line, this business owned by Thomas Hughes dealt in lime and cement, coke and coal, rough and dressed lumber, laths, shingles, sashes, doors, moldings, paints, oils, stains, and general building materials, as well as grain. It remained in business for more than 50 years.

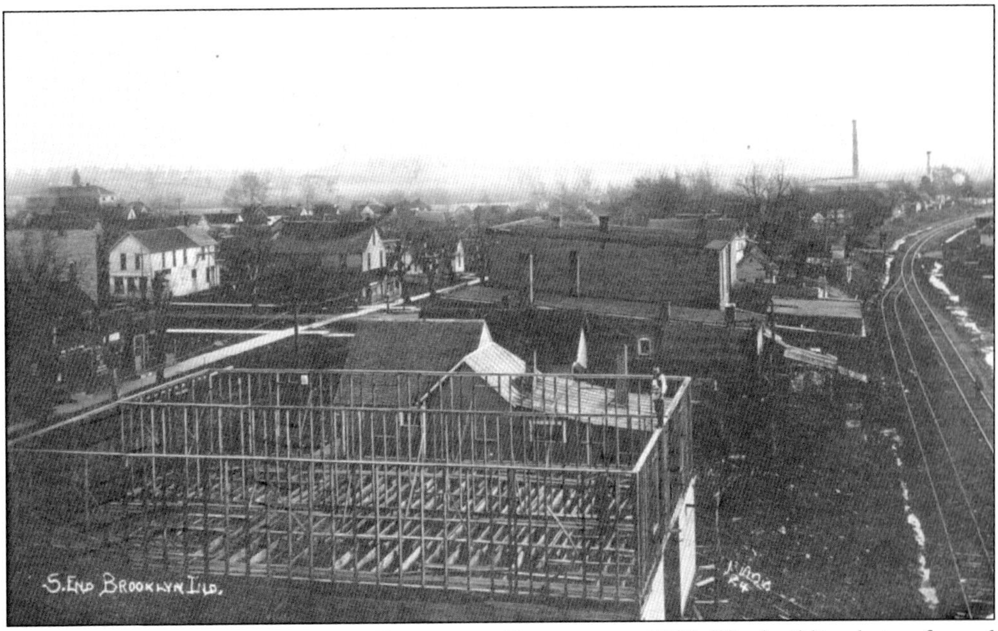

LOOKING SOUTH FROM HUGHES ELEVATOR, BROOKLYN, 1910. The building being framed appears to be part of the lumber and grain company. Main Street is at left, and the Pennsylvania Railroad is at right. The public school can be seen in the distance at left, the commercial buildings on Main Street at center, and the smokestacks of the Brooklyn Brick Company in the distance at right.

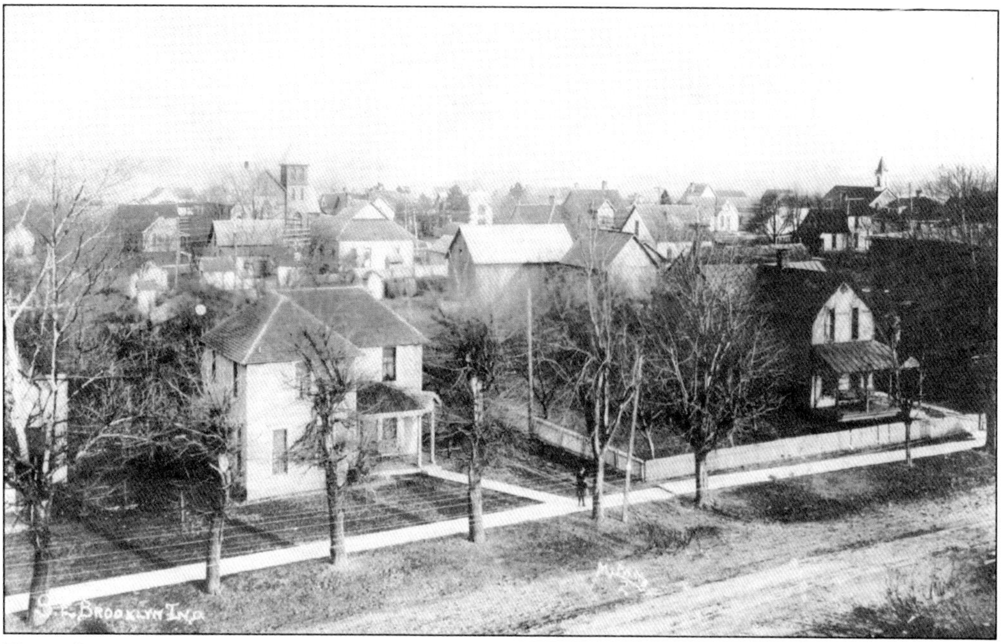

VIEW LOOKING EAST FROM HUGHES ELEVATOR, BROOKLYN, 1913. The Methodist and Christian churches, left and right, respectively, are landmarks on the appropriately named Church Street. The sender of this card writes, "The sale is over and we can fix up the house now. I wish we had a car, may be we can after a while. Wayne's stuff brought $200."

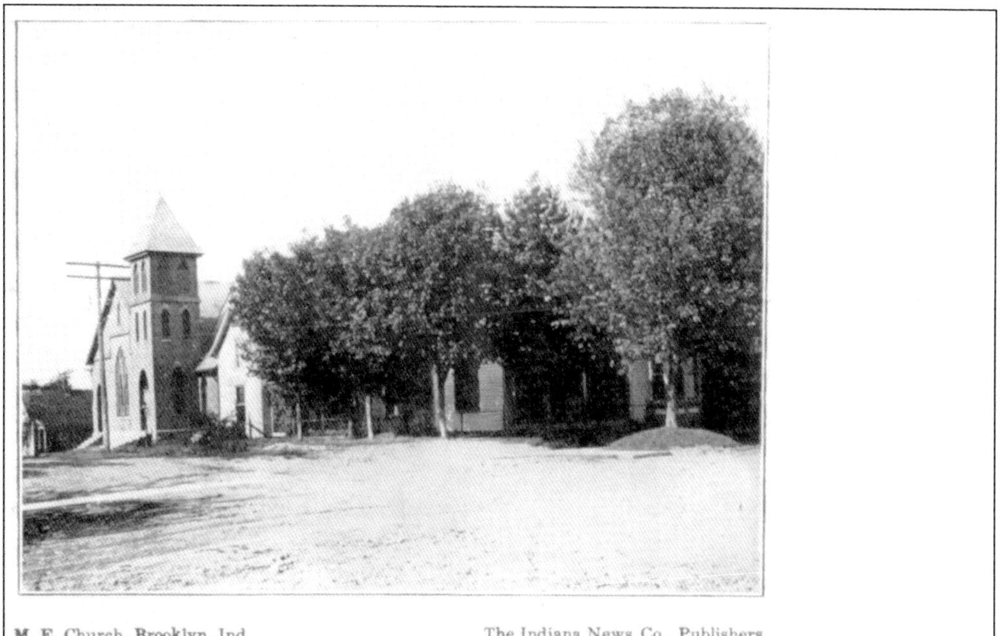

BROOKLYN METHODIST EPISCOPAL CHURCH, C. 1908. The construction of this brick church was begun in 1869, with dedication taking place the following year. The congregation disbanded in 1969.

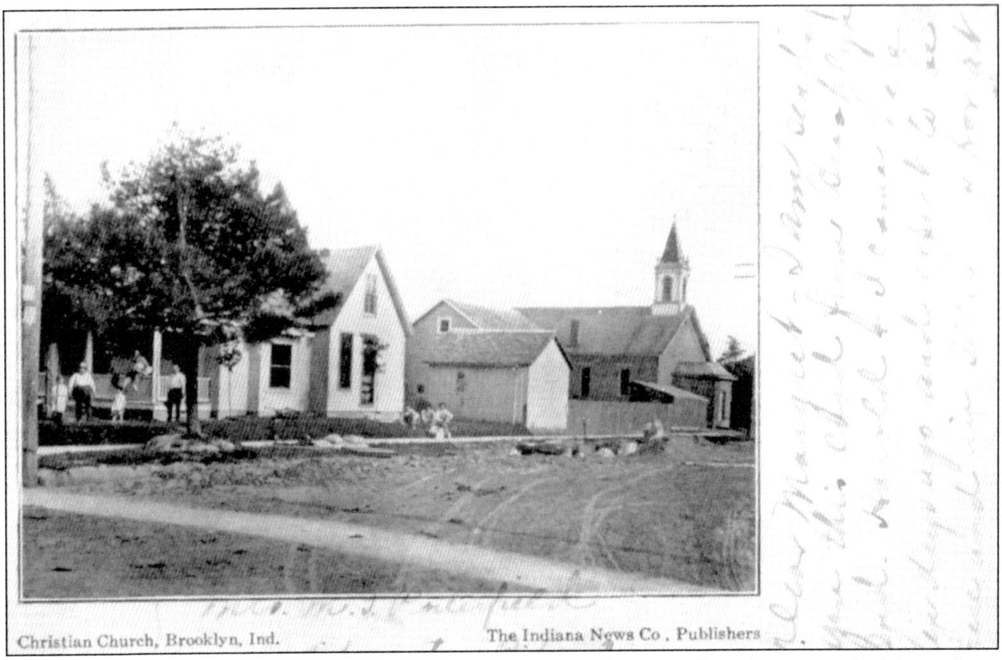

CHRISTIAN CHURCH, *c.* 1908. Built about 1872, the Christian church attracted visitors from nearby Bethany Park, owned and operated by the Disciples of Christ. In 1925, a basement was dug and a kitchen, dining room, and classroom added. Stained-glass windows were installed in 1930. Later expansions included the 1953 fellowship hall and, in 1971, a large educational wing.

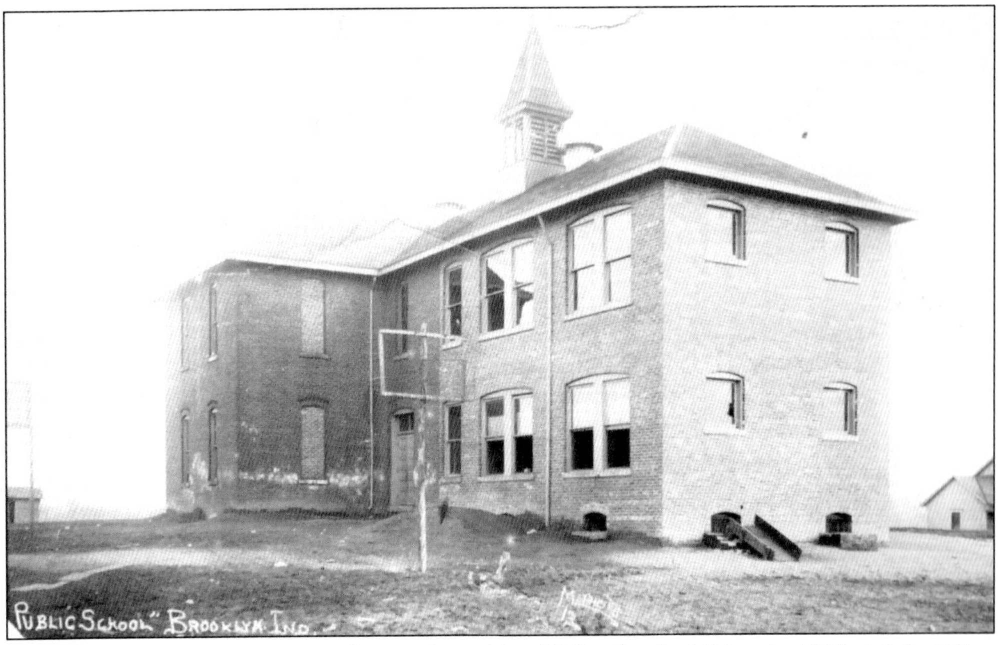

BROOKLYN SCHOOL, 1911. Built in 1885, with a high school addition in 1909, this building burned in the spring of 1916. The Clay Township advisory board refused to fund a new building, arguing that the incorporated town of Brooklyn should alone bear the cost. Trustee Fred Fields sued, the jury sided with him, and a new school was built. It has been converted into apartments.

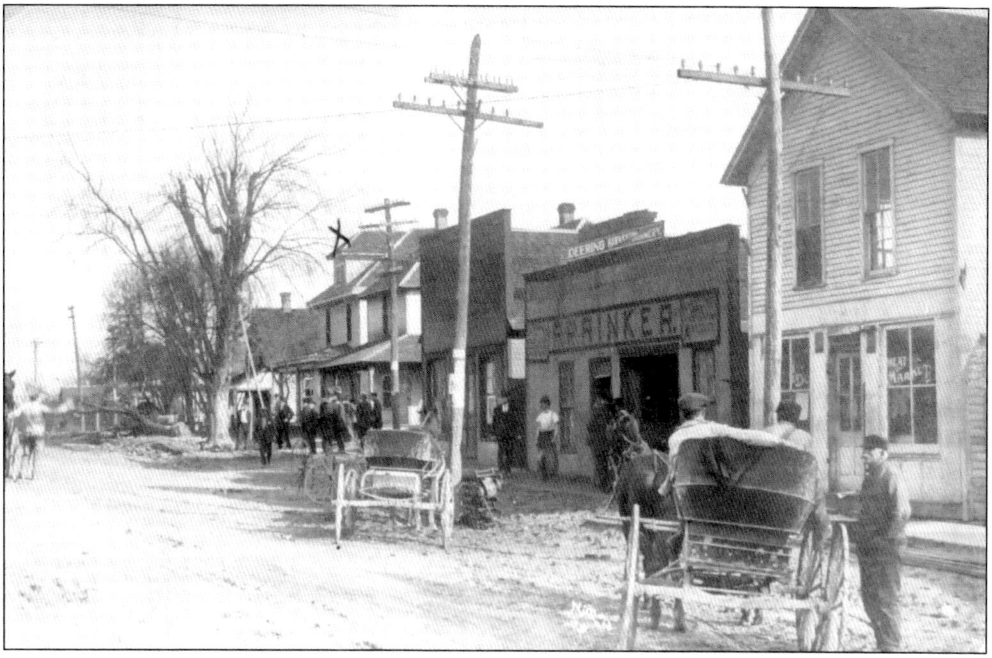

MILL STREET, BROOKLYN, 1910. Extending east from Main Street to White Lick Creek, Mill Street was characterized by a blending of homes and businesses, including Roy P. Rinker's blacksmith shop. Rinker was also an implement dealer carrying the Deering line manufactured in Indianapolis. The windows of the two-story building at right advertise a meat market. The meaning of the *X* over the house at center is not known.

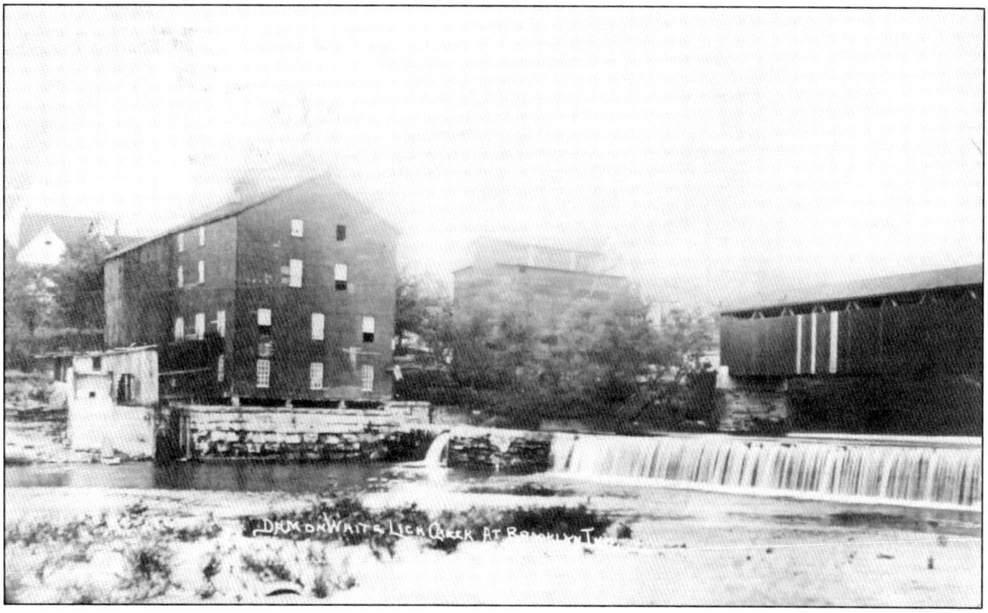

BROOKLYN MILL, DAM, AND COVERED BRIDGE, 1911. The massive stone gristmill, built by William and John Paddock in 1852, was removed in 1924. The covered bridge, built in 1876, was being dismantled in 1948 when it fell victim to fire. At the time, it was being replaced by a "new convenience in concrete." The dam, too, no longer exists.

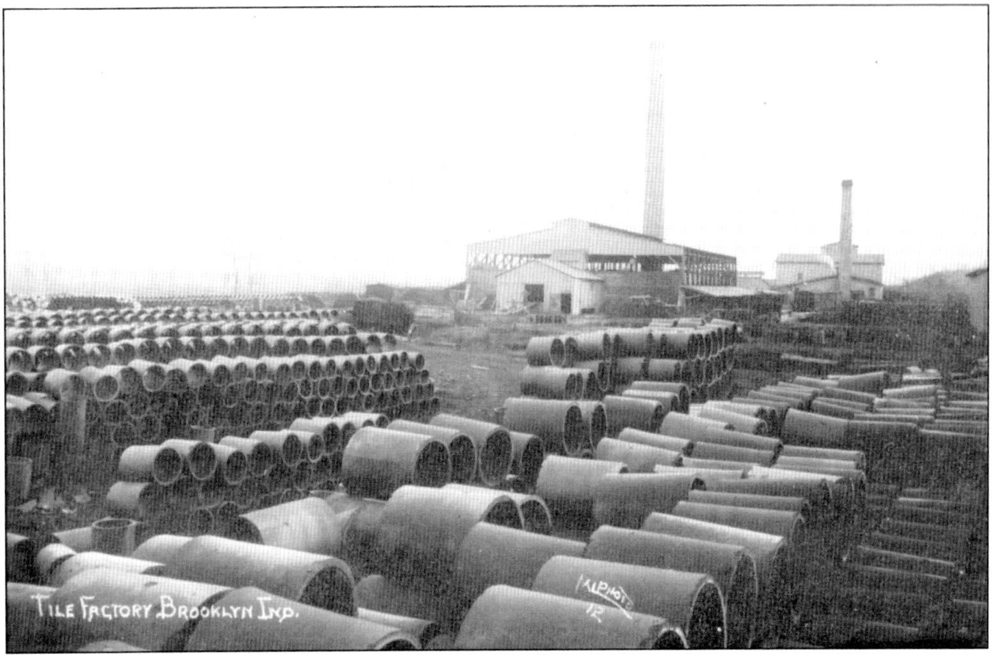

INDIANA DRAIN TILE COMPANY, C. 1915. Joseph M. Powell established this business just south of Brooklyn in 1904 for the manufacture of farm drain tile. The plant pictured here was built in 1914. Structural building material such as flue lining and tile block was added after World War II.

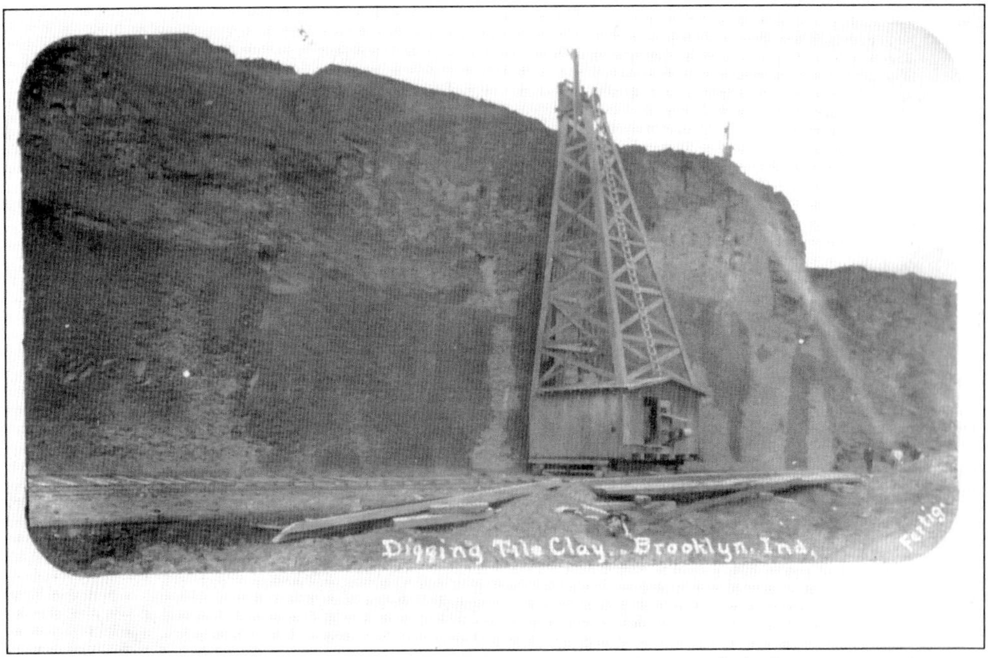

DIGGING TILE CLAY, C. 1915. Powell invented a planer used to cut shale from Mount Aetna, a large outcropping south of Brooklyn that was once the second-highest elevation in Indiana. The Dinky, a narrow-gauge railroad, carried it to the pulverizing mill. By 1954, daily production of tile surpassed 100 tons, and Mount Aetna was little more than a slope.

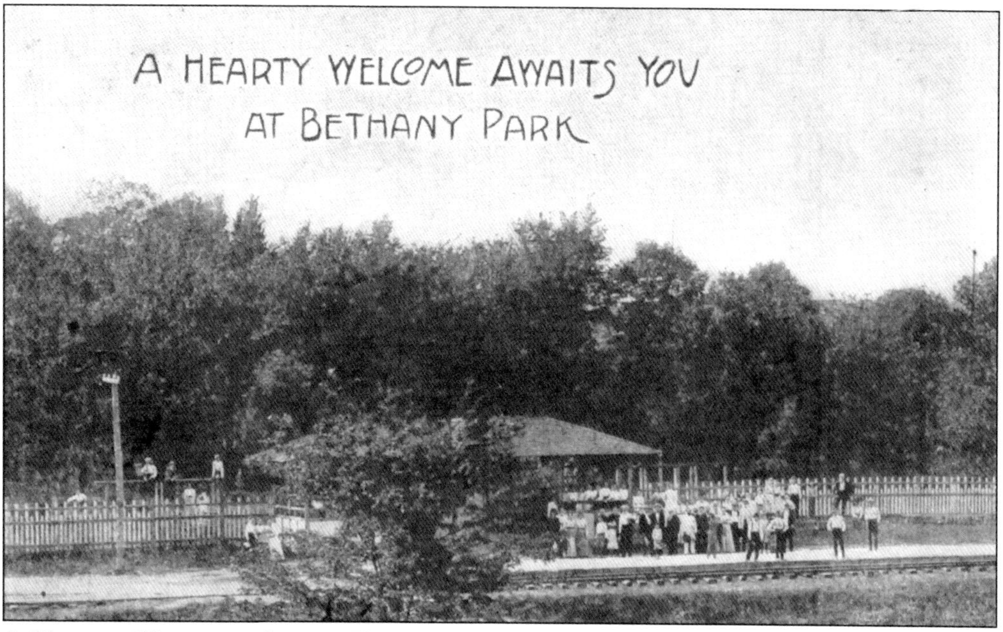

A HEARTY WELCOME AWAITS YOU AT BETHANY PARK, 1910. Organized by the Disciples of Christ in 1883, this nearly 40-acre recreational, educational, and cultural oasis southwest of Brooklyn held its first "moral assemblage" in August 1884. Thousands flocked to Bethany Park and set up tents on the grounds or took rooms in the hotel. Men and boys pitched their bedrolls in the huge tabernacle that was completed just in time.

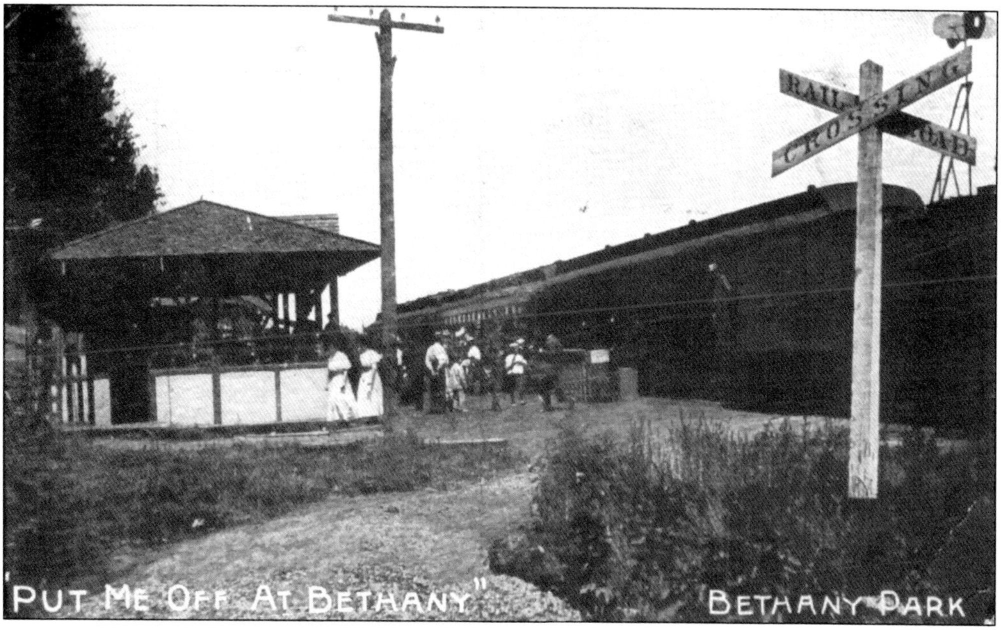

PENNSYLVANIA STATION, 1916. The reverse side of this card is an advertisement for the Bethany Assembly Chautauqua held on July 26–August 18, 1916. The sender writes, "You see I am really at the convention. This is a lovely ch. so convenient. I am enjoying it, but feel queer with no babies to look after."

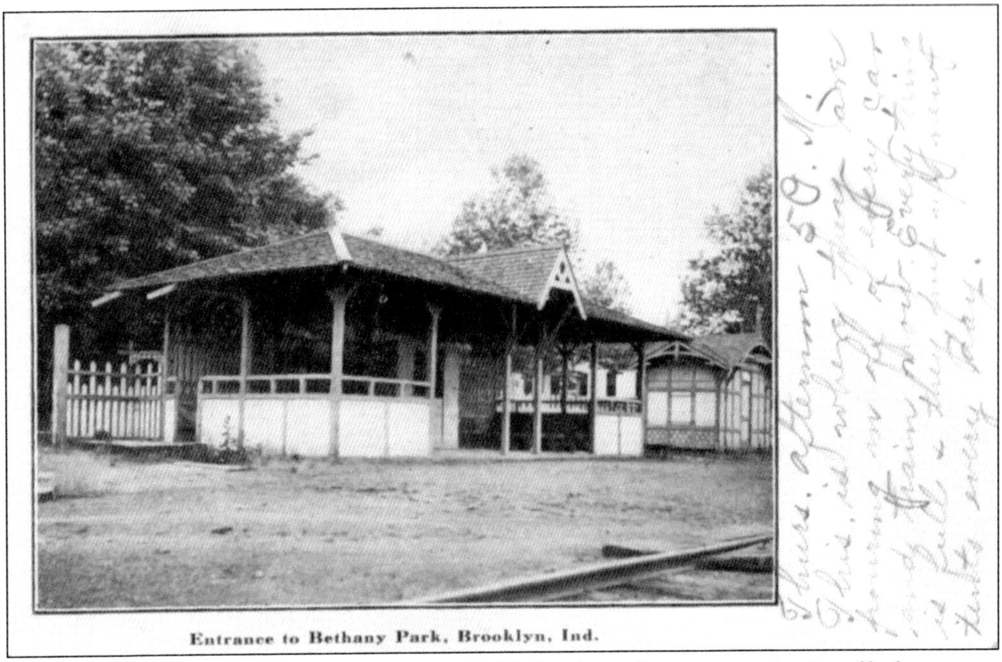

ENTRANCE TO BETHANY PARK, *c.* 1907. "This is where they are pouring in off of every car and train now. Everything is full and they put up new tents every day," writes the send of this card. "It is hard to find time to even write a postal here there is so much to see and hear. . . . This A.M. was all of the Evangelists and their helpers and it was grand to hear all those great men."

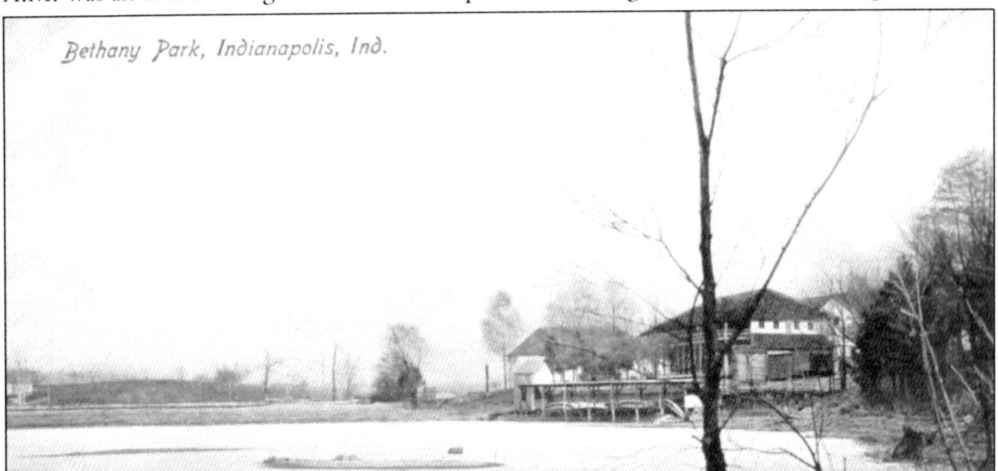

LAKE JEWEL, 1907. Within the first few years, a lake was dug and a dam built on the east side to hold back the stream- and spring-fed water. "To a lover of water what is more delightful than a row on Bethany's lake, with its placid waters lined with rich foliage and forest trees," extolled an 1897 publication. This card incorrectly places Bethany Park in Indianapolis, proving that sometimes the information on cards can be misleading.

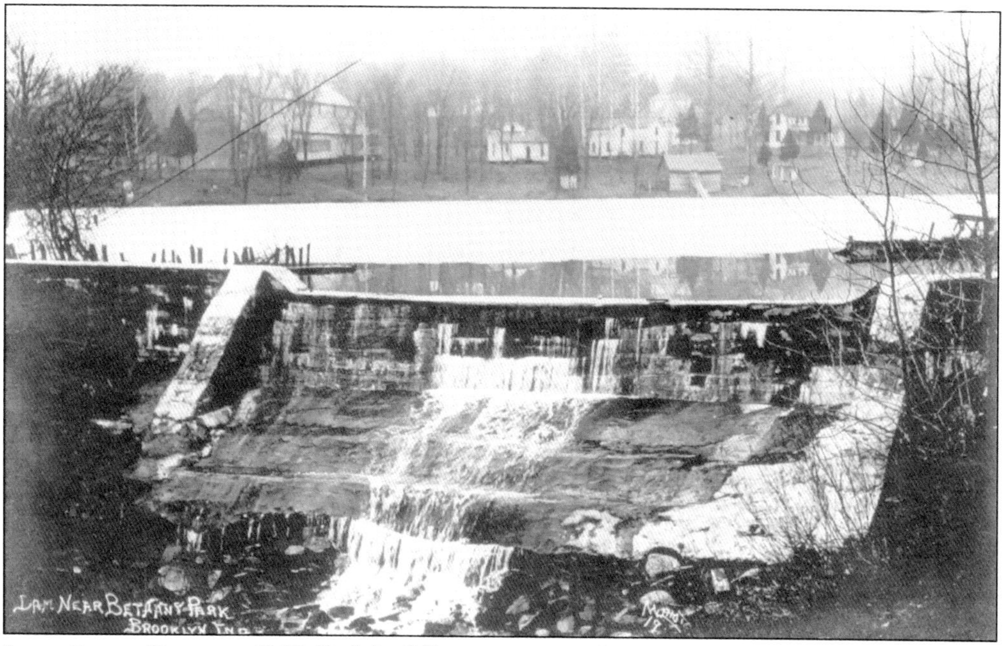

LAKE JEWEL DAM, C. 1909. Park buildings appear on the west shore of the lake. The sender, Cordelia, writes to Mrs. W. A. Johnson of Franklin, "Here is a little peep of Bethany Park. I wish you a Happy Birthday." The identical scene appears on the Brooklyn multiview card on page 81.

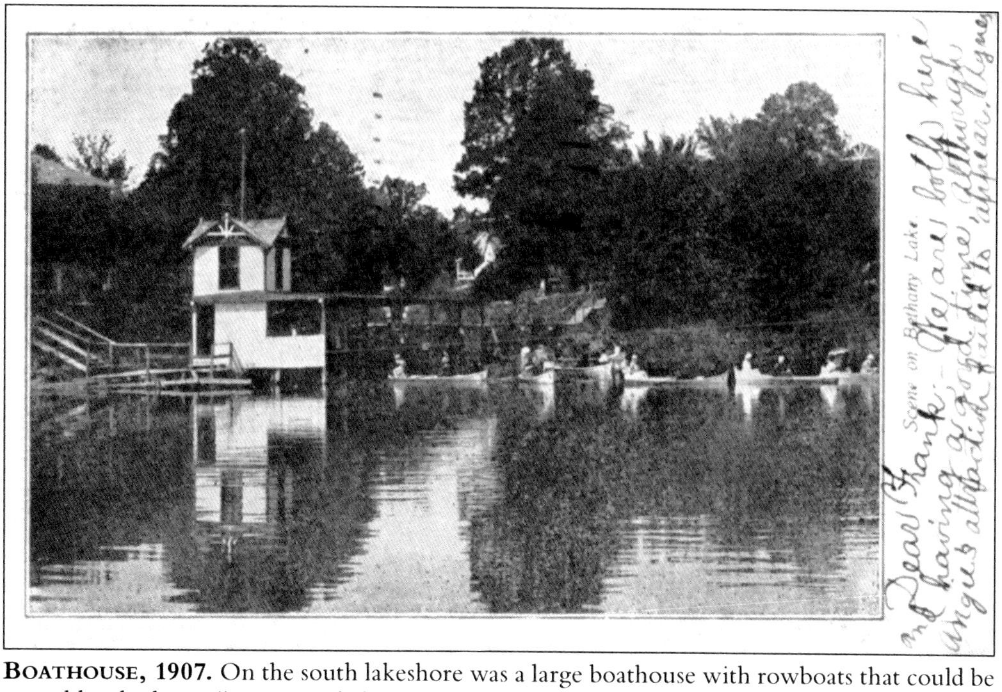

BOATHOUSE, 1907. On the south lakeshore was a large boathouse with rowboats that could be rented by the hour. "Dear Frank," writes Agnes, "We are both having a good time, although Angie's attraction failed to appear." Bethany Park was undoubtedly the meeting ground for many couples whose first sight turned to love.

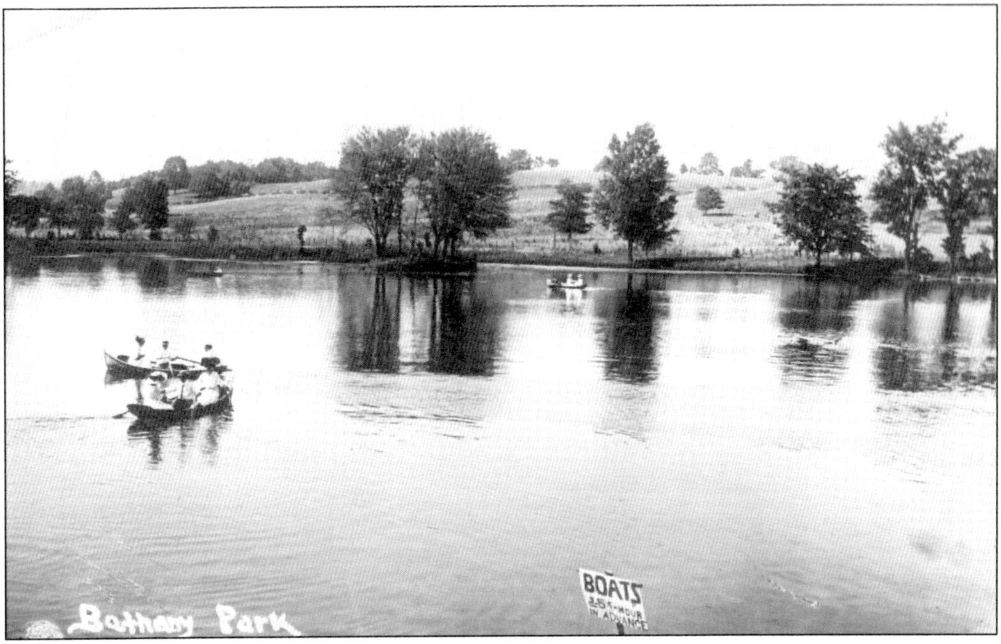

BOATING ON LAKE JEWEL, 1912. The sign reads, "Boast 25¢ an hour in advance."

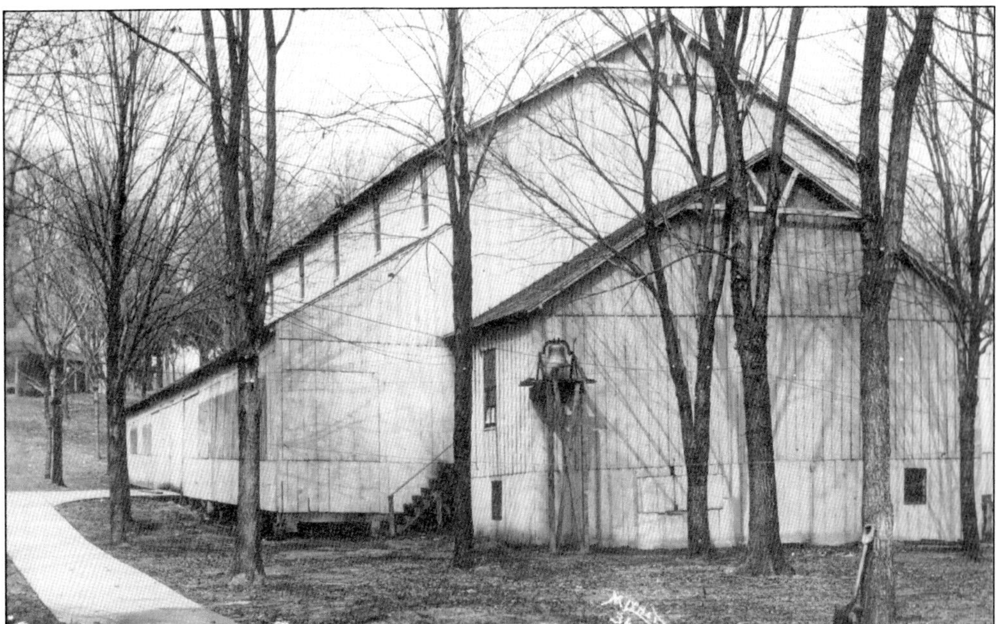

BETHANY PARK TABERNACLE OR CHAPEL, 1913. "We must not forget to mention the great tabernacle, with its splendid auditorium capable of seating 2,000 people, and one of the best in the country," boasted the *Bethany Assembly Supplement* of 1897. "This auditorium was built not only for conventions, lectures, and musical entertainments, but in fact, for public gatherings of all kinds. Its acoustic properties are perfect. It is well lighted and ventilated, so that it makes a most desirable place for what it is designed."

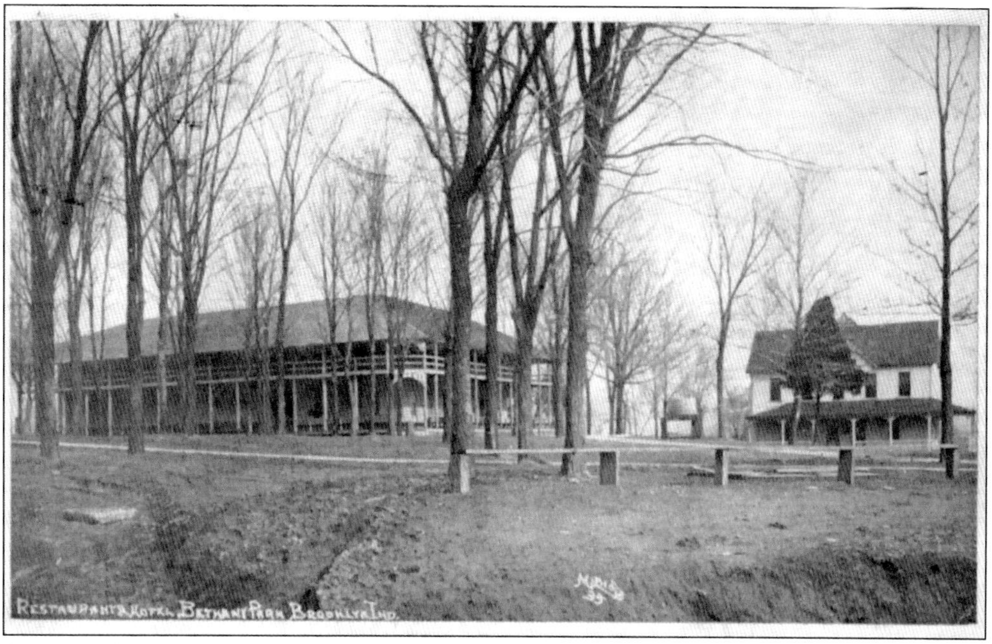

BETHANY PARK RESTAURANT AND HOTEL, *C.* 1910. The hotel, with its broad inviting verandas, had 50 rooms and a restaurant and dining room. It was built in 1884, in time to welcome guests for the first assembly. The mineral water sanitarium at right was built about 1886. A drinking fountain, whose water smelled like rotten eggs, stood between it and the hotel.

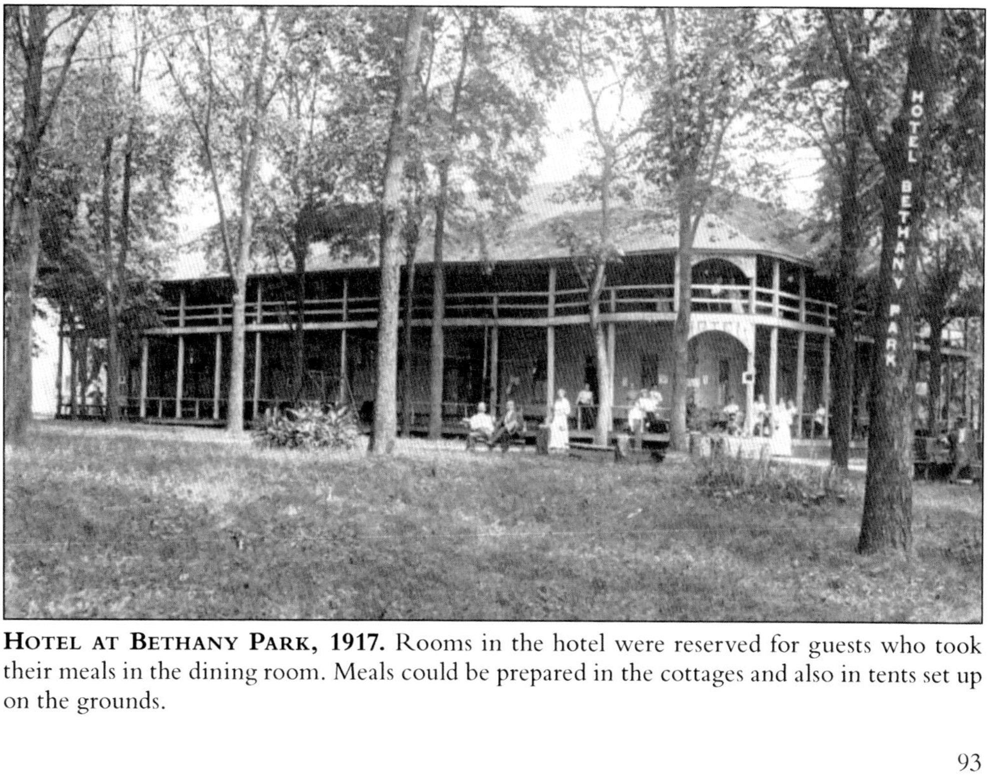

HOTEL AT BETHANY PARK, 1917. Rooms in the hotel were reserved for guests who took their meals in the dining room. Meals could be prepared in the cottages and also in tents set up on the grounds.

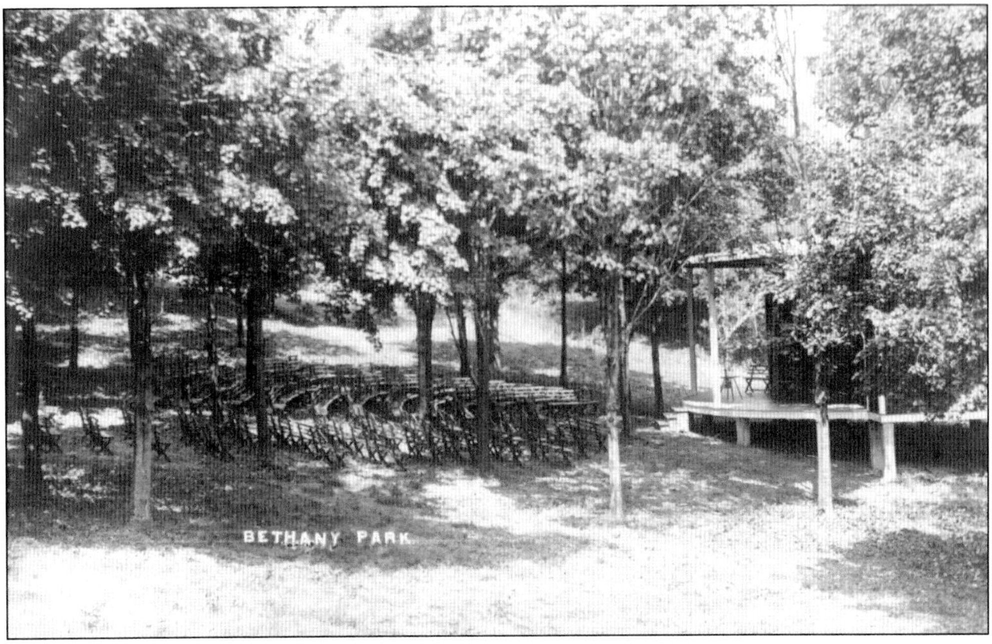

AMPHITHEATER, C. 1910. With benches aligned on the side of a slight hill and facing a covered wood pavilion, the amphitheater provided an ideal natural setting for musical performances and oratorios of all kinds. Among the noted headliners at Bethany Park were William Jennings Bryan, whose speech on the value of silver attracted some 10,000 listeners, and musicians John Philip Sousa and Arthur Rubinstein.

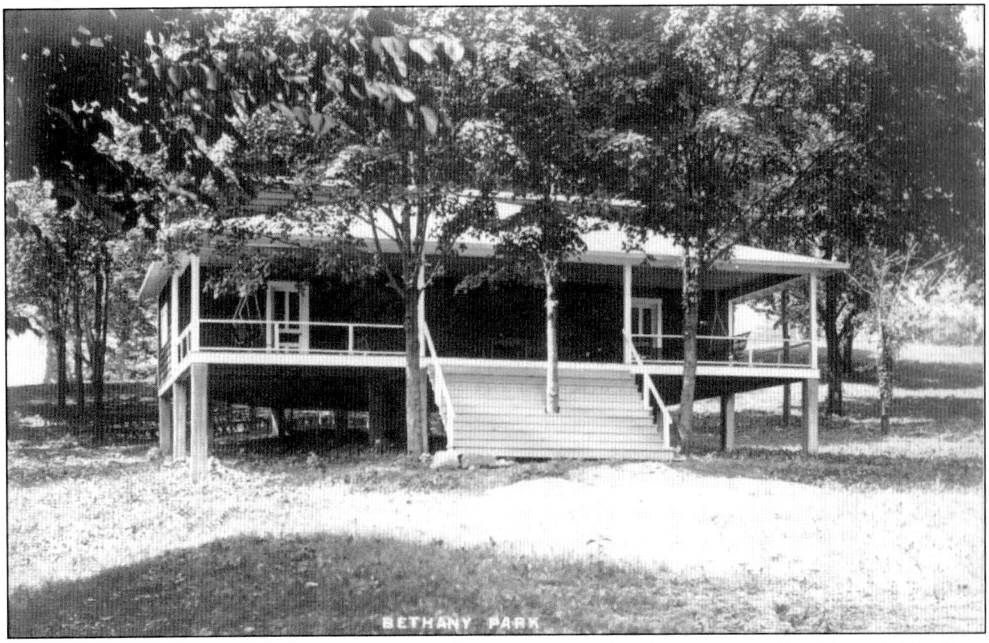

SINGER'S PAVILION, C. 1910. The amphitheater seating faced a stage on the Singer's Pavilion built by W. E. Hackleman, who served as assembly president from 1915 to 1923 and again in 1927. A publisher of hymnals and manuals for singing instruction and training, Hackleman taught singing, sight-reading, choral direction, and related sessions on the Singer's Pavilion.

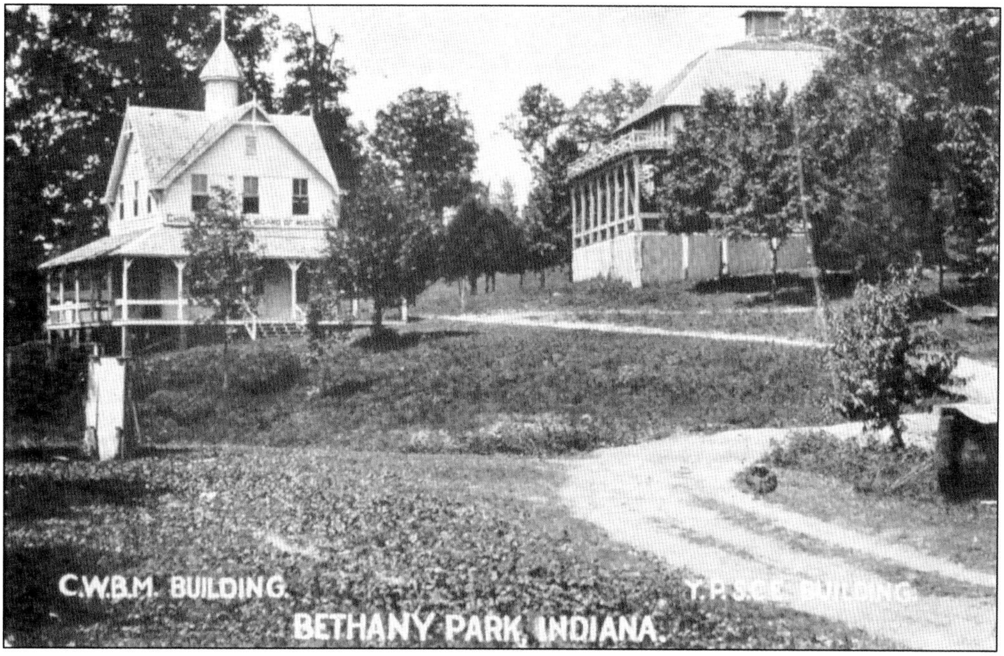

WOMEN'S AND YOUTH ORGANIZATIONS BUILDINGS, 1908. These wood buildings were an important part of Bethany Park, serving the Christian Women's Board of Missions (CWBM) and the Young Peoples Society of Christian Endeavor (YPSCE), respectively, of the Disciples of Christ. They overlooked a lagoon known as the goldfish lake south of Lake Jewel.

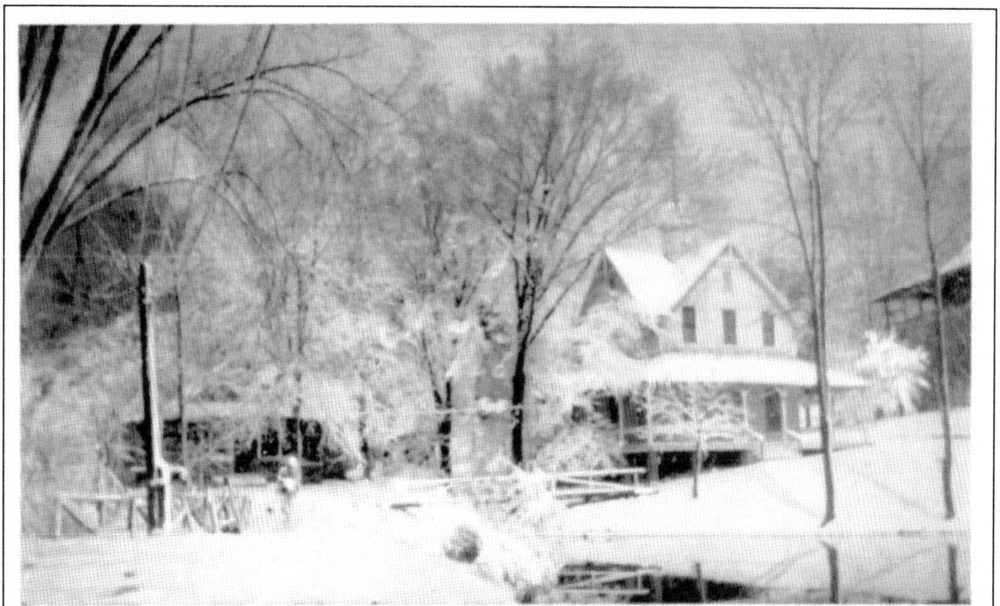

WINTER SCENE, CHRISTIAN WOMEN'S BOARD OF MISSIONS, BETHANY PARK, c. 1930. The bridge spans the small goldfish lake and then proceeds to Franklin Avenue, a cement sidewalk lined with cottages. Postcards with winter views are not common.

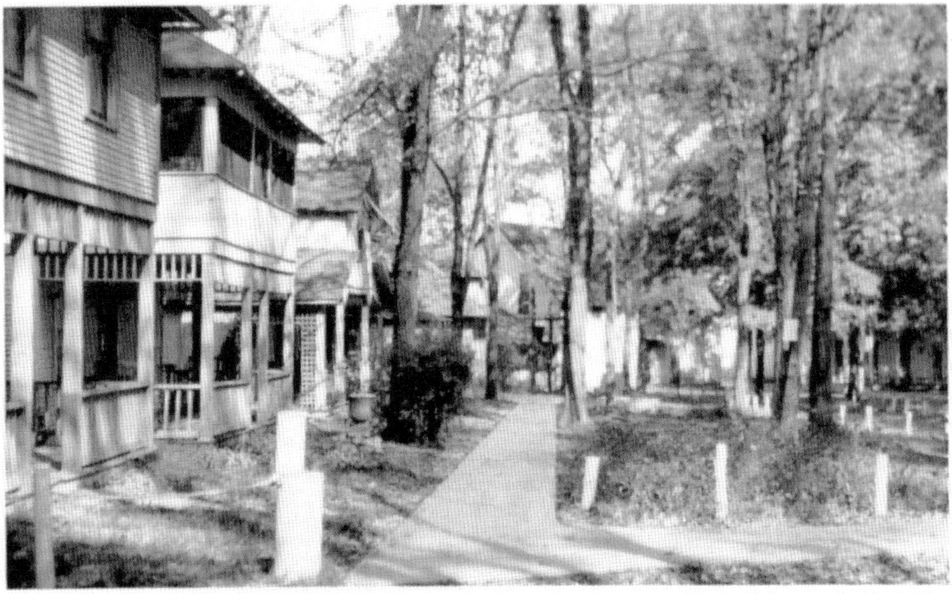

COTTAGES ON FRANKLIN AVENUE, *C.* 1930. Cottages were at first owned by the assembly and rented to guests, but it was not long before privately owned cottages, such as those on Franklin Avenue south of Lake Jewel, were built as seasonal residences. By the mid-1920s, however, interest in Bethany Park on the part of both cottagers and guests had waned. Forty years after the first triumphant assembly, Bethany Park was approaching both deterioration and obsolescence.

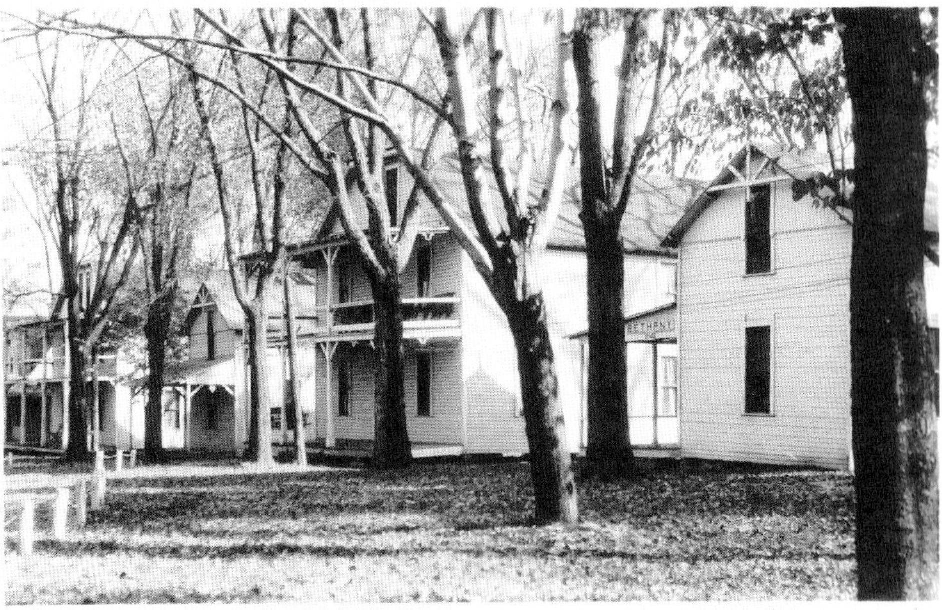

COTTAGES ON FRANKLIN AVENUE, 1938. The sender of this card provides a glimpse of a day at Bethany Park: "The bell rings every morning at 6 and we have to jump out of bed and go out on the porch and take setting up exercises for a minute. Just one way of waking up. Everything is run by bells and you have to be on time. We're having a good time but it is strenuous."

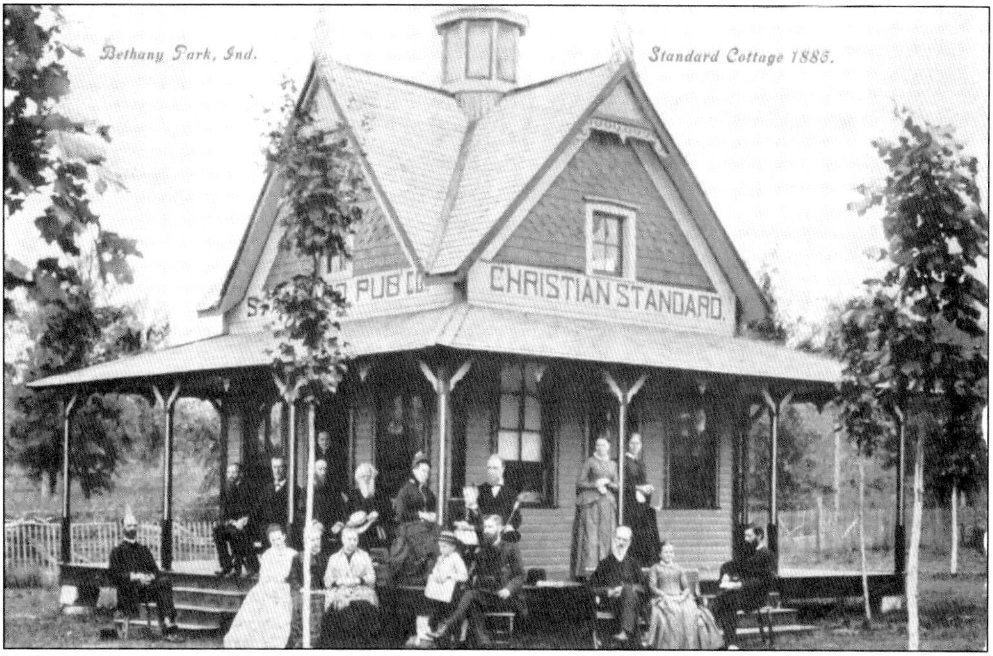

CHRISTIAN STANDARD COTTAGE, *c.* 1907. Built in 1886, this cottage was a retail outlet operated by the Cincinnati-based Christian Standard Publishing Company, a producer of religious books and hymnals. It was among the very earliest cottages built at Bethany Park and served as the first official post office. It may have included a printing press that turned out Bethany Park literature.

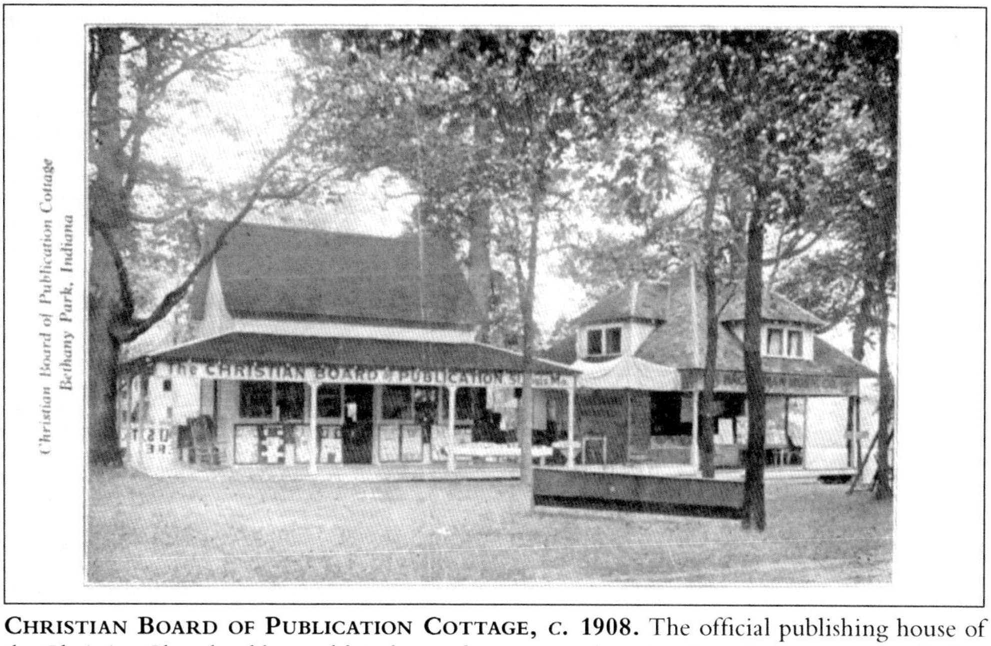

CHRISTIAN BOARD OF PUBLICATION COTTAGE, *c.* 1908. The official publishing house of the Christian Church sold pamphlets, hymnals, sermons, devotionals, and an assortment of other materials. It was one of three small stores specializing in religious publications at Bethany Park. To the right is the Hackleman Music Company store.

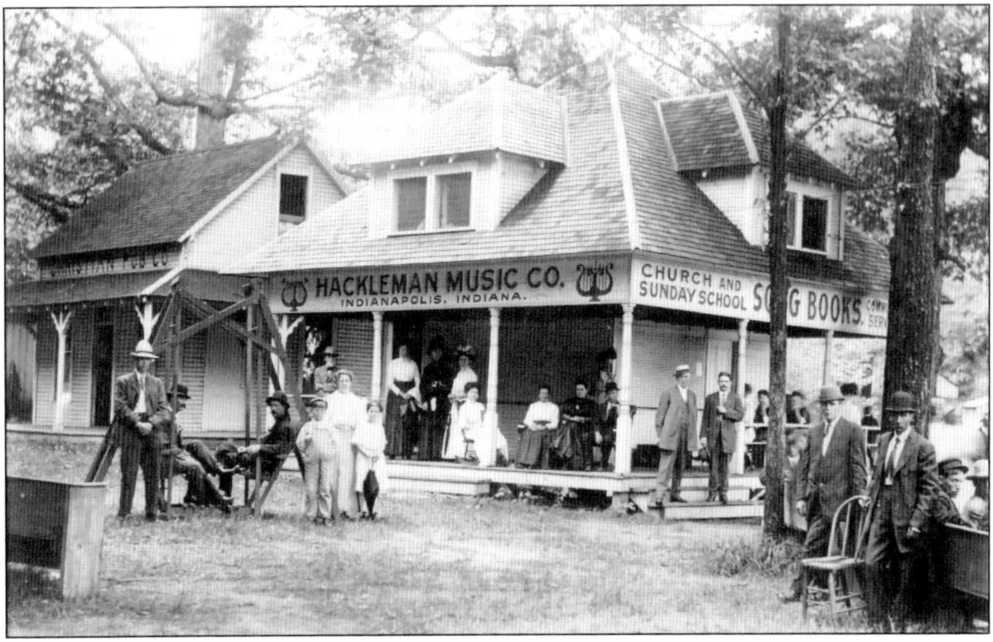

HACKLEMAN MUSIC COMPANY, *C.* 1910. Located in the Majestic Building in Indianapolis, Hackleman Music Company, owned by W. E. Hackleman, produced church and Sunday school songbooks. Hackleman drew inspiration for his life's work from Colossians 3:16: "Let the Word of Christ dwell in you richly. Teaching and admonishing one another in Psalms, and Hymns, and Spiritual Songs, singing with Grace in your hearts and unto God."

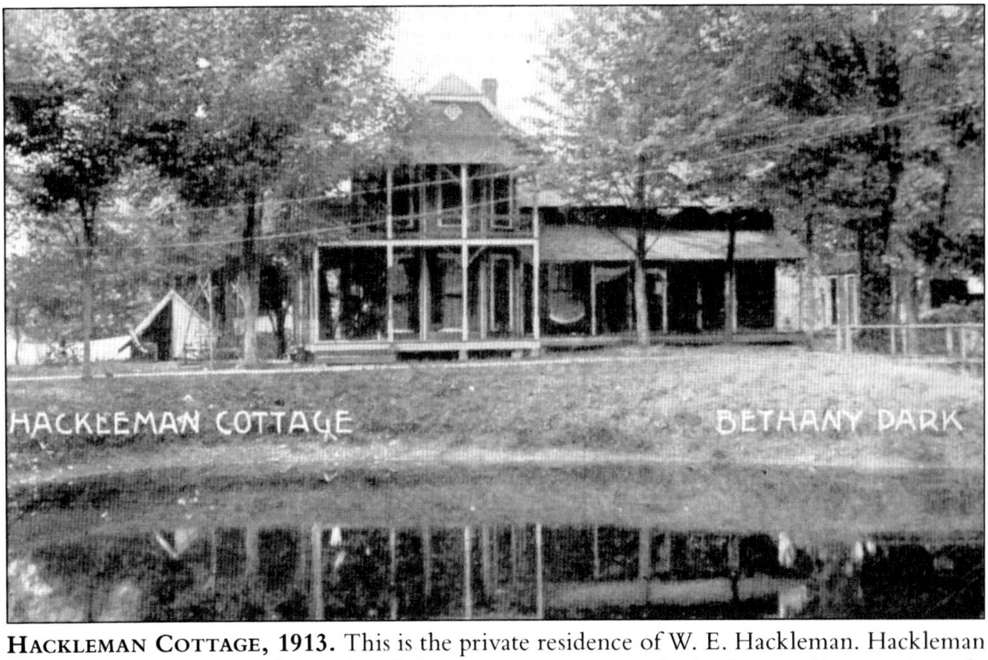

HACKLEMAN COTTAGE, 1913. This is the private residence of W. E. Hackleman. Hackleman achieved notoriety for "Hackleman's Folly"—an excursion steam wheeler that was disproportionately large for little Lake Jewel. For 15¢ passengers could see the cottages, cattails, and two islands from the steamer's deck. Note the tent set up behind the cottage.

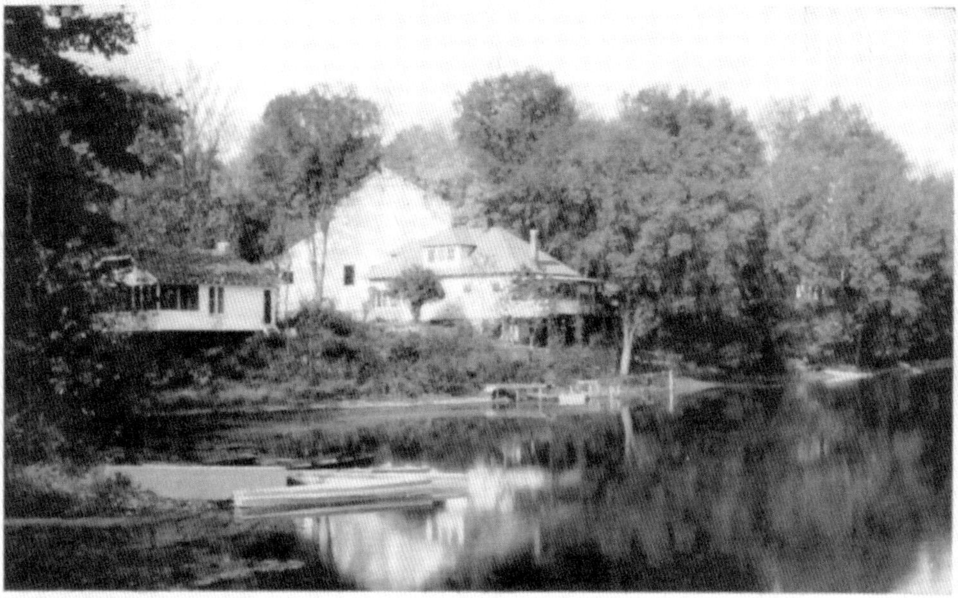

Lake Jewel with Park Buildings, 1944. By the 1940s, Bethany Park was in decline. Church leaders had begun debating its fate when the centerpiece hotel burned to the ground on a bitter winter night in 1952, forcing the park's abandonment. The tabernacle was demolished the following year. This was the end of Bethany Assembly.

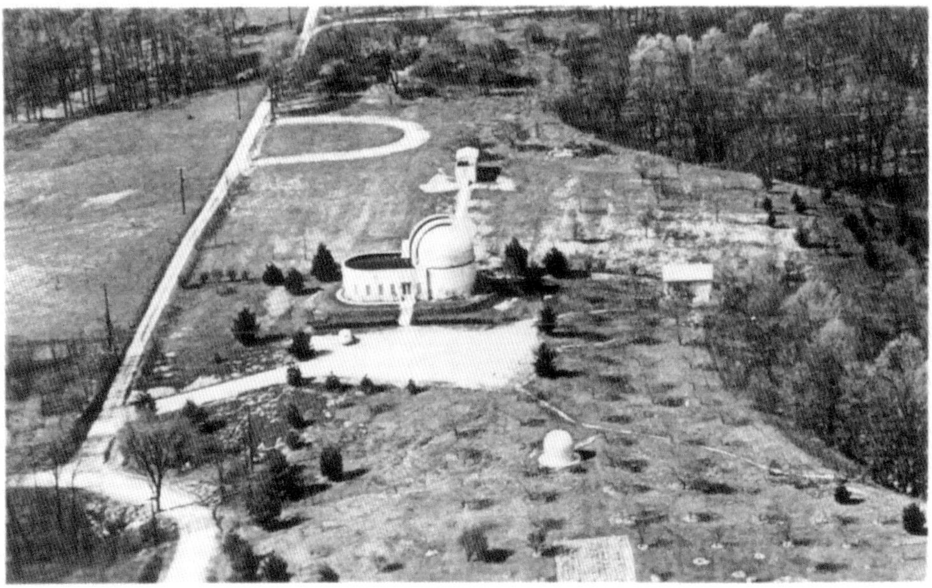

Indiana University's Goethe Link Observatory from the air, looking north.

Goethe Link Observatory, Aerial View, Clay Township, c. 1950. Located northwest of Bethany Park, this observatory was built by Dr. Goethe Link in 1937. A true renaissance man, Link was a specialist in thyroid surgery, as well as a respected amateur astronomer, collegiate bicycle racer, herpetologist, and ornithologist. As an aeronaut, he was cowinner of the 1909 national balloon race held in conjunction with the inaugural Indianapolis 500.

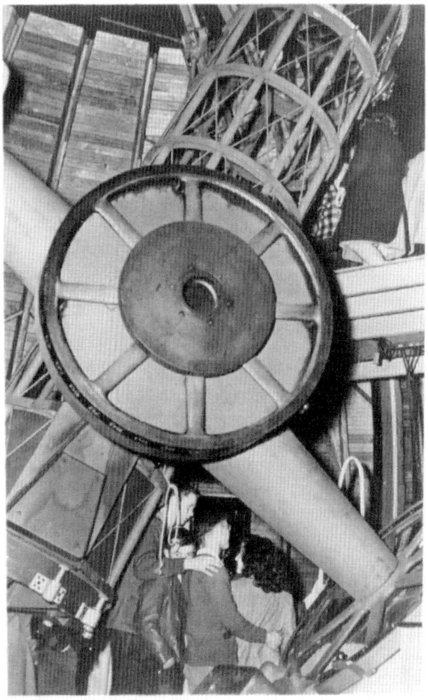

36-inch reflecting telescope at Indiana University's Goethe Link Observatory on a Public Night.

GOETHE LINK OBSERVATORY, LARGE TELESCOPE, CLAY TOWNSHIP, c. 1950. In 1948, Dr. Goethe Link gave his observatory to Indiana University, a gift that led to the establishment of the doctorate program in astronomy. Now operated by the Indiana Astronomical Society, of which Link was a founder, the observatory features this 36-inch reflecting telescope. It was one of the major telescopes in the United States up until the early 1970s.

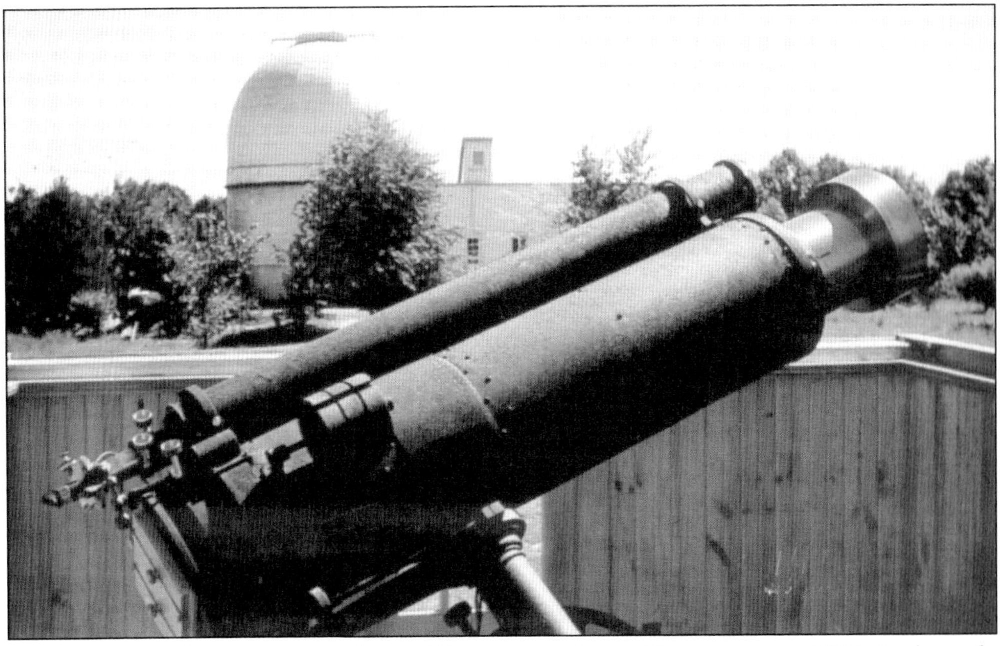

GOETHE LINK OBSERVATORY, SMALL TELESCOPE, CLAY TOWNSHIP, c. 1965. In the early 1950s, a 10-inch Zeiss refractor telescope was installed south of the observatory to locate asteroids "lost" during World War II. Asteroid 1728 was discovered in 1968 and named the Goethe Link. Immediately south of the telescope are Helen Link's daffodil beds and the Link house. Helen was a nationally acclaimed breeder of hybrid daffodils.

Five

WHITE RIVER CORRIDOR

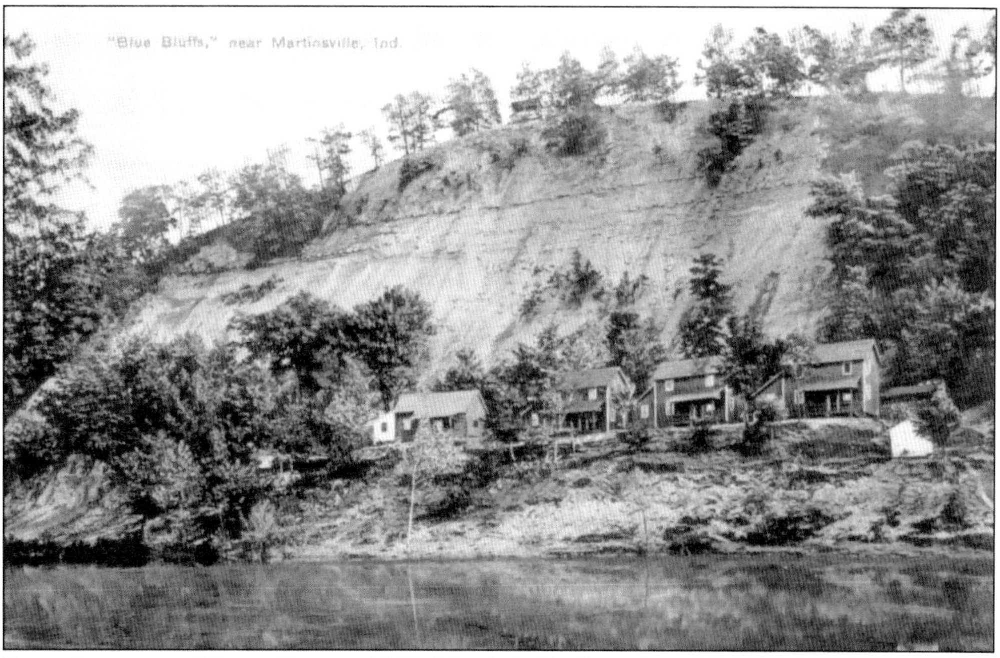

BLUE BLUFFS ON WHITE RIVER, 1909. The shale bluffs on the south bank of the White River, south of Centerton, made a perfect backdrop for this seasonal camp begun by Scotsman James Craig in 1899. An arthritis sufferer, Craig had come to Martinsville to find relief in the mineral water sanitariums. The bluffs reminded him of the hills of his native country.

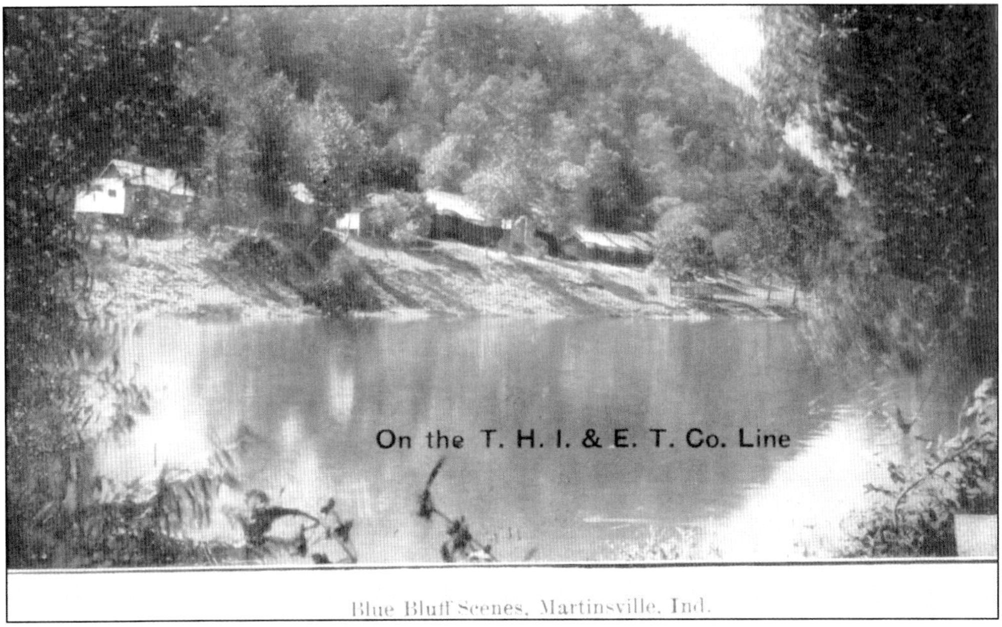

On the THI&ET Line, 1912. Visitors thronged by the hundreds to Blue Bluffs. At first they were met at the Centerton train depot—others took a horse-drawn vehicle from Martinsville—but by 1903, the interurban brought them nearly to the gates of James Craig's popular recreation area.

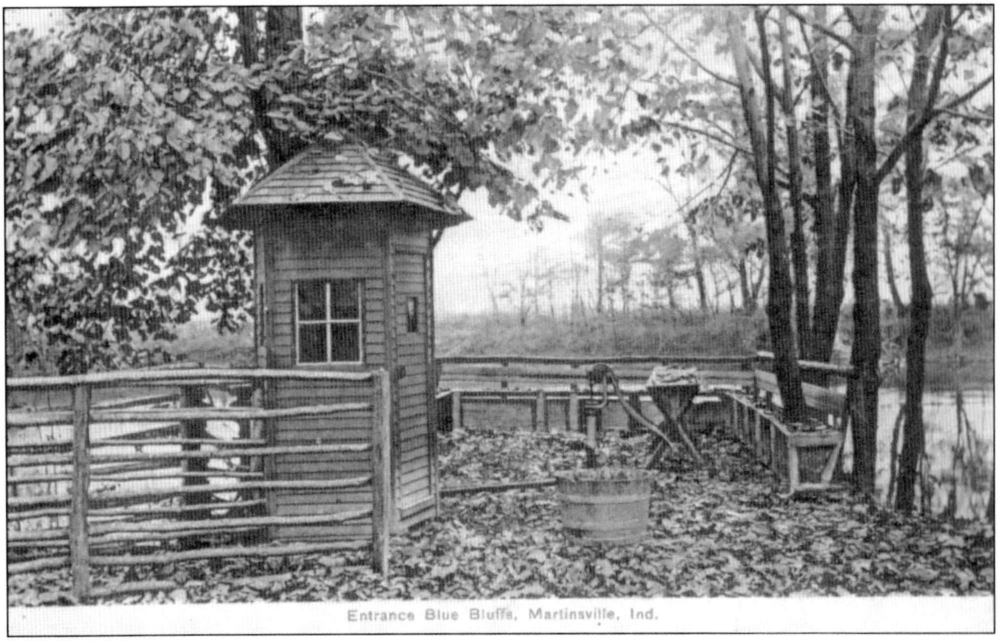

Entrance to Blue Bluffs, 1908. Adults paid a 10¢ admission charge at the gate; on an average Sunday it was customary for the park to receive 800–900 fares. Sophie writes to her friends Mr. and Mrs. Fred Starker of Martinsville, "Just having a fine time been on the water twice am going again. These bluffs are just grand. Lost my breath several times but finely reached the top."

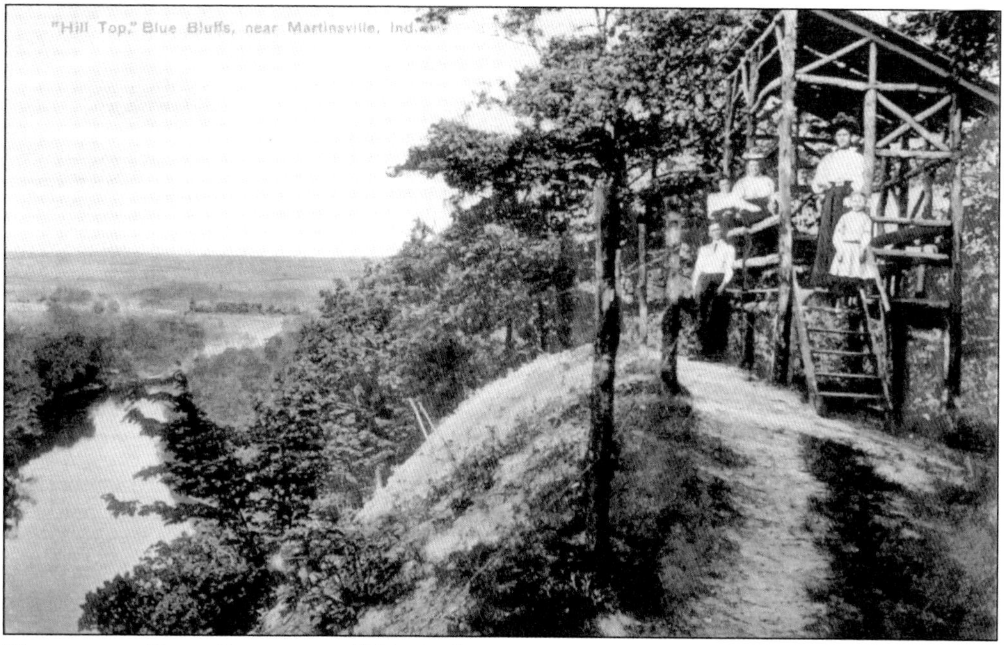

HILLTOP AT BLUE BLUFFS, *c.* 1910. Sophie entertained herself by climbing the Stairway to the Sun, a wooden staircase that led to the top of the bluffs. Hikers could rest in a rustic lookout shelter and enjoy the panoramic view before descending.

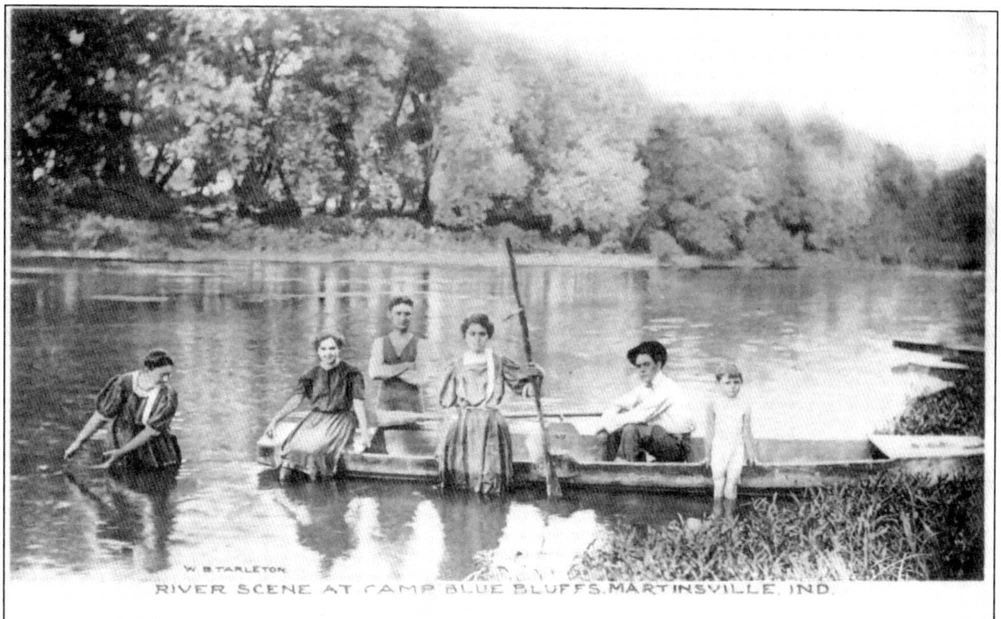

RIVER SCENE AT CAMP BLUE BLUFFS, 1907. This tinted lithograph card was published and sold by William B. Tarleton, who owned a drugstore on the courthouse square in Martinsville. Boating and swimming in the White River was fun for the whole family and a good way for Sophie and other hikers to cool down after a ramble on the bluffs.

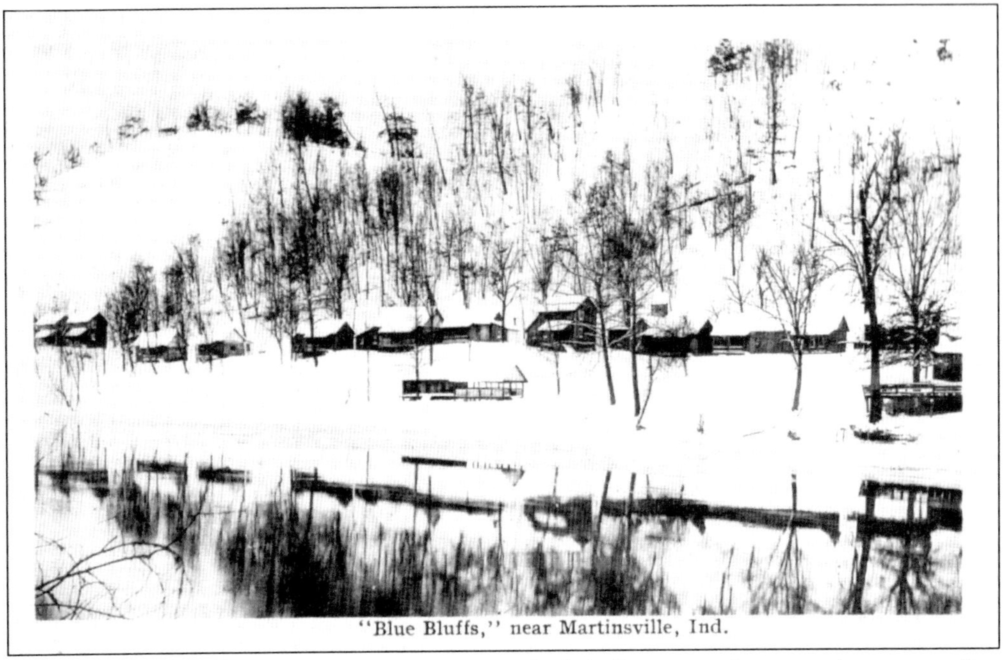

Blue Bluffs in Winter, 1918. Proprietor James Craig built cottages for seasonal use, expanding the camp with the purchase of additional acreage. A dance pavilion and refreshment stand was a popular attraction for both overnight guests and Martinsville residents who drove out for the Saturday night square dances.

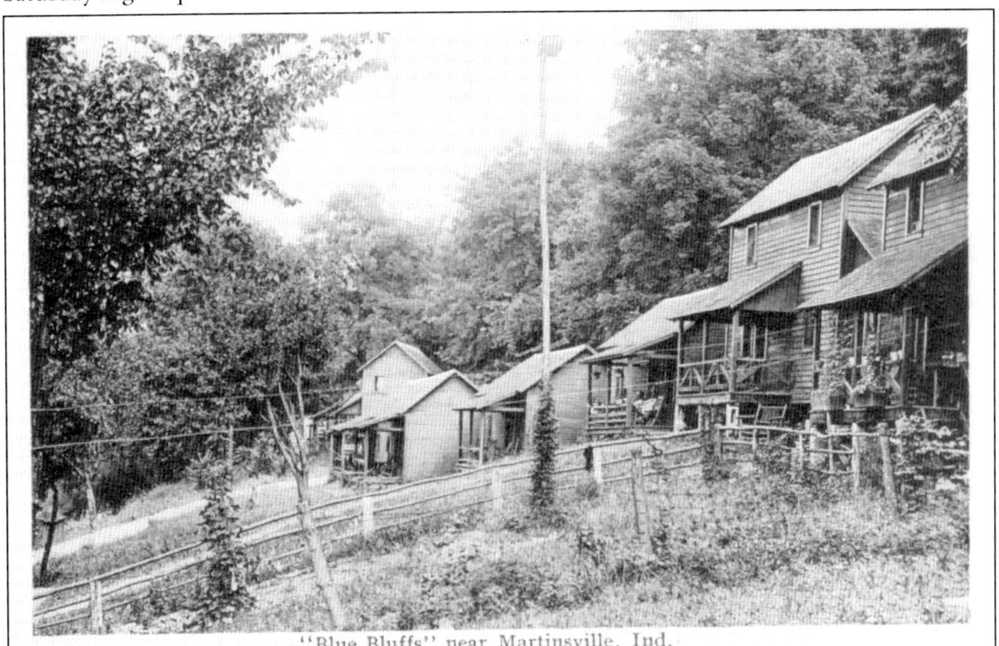

Hillside Cottages, 1908. The front porch of a cottage was an ideal place to view Fourth of July fireworks shot off the top of the bluff and out over the White River. Concession operators in the park sold great quantities of fireworks, and campers and area residents often did not get to bed until the wee hours of the morning.

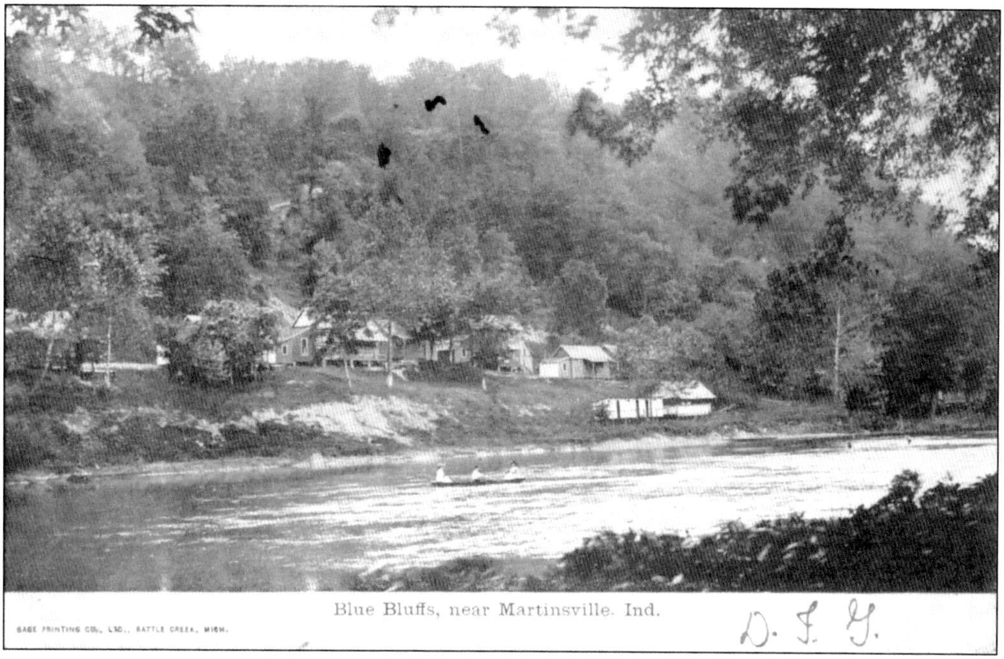

View of Blue Bluffs from across White River, 1907. Legend says that the bluffs were the wintering ground for thousands of rattlesnakes whose wriggling and burrowing among the oak and maple tree roots caused the earth and trees to come crashing down, exposing the blue shale beneath.

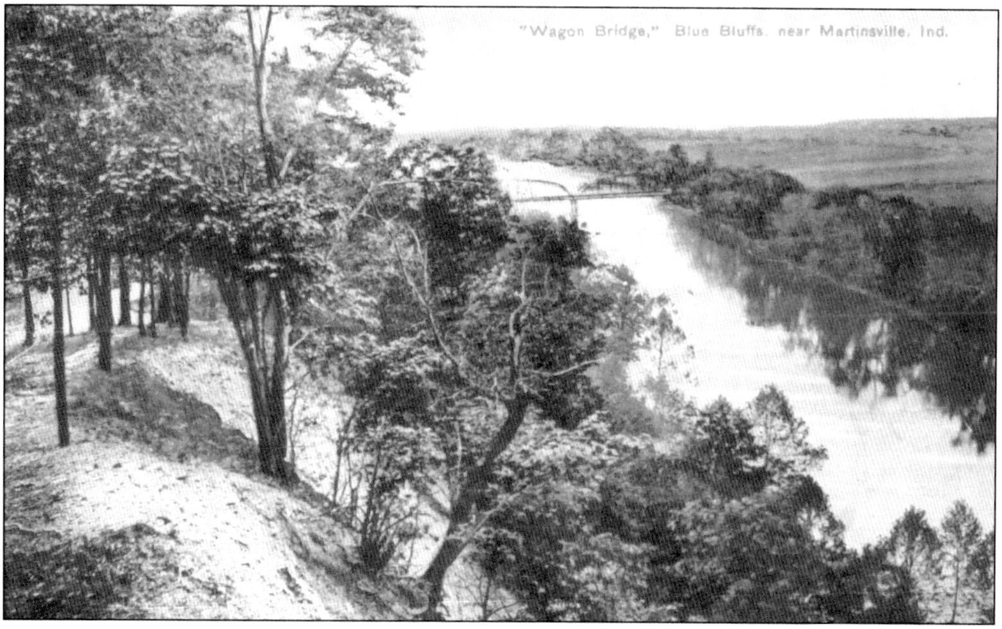

Record's Ferry Bridge at Blue Bluffs, c. 1910. Prior to the placement of this two-span iron bridge about 1890, various ferry operators, including a man named Record, shuttled people across the river. In 1971, the bridge's wood deck gave way under a loaded logging truck. Three years later, the bridge was replaced with the existing concrete span. The interurban bridge was located about one-half mile downriver.

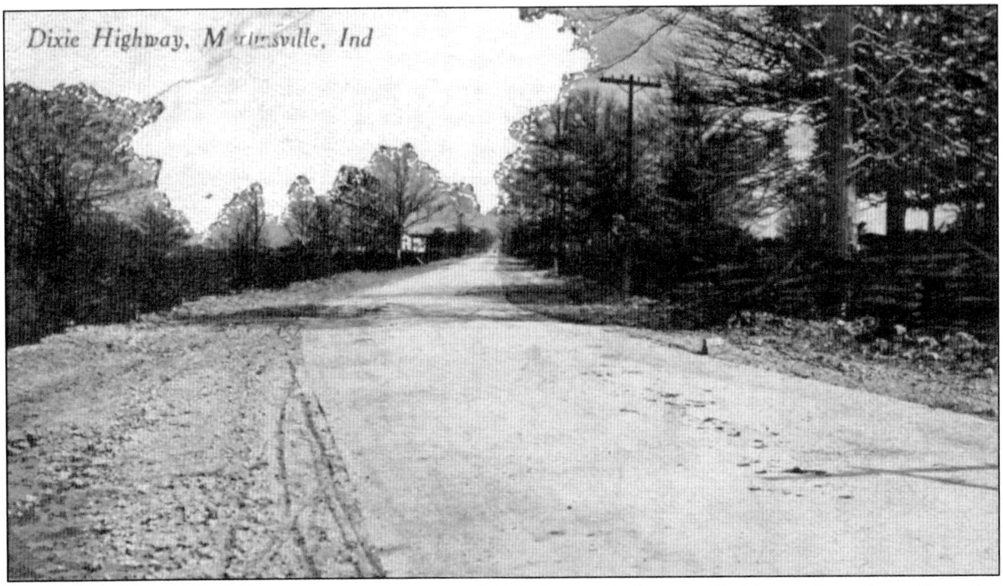

Dixie Highway, Near Martinsville, c. 1915. It was Indianapolis Motor Speedway founder Carl Fisher who conceived of a national highway connecting the Midwest with the South. Constructed and expanded between 1915 and 1927, the Dixie Highway stretched southward from Indianapolis to Martinsville, where it rounded the courthouse square and continued on to Bloomington and beyond.

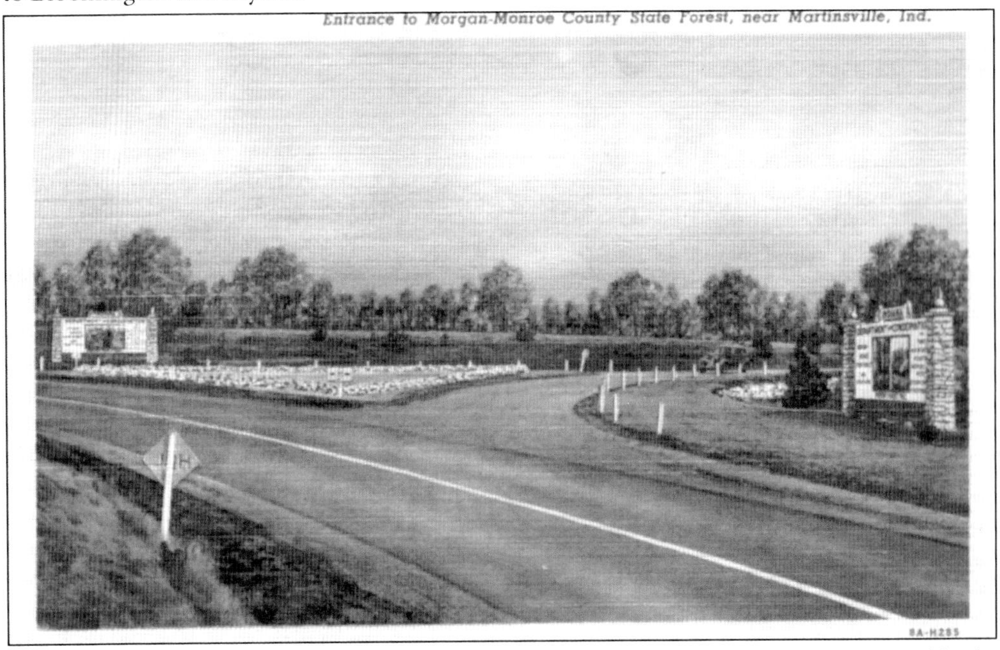

Entrance to Morgan-Monroe County State Forest, c. 1940. Motorists could take the Dixie Highway, shown here, to this beautiful state-owned recreation area. Hardscrabble farmland and wooded tracts in the south-central part of Morgan County were purchased by the state beginning in 1929. During the Works Progress Administration era (1935–1943), shelter houses, lakes, picnic areas, and roadways were constructed by the Civilian Conservation Corps. The gates were vandalized and removed in the 1960s.

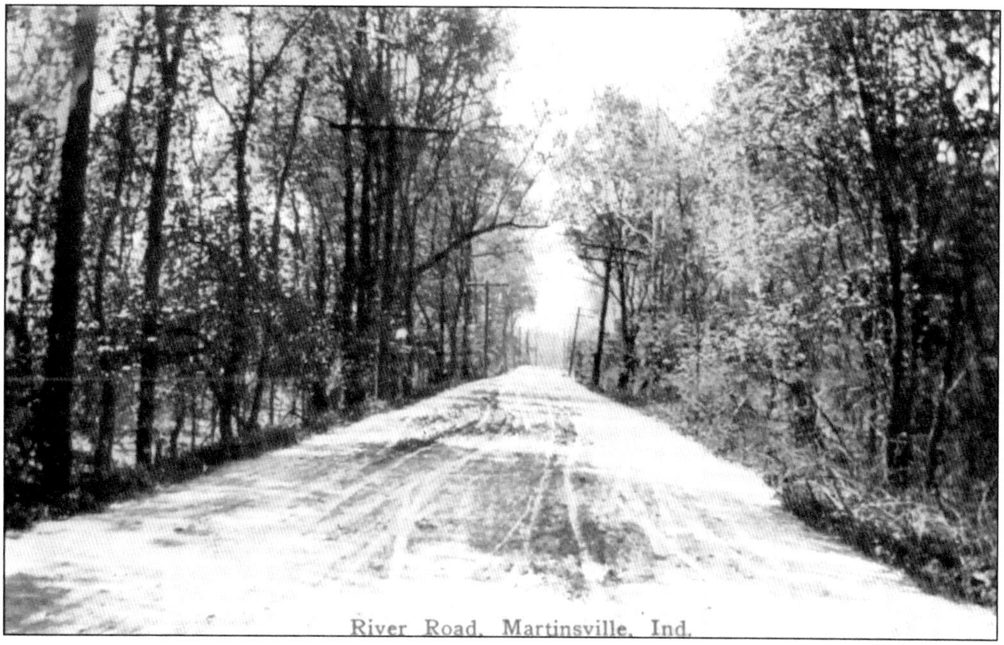

RIVER ROAD, MARTINSVILLE, C. 1910. This road extended west from Morgan Street before heading north to the bridge over the White River. Following the great flood of March 1913, it was improved with Martinsville-made Poston brick pavers, which can still be seen imbedded in the dirt alongside the State Road 39 Bypass near the county jail.

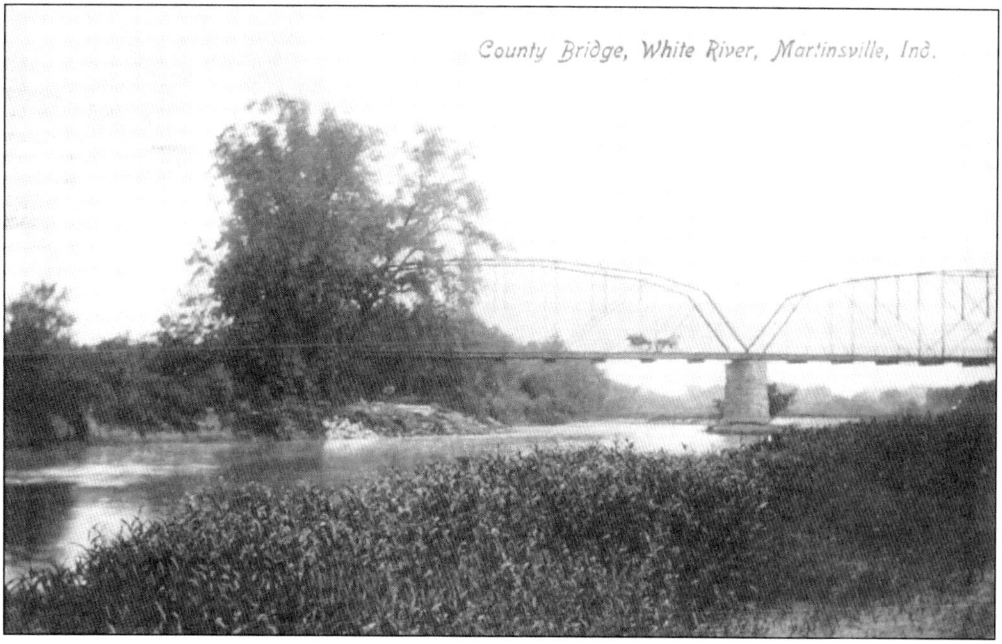

WHITE RIVER BRIDGE, NEAR MARTINSVILLE, C. 1915. The river road was carried over the White River by this single-lane, three-span metal bridge erected in 1893 at a cost of more than $10,000. It replaced a wood bridge blown down and washed away in a storm. Jerry Givan was employed to row people across the river, and later a ferryboat was used until the new bridge was placed. The existing concrete span replaced the bridge shown here in 1952.

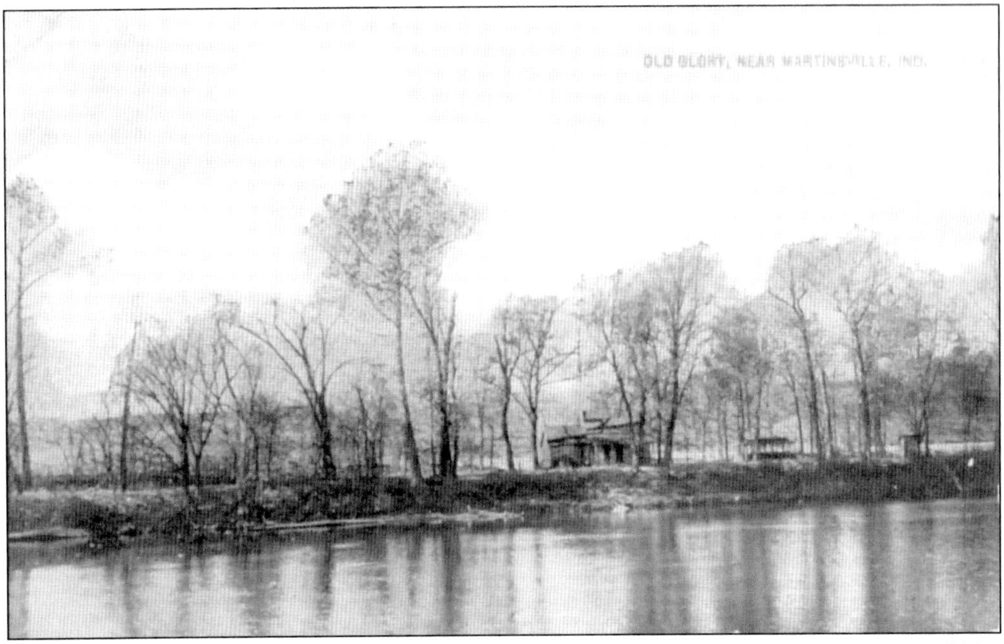

OLD GLORY, VICINITY OF MARTINSVILLE, *C.* 1912. This card published for and sold by Nutter's News Stand, on the courthouse square in Martinsville, depicts a well-known summer camp on the White River. Old Glory was owned by William M. Cain and occupied by him and his friends. In 1913, the hickory log cabin was destroyed by a fire thought to have been set by tramps. The cabin may have been replaced by an old train car known to have been on the property. Old Glory was located approximately opposite the Lake Edgewood entrance.

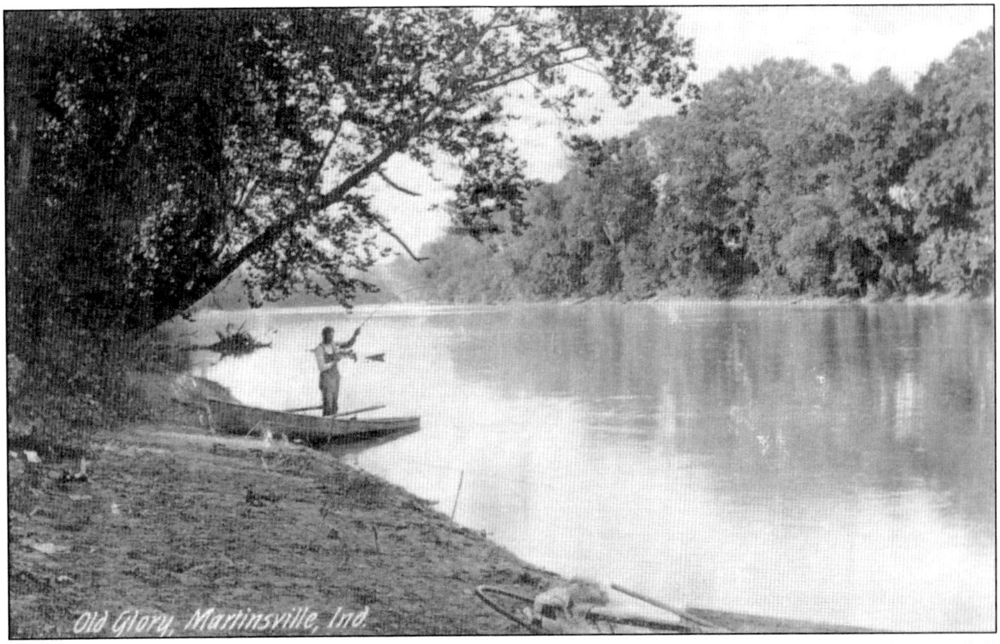

OLD GLORY, VICINITY OF MARTINSVILLE, 1908. "This is what I should be doing but ain't," says the message on the reverse side of this card.

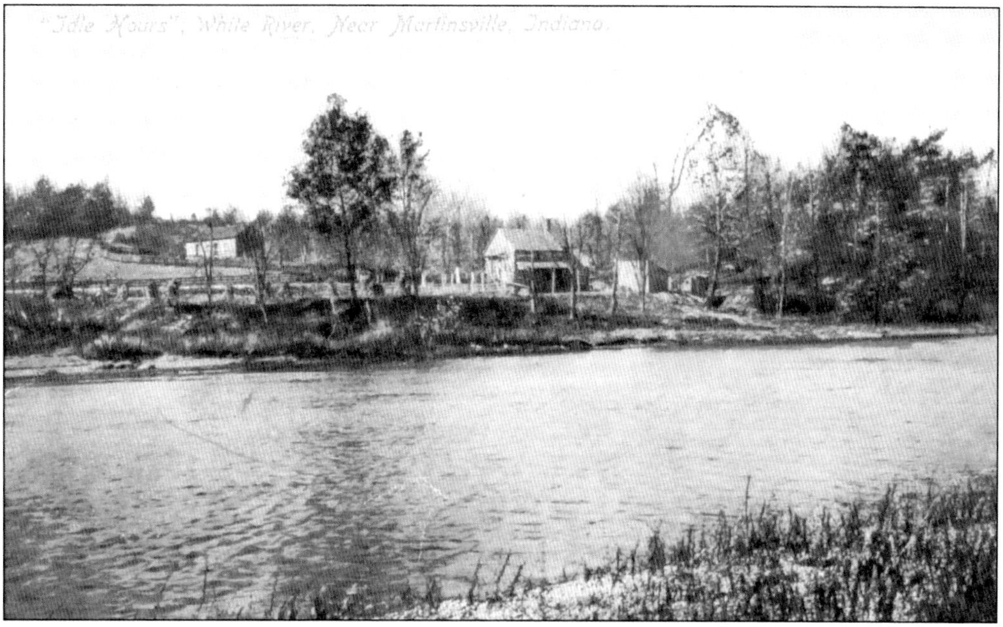

IDLE HOURS, VICINITY OF MARTINSVILLE, 1913. Little is known about Idle Hours, another fishing camp on the west bank of the White River about two miles north of Martinsville and just south of High Rock. In the absence of formal road markers, it was a landmark on the former Martinsville-Monrovia Road and a reference point for travelers, local residents, and elected officials.

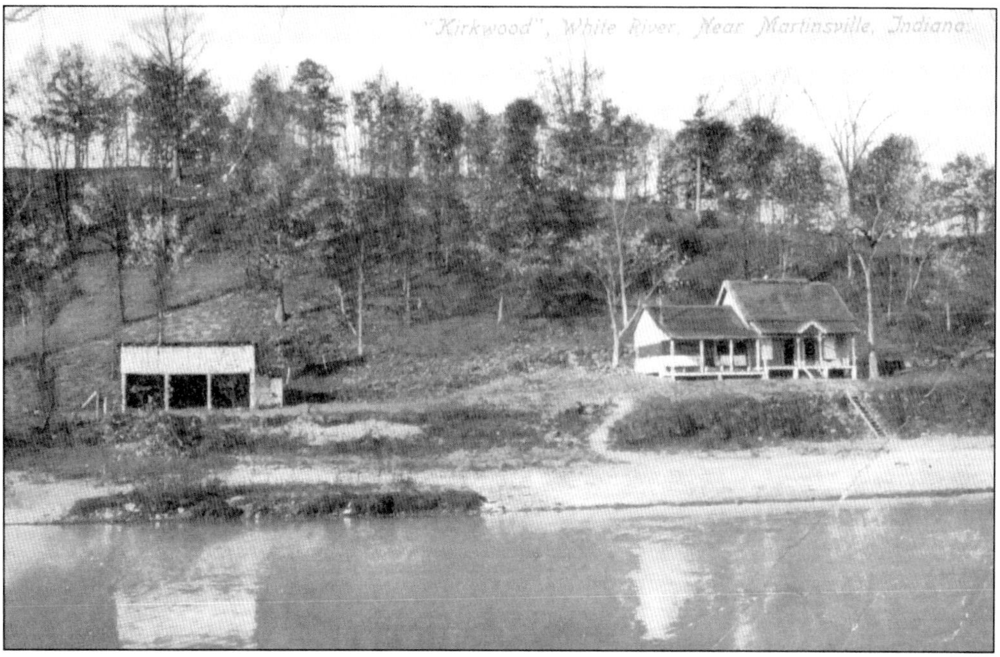

KIRKWOOD, VICINITY OF MARTINSVILLE, 1912. Yet another seasonal fishing camp on the White River, Kirkwood was located near the farm of Daniel Kirk, about three miles north of Martinsville in the vicinity of High Rock. With the construction of State Road 67 about 1939, it and other popular riverbank sites were all but obliterated.

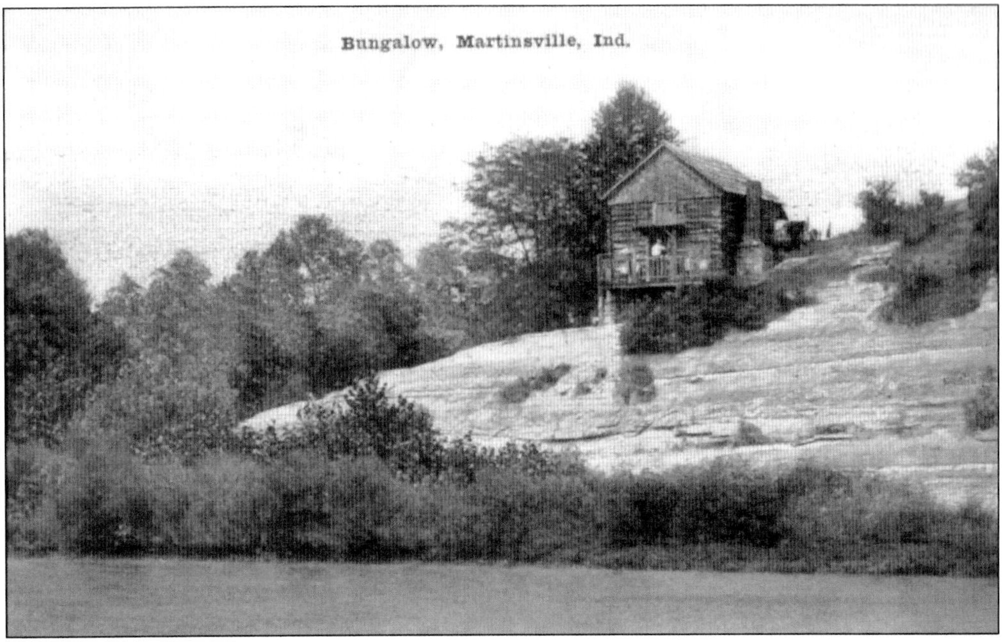

HIGH ROCK BUNGALOW, 1910. Named for the picturesque bluff rising above the west bank of the White River about three miles north of Martinsville, High Rock was once a thriving settlement with a mill and dam, a schoolhouse, and this nostalgic, two-story log house. Furnishings included all variety of rustic hickory chairs, rockers, settees, and tables. Erected by "gentlemen," the High Rock Bungalow is thought to have been associated with the Old Hickory Chair Company, its owner, William H. Patton, its major shareholders, and other prominent Martinsville businessmen of the early 1900s.

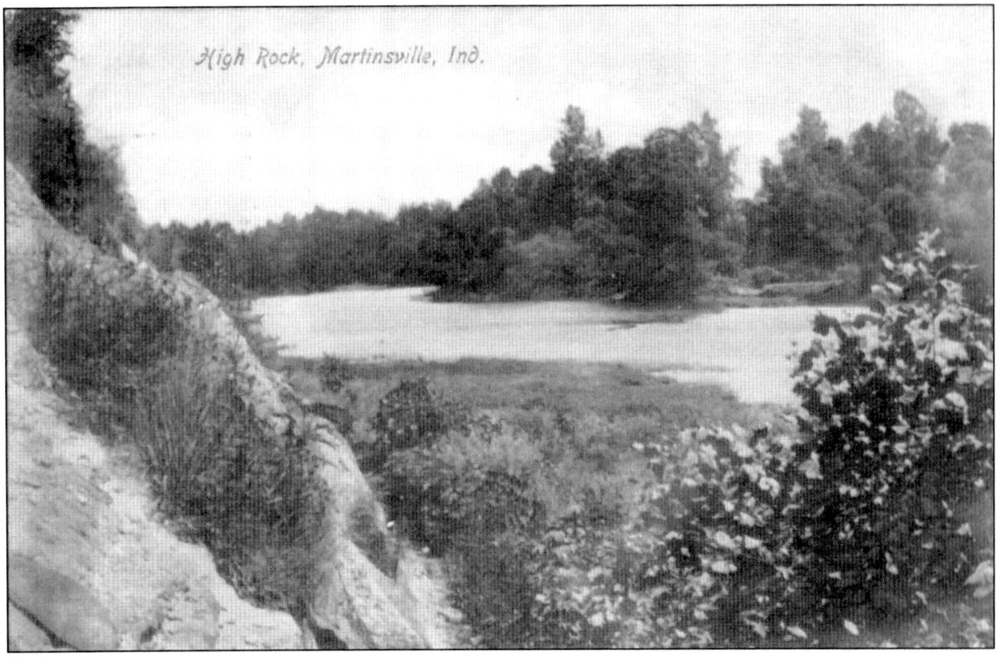

SCENIC HIGH ROCK, 1908. This view of the White River was taken from the bluff.

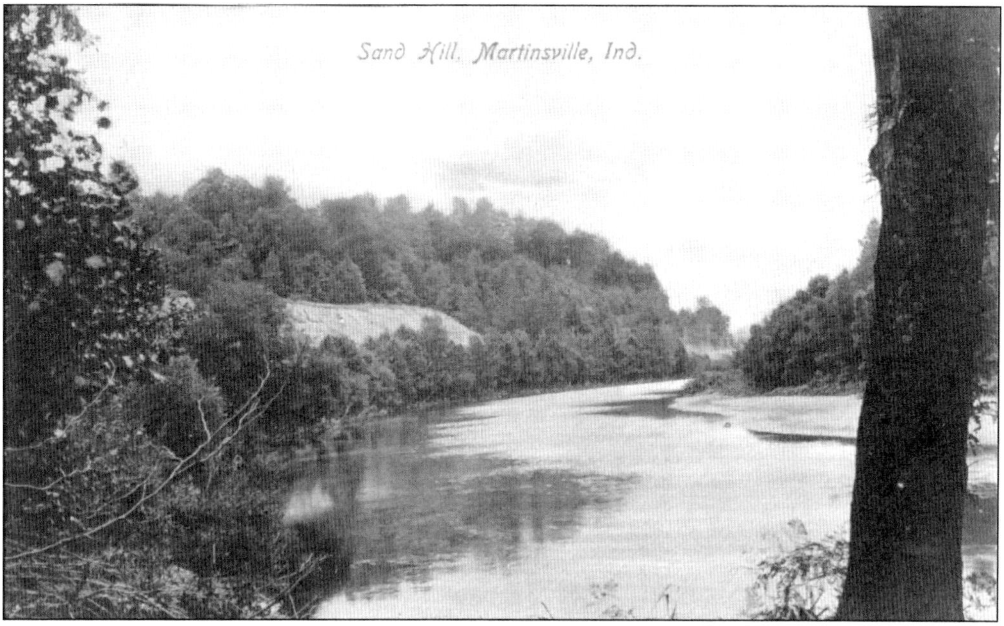

SAND HILL, VICINITY OF MARTINSVILLE, *c.* 1908. About 1886, Perry Bradford discovered fine-grained sand on the Bradford property near Sycamore Creek in Clay Township. By 1913, the Bradford Sand Mining Company had shipped more than 180,000 tons of sand, perfect for metal molding, to United States steel foundries. Member by member, the Bradford family passed away. The last surviving brother, John, donated the Bradford estate to Indiana University in 1938.

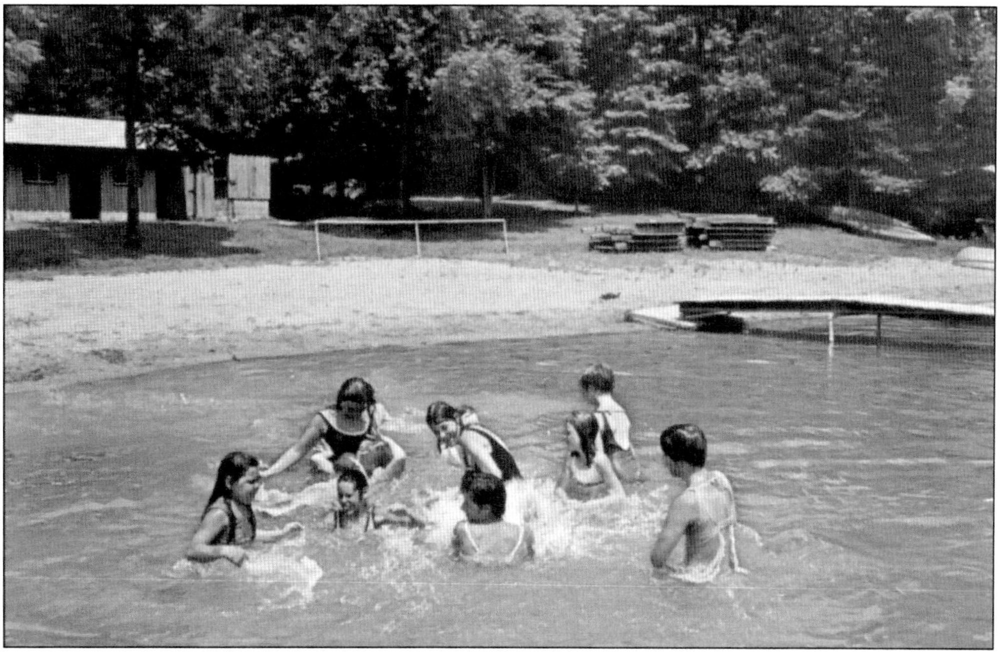

LAKE AT CAMP JAMES WHITCOMB RILEY, BRADFORD WOODS, *c.* 1965. John Bradford's gift was designated for use as a recreational and rehabilitative facility for Riley Hospital. In 1963, a 100-acre lake—the Old Swimmin' Hole—was developed for carefully supervised swimming, fishing, and boating.

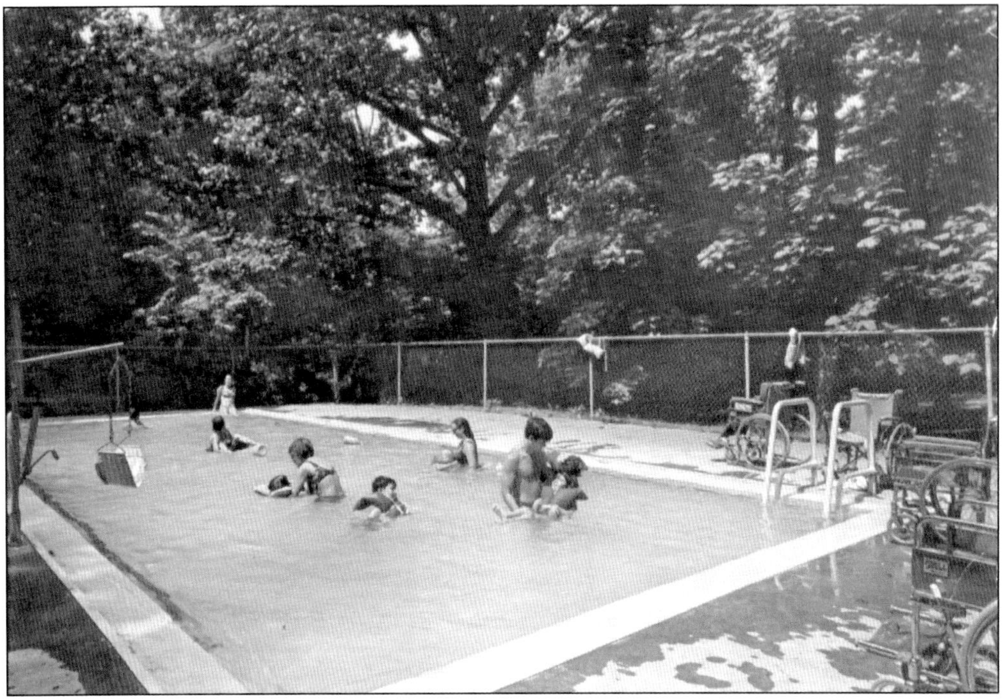

POOL AT CAMP JAMES WHITCOMB RILEY, BRADFORD WOODS, *c.* 1965. This temperature-controlled swimming pool made it possible for even the most severely handicapped campers to enjoy water sports under careful supervision.

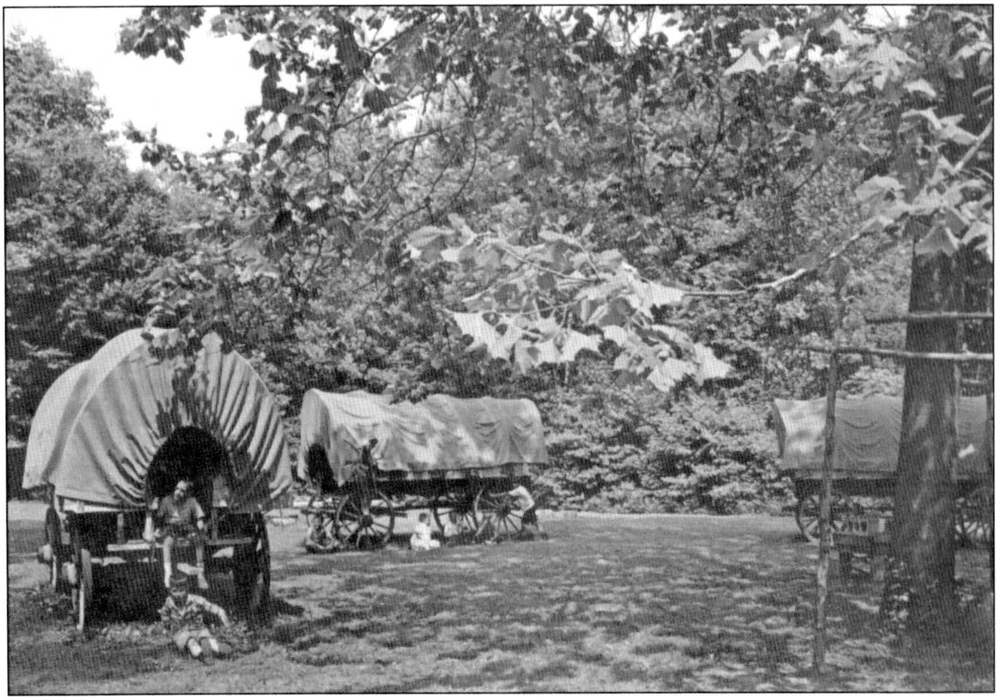

OUTPOST AT CAMP RILEY, BRADFORD WOODS, *c.* 1965. The Wagon Train was a favorite site for more active children who camped overnight with trained and experienced counselors.

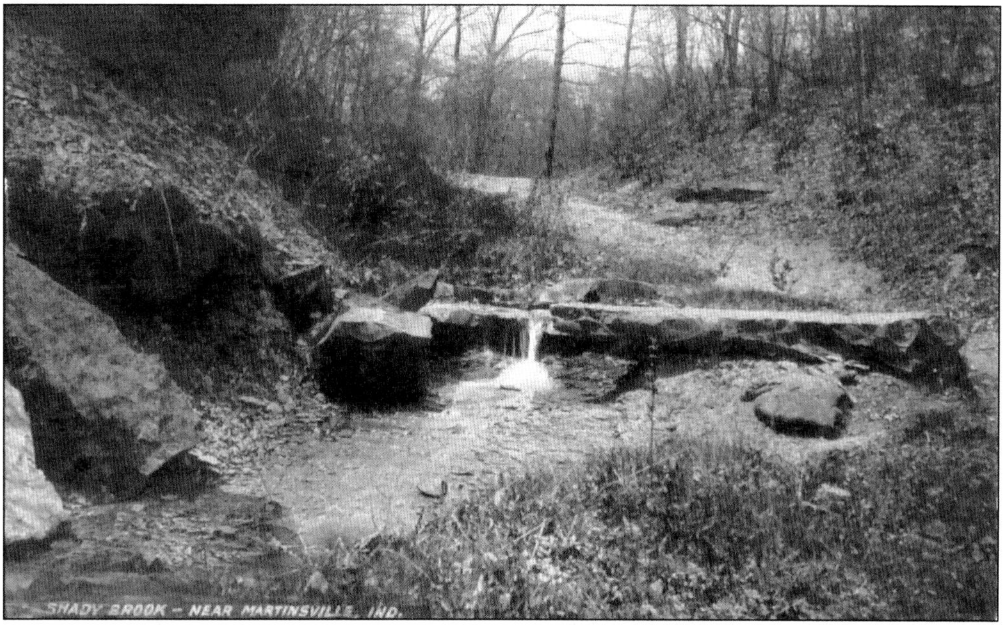

SHADY BROOK, VICINITY OF MARTINSVILLE, 1916. An area of lush and natural beauty featuring outcroppings of knobstone shale, the Sycamore Creek valley was unsuccessfully offered to the State of Indiana for a state park in 1916. "Few painters, whether they use words or colors, can justly describe [its] beauties," extolled the state geologist. The brook pictured here is believed to be in the proposed park area.

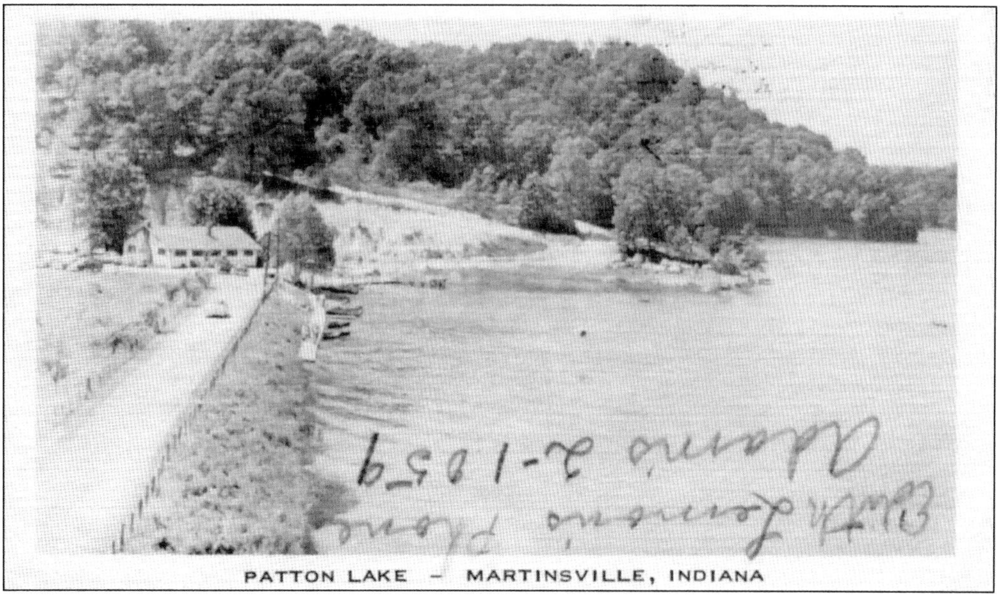

LAKE AT PATTON PARK, 1962. Located in north-central Jefferson Township, Patton Park originated as a park donated to area youth by Old Hickory owner William H. Patton. The first lake dug by area residents failed when the dam washed away. It was rebuilt, and the lake enlarged, as a federally funded Works Progress Administration project. In early years, the park was managed and operated by the Martinsville Lions Club, which sponsored popular Fourth of July fireworks displays. Gradually summer cabins became year-round residences.

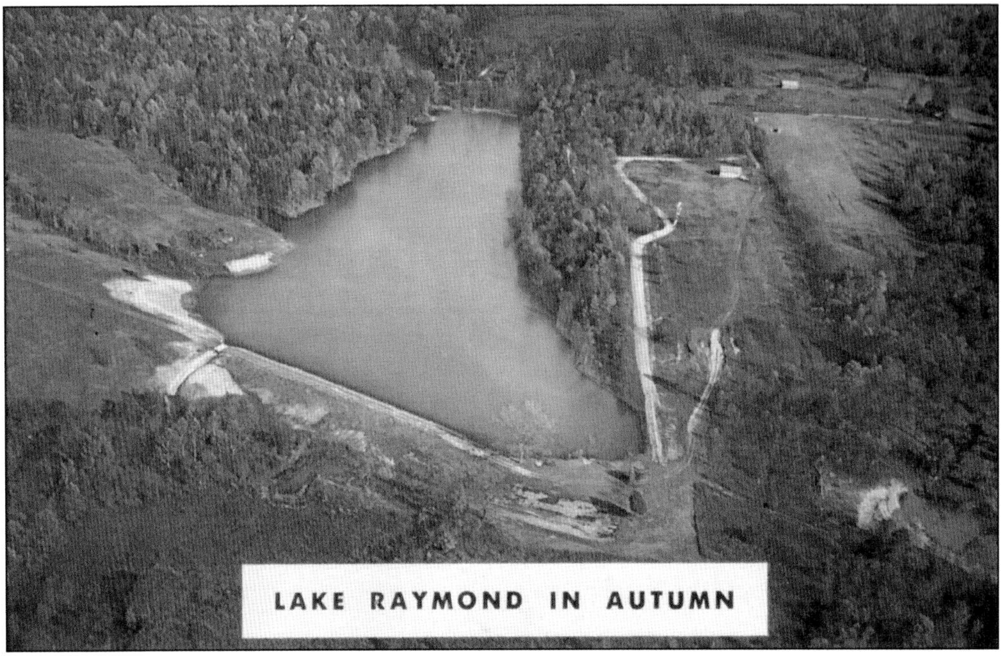

LAKE RAYMOND FISHING CLUB, ASHLAND TOWNSHIP, *c.* 1960. Raymond Ploughe began the development of this private lake as a membership-only fishing club in 1959. With his death four years later, the venture came to an end. The cottages were sold and became permanent residences.

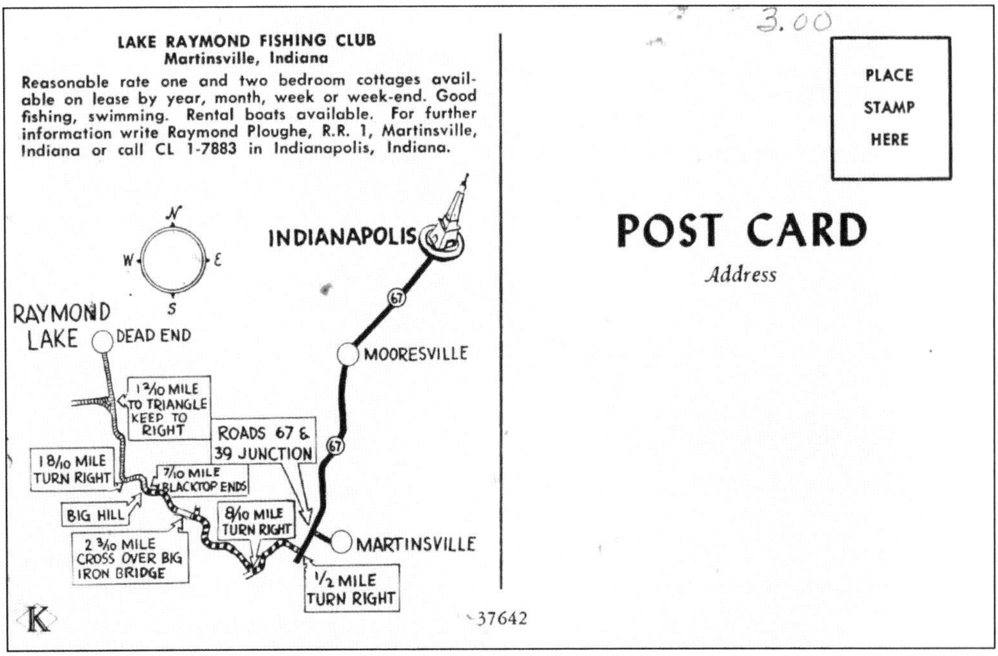

LAKE RAYMOND FISHING CLUB, REVERSE SIDE, *c.* 1960. The lake is located at the north end of Dynasty Lane about two miles west of Patton Lake.

Six

Hall, Monrovia, Eminence, and More

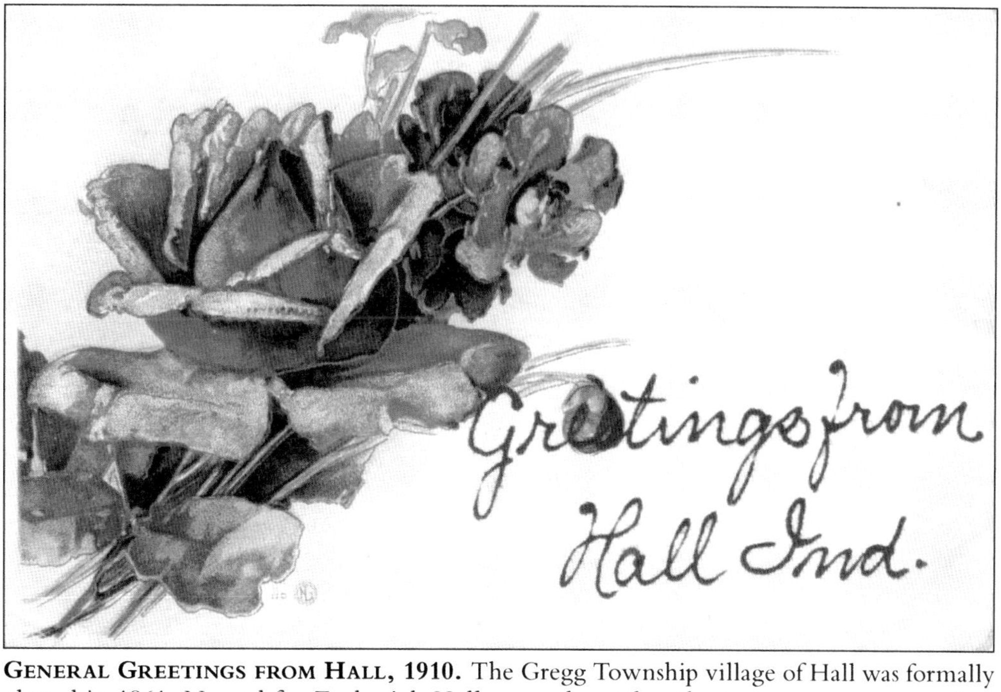

General Greetings from Hall, 1910. The Gregg Township village of Hall was formally platted in 1861. Named for Zachariah Hall, an early settler, the town grew to more than 200 people by the beginning of the 20th century. Handwriting in a kind of glitter ink or paint makes this generic card place-specific.

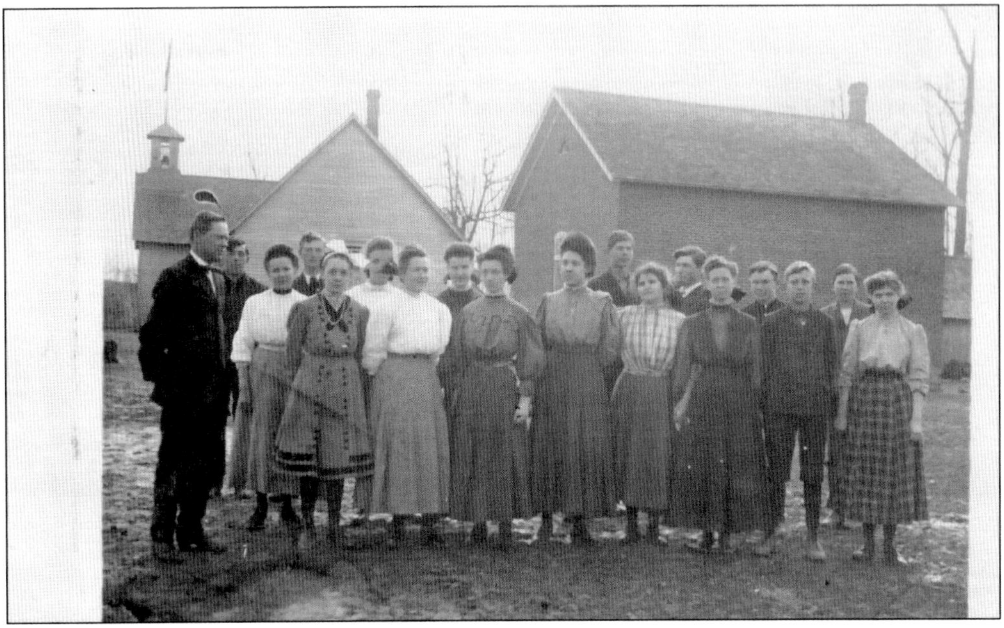

HALL HIGH SCHOOL, 1909. The one-room brick schoolhouse at right was built in 1877. The two-room frame building at left was erected in 1888 by order of the Morgan County commissioners, who regarded its predecessor as outmoded and unsafe. In 1902, however, the brick building was called back into service as Hall High School, of which the only graduate was Clyde Pearce in 1906. Both buildings were replaced in 1910–1911.

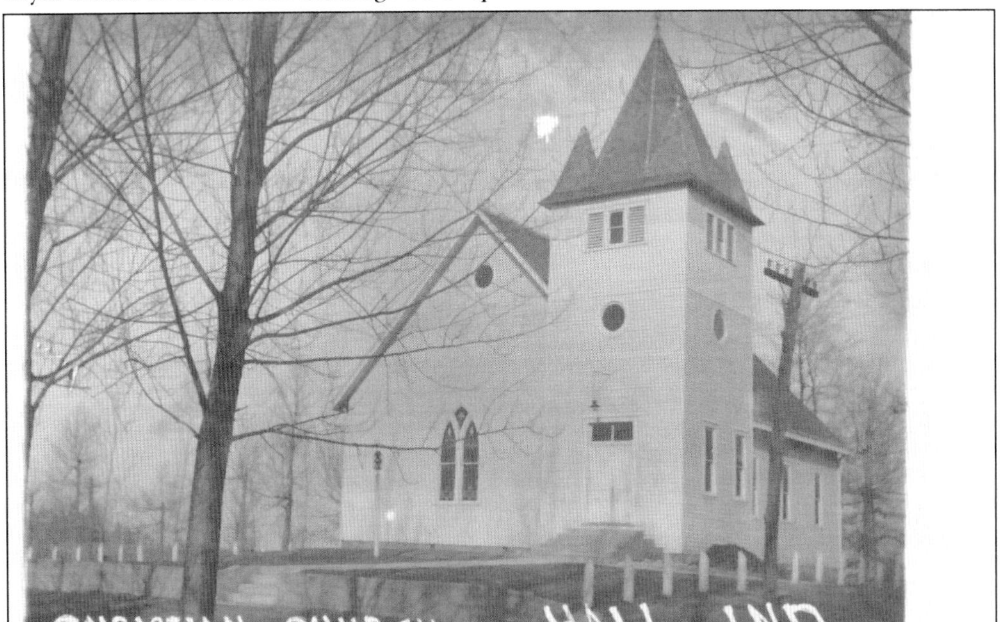

MOUNT PLEASANT CHRISTIAN CHURCH AT HALL, 1908. Organized in 1832, this church was originally located adjacent to the Mount Pleasant cemetery east of Hall. In 1853, the congregation moved to town. The church pictured in this real-photo postcard, and which exists yet today, was completed in 1901.

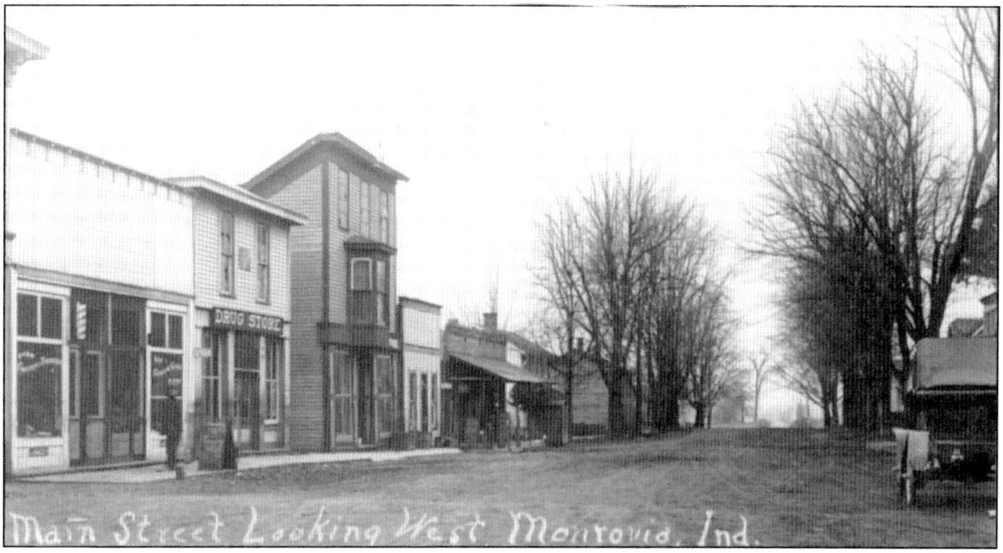

MONROVIA, SOUTH SIDE OF MAIN STREET, LOOKING WEST FROM WATER STREET, 1913. Postcards of Monrovia are very scarce. This one has a message written in French and was mailed from Monrovia to Lyon on August 13, 1913. It was purchased on eBay from a seller in France. The frame buildings shown here were destroyed by fire on April 12, 1916. Lost were, from left to right, Henry Brooks's confectionery (the barber pole represents Brooks's former profession), Columbus McMorris's drugstore, Charles Daily's harness shop, and Harlan Kenworthy's hardware store, occupying both the one-story frame and brick buildings at center.

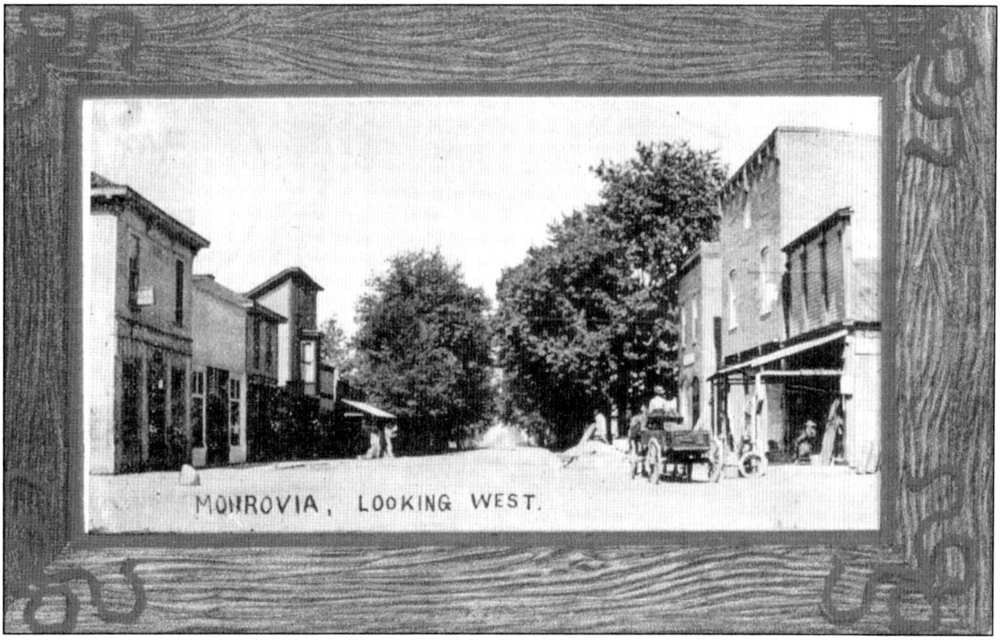

MONROVIA MAIN STREET, LOOKING WEST, C. 1910. The buildings on the north side of the street appear in this view of the same block as shown above. The Monrovia National Bank is the two-story brick building at rear. Next to it is the Gentry building owned by Harrison Gentry; the Knights of Pythias lodge occupies the second floor. The frame building may be August Olsen's blacksmith shop and garage.

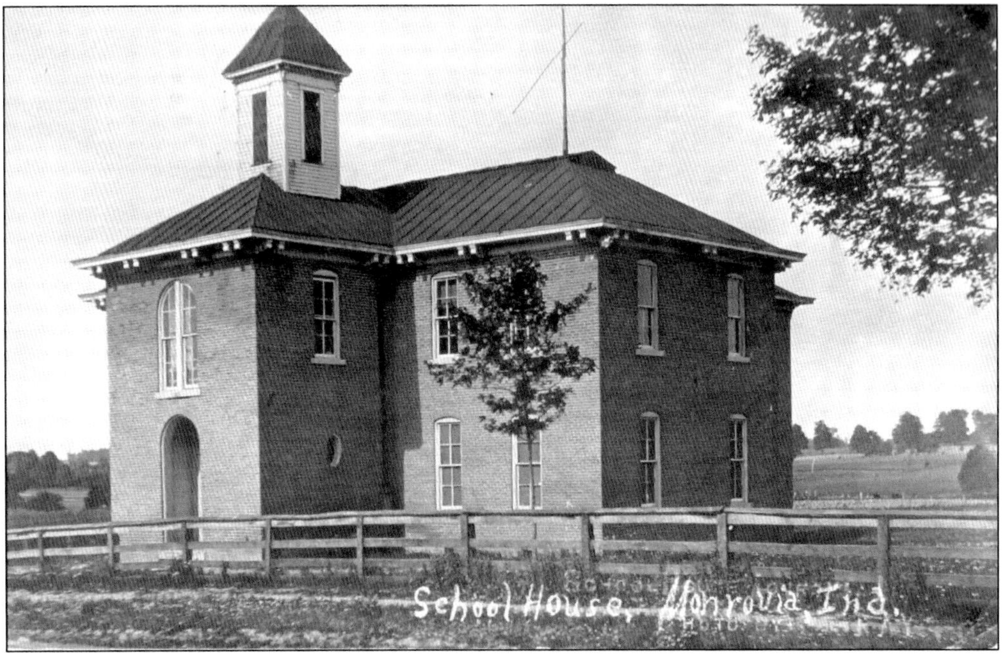

MONROVIA SCHOOL, 1906. In use from 1881 to 1912, this brick school building was the second to be located at Monrovia. The class of 1884 was the first graduating class. It was located on the west side of State Road 39, on the site of the current Citizens Bank and opposite the present-day school complex.

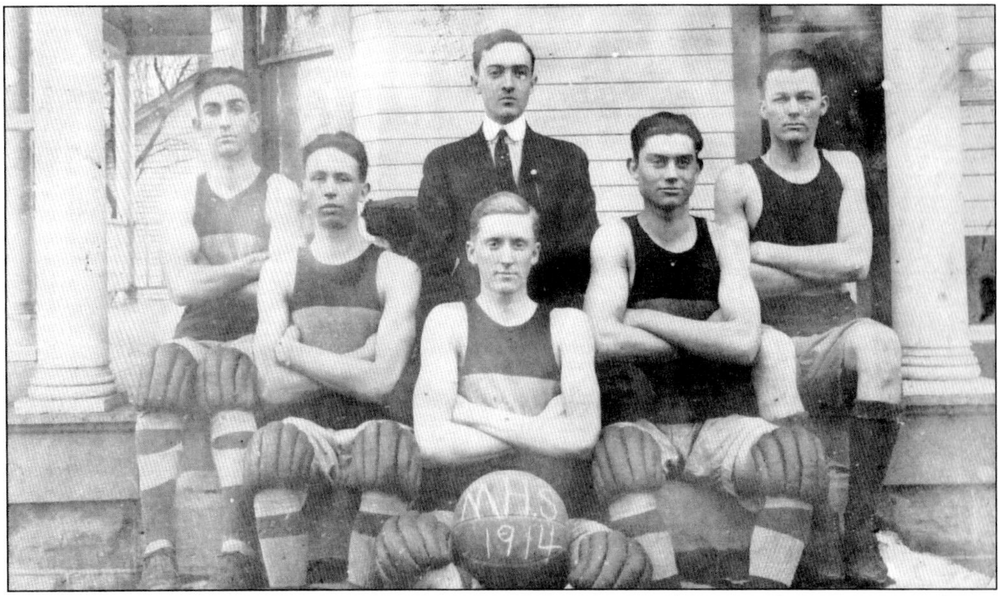

MONROVIA HIGH SCHOOL BASKETBALL TEAM, 1914. From left to right are Don Rushton, Ira Hinshaw, Clair Shields, Raymond Bray, and Paul Allen with coach Wallace Bain at rear. Missing are teammates Roy Dillon and Willis Richardson. Among the state's best, the team lost in the first round of the 1914 state tournament. Monrovia has produced a number of notable basketball players, including 1926 graduate Branch McCracken, who went on to play and coach at Indiana University.

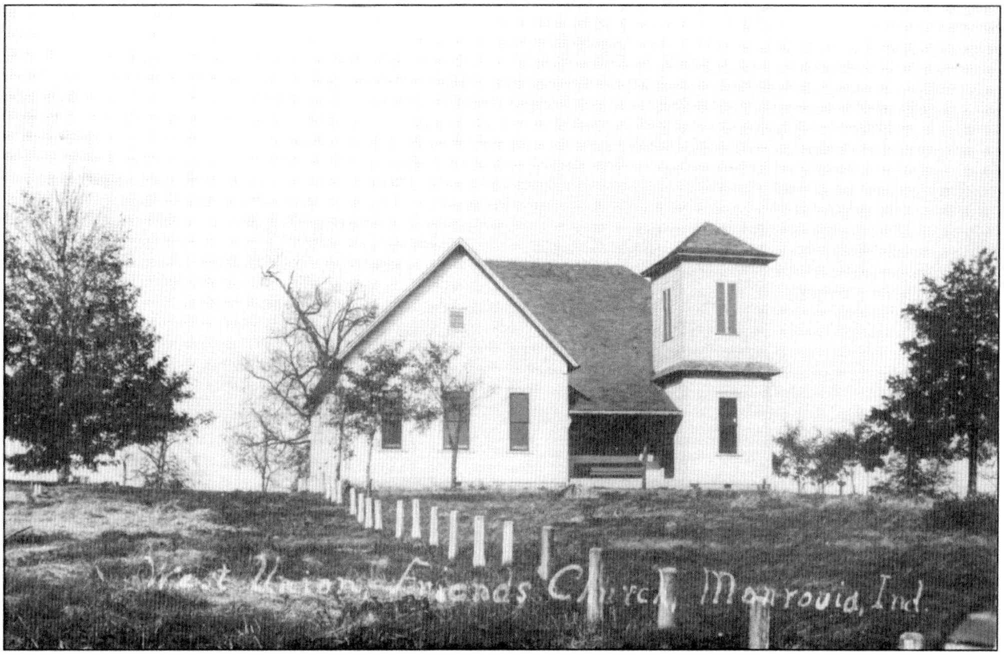

West Union Friends Meetinghouse, East of Monrovia, 1914. One of Morgan County's oldest surviving religious buildings, this church was built in 1856, with an addition completed in 1868 to accommodate the quarterly meeting. Updating and remodeling occurred in 1905. The earliest burial in the adjacent cemetery was Deborah Allen in 1832, the same year that Friends from North Carolina organized the church.

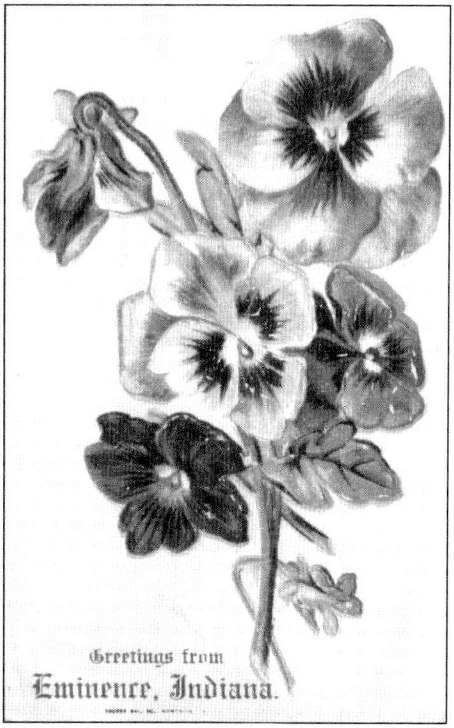

Generic Greetings from Eminence, 1908. No postcards with views of Eminence have yet been found. This general greetings card could be imprinted with any place name or heartfelt message. In the Victorian period, pansies symbolized loving thoughts.

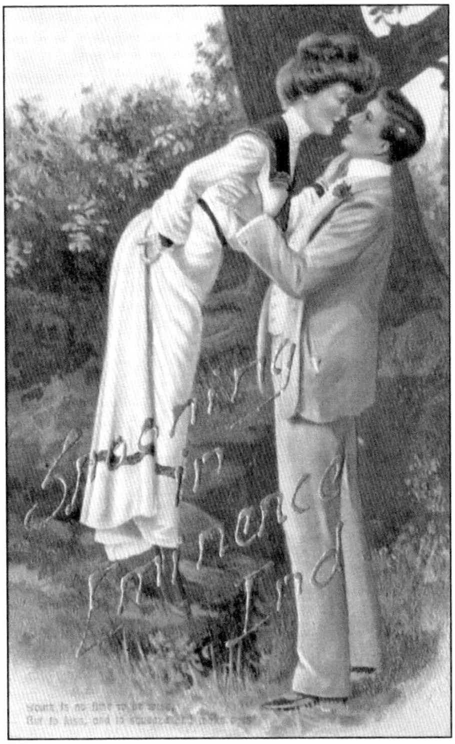

GENERIC GREETINGS FROM EMINENCE, 1910. In years past, *spooning* was a slang term for kissing and cuddling. The printed message at the bottom reads, "Youth is no time to be wise, / But to kiss, and to squeeze and make eyes."

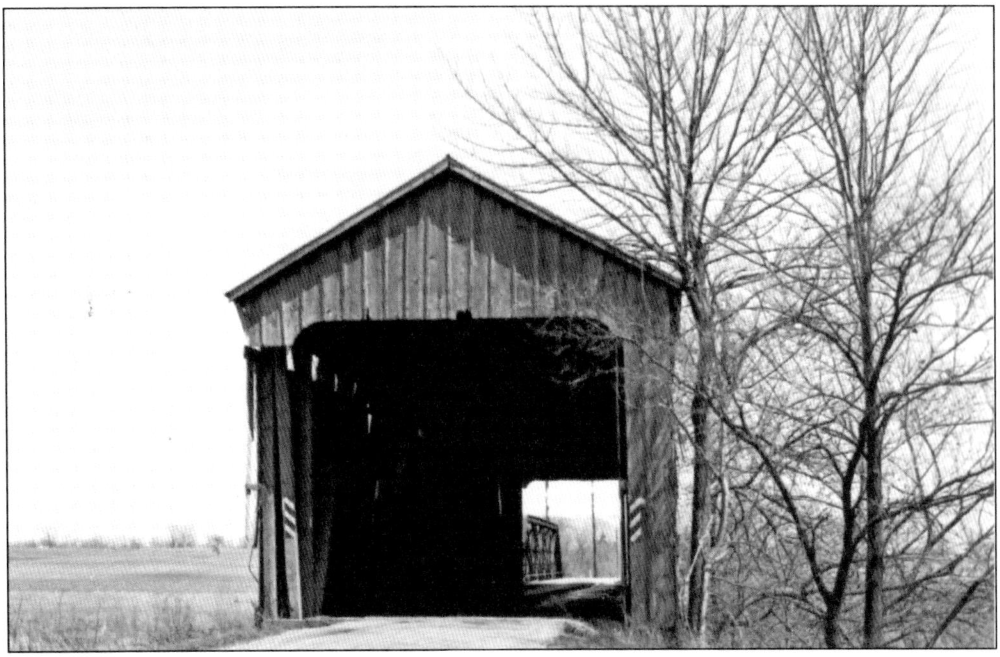

PARKER/PETE COX COVERED BRIDGE, *C.* 1965. Spanning Mill Creek west of Eminence and connecting Morgan and Hendricks Counties, this Howe truss covered bridge was built in 1886. Negotiations for the preservation of Morgan County's last surviving covered bridge came to naught when it collapsed in a storm on November 26, 1979. The bridge originally consisted of two covered wood spans, one of which was replaced by an iron truss, as seen here.

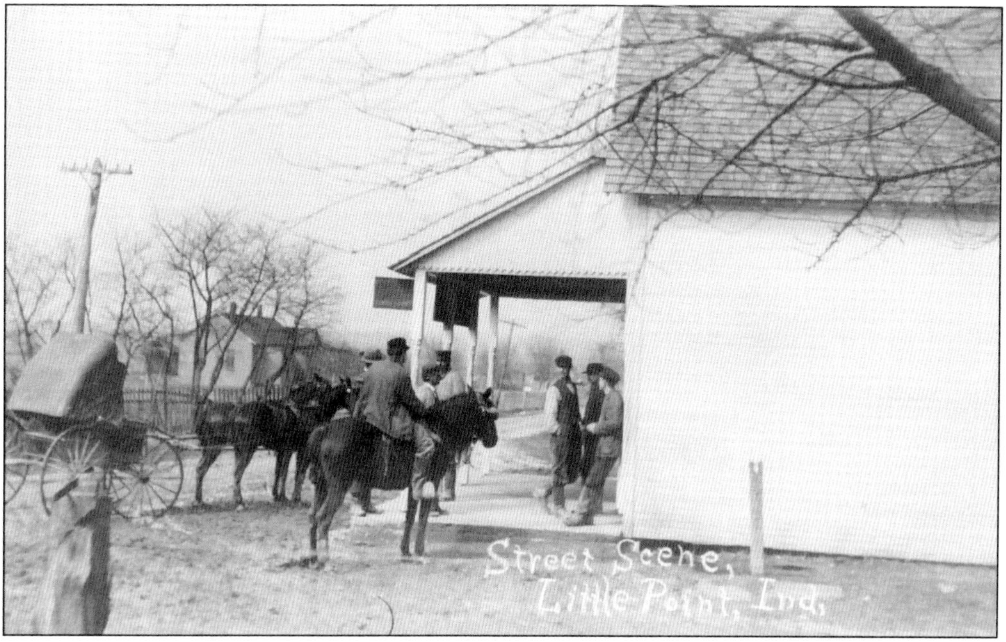

DRY GOODS STORE, LITTLE POINT, *C.* 1910. Apparently a popular meeting spot for loafers and local residents, this store, believed to be operated by Marion McClain, was located on the east side of Little Point Road just north of what is now State Road 42. The sign hanging from the porch roof reads, "Good Goods."

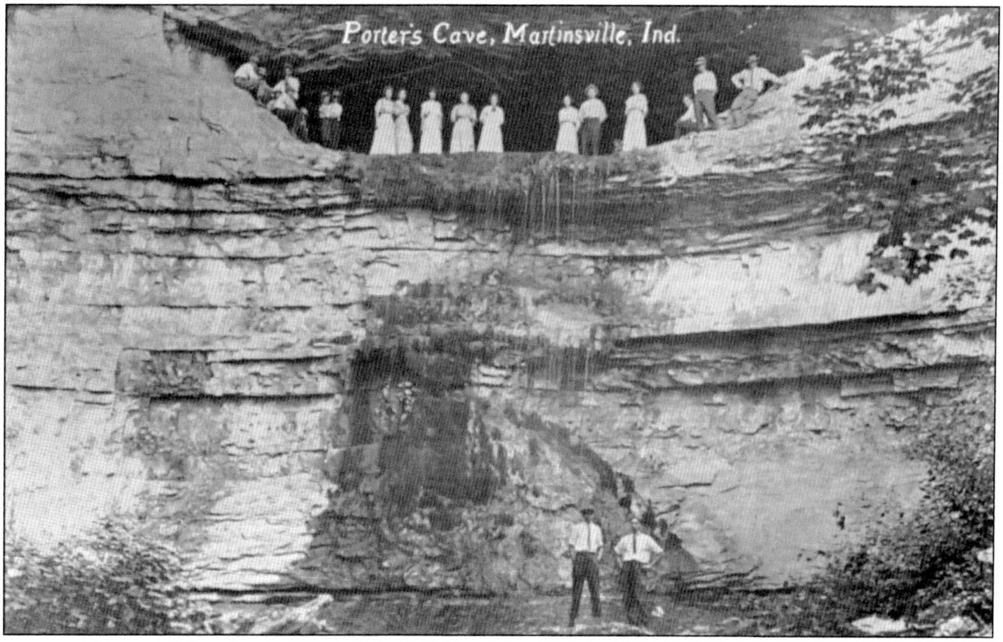

PORTER'S CAVE, VICINITY OF LEWISVILLE, 1917. Although this postcard identified the cave's location as Martinsville, it is actually about two miles south of Lewisville and just over the Morgan County line in Owen County. The natural beauty and mystery of the cave made it a popular destination for family picnics and reunions, as well as day trips for guests at Martinsville's sanitariums.

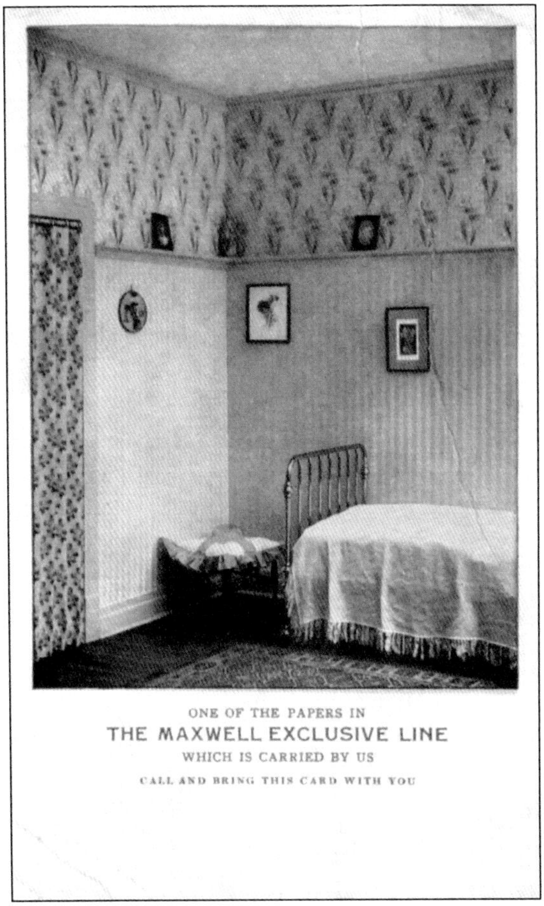

LEWIS AND COMPANY STORE, LEWISVILLE, *C.* 1915. In 1880, gristmill operator Henry Lewis and two partners erected a two-story brick building and opened the Lewis and Company store. Within a few years, Lewis was sole owner and dealer in sundry items: hardware and harnesses, dry goods and groceries, building supplies, and general home furnishings, such as the wallpaper on this trade card. In 1905, Lewis was joined by his son Perry. In 1952, Perry's own sons, Junior and Wayne, took over the business. The store building and its contents—including the old Regulator clock, safe, and even the telephone switchboard and cash register—were sold at a four-day auction in 1982. Closing the door on the Lewis and Company meant closing the door on Lewisville, which once boasted a shoe store, two blacksmith shops, other stores, and, later, a service station. Several of the building's subsequent owners have tried to operate a store but never with much success.

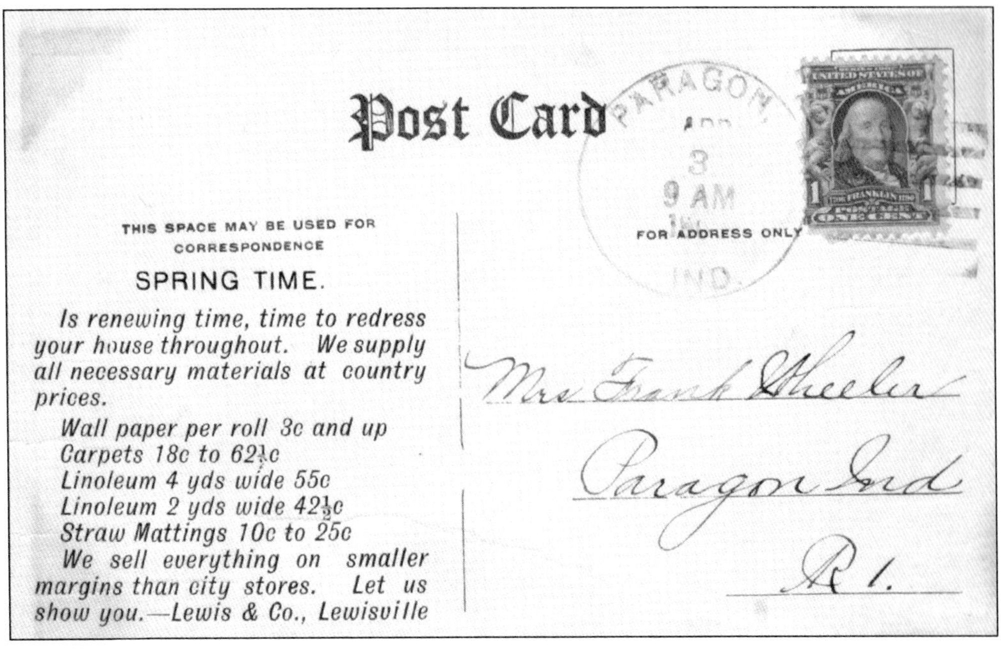

Index

SLEDDING IN WAVERLY, 1910. In this photograph by Joseph Counsilman, boys double up on wood sleds with steel runners, making for a fast ride on an icy hillside. The area north of Waverly was once known as the Bluffs, but as a result of a century of sand and gravel mining, the hills that influenced its name have disappeared.

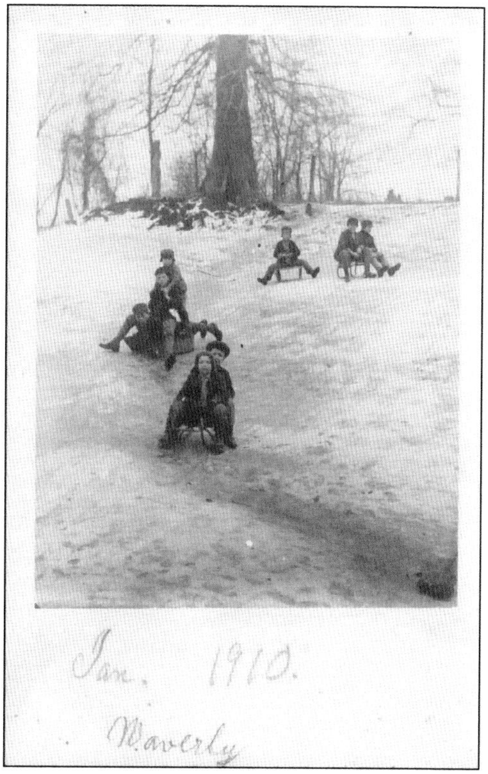

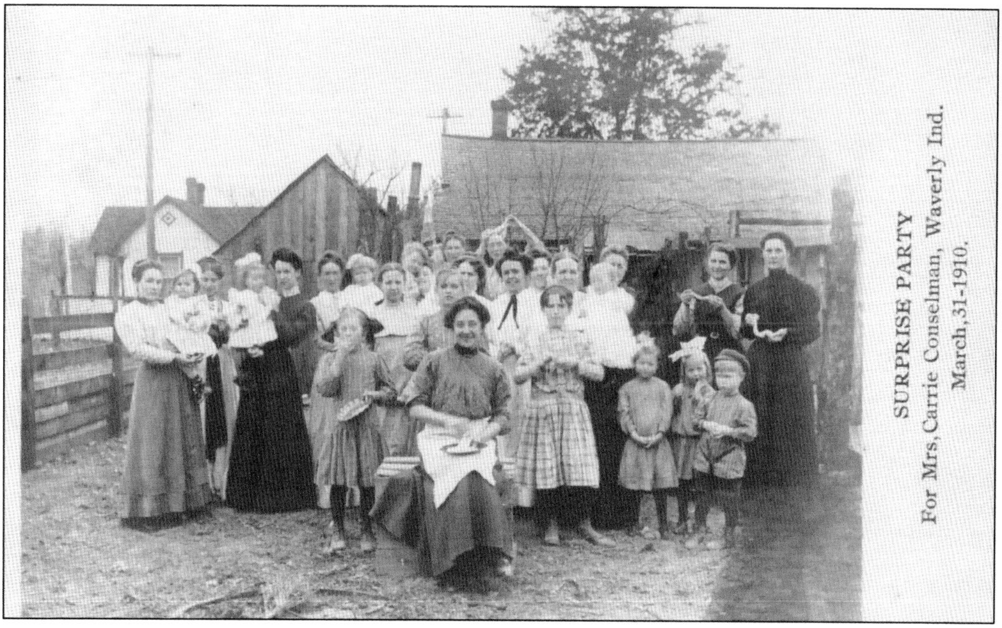

SURPRISE PARTY FOR CARRIE, MARCH 31, 1910. The second wife of Waverly photographer Joseph Conselman/Counsilman, Carrie is feted with a taffy-pulling party attended by women and children. Note that someone has used a lead pencil to obscure a person standing third from right. Carrie Counsilman would later divorce Joseph, whose itinerant travels and variety of colorful business ventures made marriage a trying adventure in itself.